Principles of Examining

Principles of Examining

James M Thyne, MA, MEd, FBPsS

Principal Lecturer in Psychology
Jordanhill College of Education, Glasgow

 UNIVERSITY OF LONDON PRESS LTD

ISBN 0 340 18073 0 Boards
ISBN 0 340 18074 9 Unibook

University of London Press Ltd
St Paul's House, Warwick Lane, London EC4P 4AH

Printed in Great Britain by
Hazell Watson & Viney Ltd
Aylesbury, Bucks

Preface

This book describes the basic techniques of examining: the setting of questions (including 'objective' questions), the marking of answers, the scaling, comparing, and combining of marks, and the evaluating and reporting of results. Throughout, however, the emphasis is upon the principles underlying technique rather than upon statistical theory. For one thing, it is only by reference to principles that techniques can be properly designed and profitably applied. For another, it is possible and often necessary for the teacher or lecturer to become a competent examiner without first becoming a statistician. For these reasons the main text contains no formulae, though there is an Appendix in which some statistical formulae are described. Also, although the argument is intended to be rigorous and to make no concessions to loose thinking, it is assumed that for some readers the skills of examining will be new, and so the subject-matter is presented accordingly, the more technical comments and references being indicated by number in the text and given as notes in another Appendix. The omission of these Appendices is, of course, at the reader's discretion, for they are not essential to the main theme.

In addition to its method of presentation, what novelty the book has is likely to be found less in the techniques it describes than in its treatment of the underlying principles, particularly in respect of Validity. We have adopted the view that Validity is the ultimate necessity, and that Reliability is a *condition* of Validity –a necessary condition but by no means a sufficient one. This view is not novel, though it is often forgotten or misunderstood, as when it is stated that an examination must be both valid and reliable–which is illogical. The implication of the view we have adopted is that if Reliability is a necessary but insufficient condition of Validity, one must seek out and establish further conditions of Validity, each of which is necessary and all of which, together, are sufficient. This we have tried to do.

That task has been undertaken not merely in the interest of theoretical tidiness, desirable as that is, but on the ground that its conclusions will provide a sounder basis for technique: the more rigorously one specifies the conditions Validity demands, the more guidance one gets in the practical business of designing valid examinations. On this ground we have gone so far as to suggest that, for examinations if not for standardised tests, the traditional concept of Reliability has outlived its usefulness (particularly in respect of criterion-referenced evaluation), and that the multiplicity of things 'reliability' has come to mean should be regrouped to become aspects of more practicable conditions.

We are not making an appeal for more examinations. It is quality, not quantity, that matters. The difference is pertinent, for while examinations are certainly susceptible to criticism on many counts, many of the criticisms commonly levelled at them are applicable, not to examinations as such, but to examinations of poor quality—which fail to fulfil their proper functions, or aim to fulfil functions for which they are inadequate. It is one of the purposes of this book to make explicit what examinations may legitimately be expected to do and how they can be designed to do it.

Acknowledgments are due to many people, but especially to the authors of the works cited; to the many hundreds of students who, as examinees, have given me firsthand experience of the practical problems of examining; and to my colleagues, past and present, in Jordanhill College of Education, for whose patient and encouragingly critical comments I am most grateful.

JMT

Contents

PART THREE   *Setting questions and marking answers*

PART ONE

The meaning of examination results

1 What is a good examination?

Validity

To propose principles of examining is to imply that their observance will make for better examinations. But while examinations assess their candidates as better and worse, in what sense can such a judgment be passed on examinations themselves?

Every examination's results are assessments of the candidates who sit it, but every examination is set for a purpose: to find out how much the candidates know about a certain topic, to test their application of knowledge to some practical task, to select them for higher education, to evaluate their fitness to be granted a degree, and so forth; and it is by reference to the purpose to be served by an examination that the examination itself becomes susceptible of assessment, and that in two ways.

In one sense, an examination is good to the extent to which it produces results of the kind its purpose has prescribed. It would be a bad examination if, aiming to assess the candidates' understanding of some issue, it indicated only how much they had committed to memory. Likewise, it would be a bad examination if, aiming to discover the candidates' factual knowledge of some topic, it provided them with the very facts they were supposed to recall, and asked for examples of application. That one of these purposes might be preferred to the other is beside the point, namely that in this sense an examination is good to the extent to which the results it produces are of the kind prescribed by whatever purpose the examination actually has. Whether it *should* have had that purpose is another matter, considered in a moment. In this first sense of goodness the purpose itself is not on trial, and the judgment of an examination is essentially a judgment of it as a means of producing results which are in accord with its actual purpose.

In a second sense, however, what is crucial is the goodness

of the purpose itself. In this sense, no matter how well the examination fulfils its actual purpose it cannot be good if the purpose is bad, because the badness of the purpose will reflect upon any means of fulfilling it. For example, an examination which adequately fulfilled the purpose of selection for secondary education would be good in the first sense, by reference to its adequacy as a means, but it would be bad in the second sense if selecting pupils for secondary education were itself a bad purpose.

The former sense presupposes a judgment of means, the latter a judgment of ends. Accordingly, how an examination can be designed to produce the kind of results its actual purpose requires is a technical problem, whereas what purposes examinations ought to have is a problem in educational, social, moral or political philosophy. Obviously, *both* sorts of goodness are of very great importance. The results of an examination which was technically excellent would be very much worse than useless if they were applied to a purpose judged to be educationally deplorable, or if the very conducting of the examination had disastrous effects upon the school or college curriculum. In an educational context, therefore, the purposes for which examinations are held must be closely scrutinised. But, no matter how desirable the purpose might be, the results of a technically inefficient examination could have disastrous effects too. Related as they are, however, the judgment of means and the judgment of ends are essentially different; and any book attempting to deal with both issues would have to be two books in one. This book is concerned only with the judgment of goodness in the first sense, with the goodness of examinations as technical instruments; but it will be appreciated, from what we have just said, that in restricting this book to the evaluation of means we are in no way underestimating the importance of the evaluation of ends. It is simply that that is not what this particular book is about.

The answer here, then, to 'What is a good examination?' is that an examination's goodness is the extent to which the results it produces are in accord with whatever purpose the examination has.

That description can be contracted to one word – 'validity', because its current meaning covers the three basic aspects of our answer. First, validity (as the term is used) depends upon the particular purpose of the examination: as has been illustrated, an examination which was highly valid for one purpose (say testing rote-recall) might have little or no validity for some other purpose (such as assessing understanding). Second, validity is not all-or-nothing but a matter of degree: since no examination is likely to be perfectly valid, strictly we should ask, not 'Is it valid?', but 'How valid is it?' Third, since it is the examination's results which are to be in accord with the examination's purpose, strictly it is to the results of an examination that 'validity' refers.[1]

The examiner's basic aim, then, must be to maximise the validity of the results of his examinations, and this he can do only by means of the procedures in which examining consists and which produce these results – the procedures involved in setting questions, marking answers, combining marks, and so forth. Not every possible procedure of examining will of course produce results of maximum validity; questions can be set and answers marked in such a way that the results will bear little or no relation to what the examination's purpose requires. Obviously, if the procedures of examining are to produce highly valid results, certain conditions must be imposed upon them. The examiner must therefore know these conditions, so that in designing, selecting, or employing any procedure of examining he can ascertain whether it conforms to them.

These conditions are described in the next chapter, but since an account of them must refer to the procedures which are to conform to them, we must first look at the intrinsic nature of the procedures themselves, and ask, 'What is an examination?'

Examining as the measuring of performance

Examinations are sometimes said to be means of assessing knowledge, comprehension, and the like, but such assessment is possible only when the candidates actually demonstrate their 'knowledge', 'comprehension', and so on. In practice, examinations do require candidates to do this, for what are commonly called 'the questions' are in effect directives, to the candidates, to demonstrate what they understand, know, can do. (Many 'questions' are not interrogative at all.) For example, 'Write an account of . . .', 'Draw a map showing ...', 'Solve ...', 'Translate ...'. In general, examination questions are *directives* to the candidates to give certain *performances*.

The next procedure, marking the answers, may then be described as assessing the performances the candidates actually give. This must of course be done by reference to the performances the candidates were *directed* to give: a performance is not awarded a high mark on the ground that it would have been a good answer to a question which was not asked. And even if the examiner were of the opinion that a certain performance should not have been asked for, he must award marks for it if it were the performance the candidate was directed to give. These points are probably obvious, but are mentioned for future use.

Now when numerical marks are awarded in an examination, a mark of 12 is intended to indicate a better performance than is the mark of 8; and if each of two candidates is awarded 7, this is intended to mean that the two candidates' performances are to count as equal. Such assessment comes under the general head of 'Measurement', in the wide sense that to measure is to assign numbers to things so as to represent their magnitudes (English and English 1958).[2]

But assessments by means of letters (such as A, B, C, D, ...) are measurements too. When two candidates' performances, in answer to the same question, are awarded respectively the marks of A and C, this is not usually intended to mean that the two performances have exhibited different, *unquantifiable*, qualities. It means that the 'A' performance displays *more* of something (elegance, perhaps, or style, or insight, or organisation–or even length), or that it is *higher* in some respect, or goes *farther* in some way, than the 'C' performance. Letters too refer to magnitudes, and so marking, generally, is in effect the measuring of performance.

Finally, it is customary to combine the marks each candidate has obtained (such as his marks for the various questions) to produce his 'final mark'; and the whole set of these composite measures constitutes the 'results' of the examination.

There are two main advantages of envisaging examinations in 'performance' terms. First, the interrelatedness of the constituent procedures is more readily apparent: the questions are directives to *give* certain performances; the marking is the *measuring*, and the marks are the *measures* of these performances; the adding of marks is the *combining* of those measures; and the results are the *composite* measures so produced. Second, the view of the results as composite measures of performance simplifies the deduction of *conditions* to which examination procedures must conform if the results they produce are to be of maximum validity. These deductions are made in the next chapter.

Marking-Consistency

This chapter establishes four conditions which must hold if examination results are to be of maximum validity.

We begin with a condition deriving from a presupposition of all purposes of measuring, namely that the measures within one series are *comparable* with one another, in the sense that (for instance) 64 represents a greater *magnitude* than does 63, that 47 and 47 represent equal magnitudes, and so on.[3] If the measures

LADIES !
BE AS SLIM
AS YOU LIKE
with our
PATENT EASY-STRETCH
ELASTIC
MEASURING TAPE

within a series are *not* comparable in this way they will be of no use for any purpose, and so to the extent to which they fall short of being comparable they will be lowered in validity.

This would happen if the measuring instrument were *inconsistent* in measurement, a point aptly illustrated by Wesman's (1952) example of an elastic ruler. With such an instrument, one and the same thing is just as likely to measure 44 units as 27–or even 73. The crux of the illustration is that if one and the same thing may have any of several different measures, we cannot assume that something measuring 44 units is of greater magnitude than something else measuring 27–not if these two measures are just as likely to represent one and the same magnitude. An instrument changing the meaning of its units in this way would therefore produce measures which were not comparable and were therefore reduced in validity.[4]

To an instrument of that kind, and also to the measures it produces, the term 'unreliable' is often applied, but as the example illustrated, the essence of reliability is consistency. The same term, with the same meaning, is customarily applied to the marks produced by an examination or test. Cronbach (1960) says, 'Reliability always refers to consistency throughout a series of measurements.' Wiseman (1961) has suggested (see also Cox 1969) that the term 'consistency' might well be used instead, and we propose to adopt that suggestion. Why use even the conventional term, 'reliability', if what it means is indicated better by 'consistency'? We may nevertheless speak of *degrees* of consistency, because some series of marks may be more inconsistent than others.

The condition implied in our discussion might therefore be expressed by our saying that the marks must be consistent, but it will be more practical if expressed in terms of the test which has to be applied to find out to what extent consistency has been achieved.

The only test for consistency of this sort is to have the same performances marked again and to compare the two sets of results. It would be no proof of inconsistency to find that *different* things had differing measures. Inconsistency becomes apparent only when the *same* series of things is measured again and found to have different measures.

If, then, an examiner marked all the candidates' answers to one question, the marks being recorded but not written on the scripts themselves, and the scripts he marked were continuously shuffled back into the bundle until every answer had been marked twice, any inconsistency in marking would be revealed. Since the written answers do not alter, any changes in candidates' marks would exemplify inconsistency in marking, and the greater the divergence between the two sets of marks the greater the inconsistency would be.

What is not always made clear, however, is why inconsistency of this kind lowers validity. It is sometimes said that if the same group of performances is assigned two contradictory sets of marks, neither set can be regarded as reliable. This may be true, but does not explain why *validity* is thereby lowered. The explanation is that the discovery of inconsistency *between* the two sets of marks (for the same scripts) is but a means (though the only means) of discovering inconsistency *within* each of the sets. Unless we make the very unlikely assumption that the marker consistently used a new system of marking *only* when meeting every script for the second time, we must assume that he was an inconsistent marker; that is, that there were inconsistencies *throughout*—and in particular within the set of marks awarded first time round. And it is inconsistency *within* a series of measures which lowers their validity because (as has been noted) by their thus being not comparable the measures will fail to fufil *any* purposes for which measures are to be used.

Essentially the same test is applicable to scripts shared by a team of markers, each marking one bundle. Even if, by the test already described, it were discovered that each examiner was *self*-consistent, there could still be inconsistency *across* them, as could be discovered by 'cross-marking'. If the examiners now exchanged bundles, and if an answer initially awarded 7 were now awarded 10, and the like, this would indicate inconsistency within the *total* series of measurements. And since the mark obtained by one candidate has to be comparable with the mark obtained by any other, no matter which examiner awarded it, such inconsistency within the total series of measures would lower their validity.

The consistency-condition may therefore be expressed by our saying that the marking must be such that the same marks will be awarded when the candidates' performances are re-marked. This may not seem much of an improvement on the first statement—that the marking must be consistent—but it does give clearer guidance for practice. If an examiner can be required to produce exactly the same results on re-marking the same performances, plainly he must have a set of rules for marking. We shall consider such rules later. For the present the aim is to establish conditions from which practical rules must be derived.

To this particular condition we propose to give the name 'Marking-Consistency': the marking must be such that the same marks will be obtained when the candidates' performances are re-marked.

Now although Marking-Consistency is necessary for maximum validity, yet it is not sufficient; other conditions also must be fulfilled. Consider two *self*-consistent examiners who produce different marks on marking, independently, the *same* set of scripts. If either of these examiners were the sole examiner, his marks would satisfy the condition of Marking-Consistency. But the two sets of marks, in this case, would be different. Then can two self-consistent but different sets of marks for the same scripts both be valid?

The answer depends upon the way in which the two sets of marks differ. They could be different yet compatible, as would happen if there were a perfect *correspondence* between the two sets—in the sense that the two examiners were in complete agreement about the relative merits of the scripts (Robert's script being top for each examiner, Charles' script being second for each, and so on), and moreover that the two examiners were in complete agreement about the relative 'distances' between successive degrees of merit—for instance that Robert's script was twice as far above Charles' as Charles' was above David's.* A parallel is provided by two experimenters measuring the temperatures of a set of objects, the one experimenter measuring in degrees Centigrade, the other in degrees Fahrenheit. The two sets of measures would be different, but there could (and should) be a perfect correspondence of the kind we mean. In such a case the two sets of measures would be perfectly compatible, the numerical differences being accounted for entirely in terms of the two different measuring systems employed. If, then (to mix the metaphor), *all* the candidates were measured on the Fahrenheit system, or *all* the candidates were measured on the Centigrade system, not only would there be no inconsistency *within* either set of measures, but neither would there be any contradiction *between* them; and so the validity of the one set would not indicate the invalidity of the other; both sets of measures could be perfectly valid.

* See also pp. 133ff. and the Note on Correlation (pp. 263ff.)

If, on the other hand, there were not a perfect correspondence between the two sets of marks, the sets would be *in*compatible–for instance if Charles came out top for one marker but sixth for the other. Obviously, two incompatible (non-corresponding) sets of marks for the same scripts cannot both be fulfilling the one purpose. True, we cannot say which of the two sets *is* fulfilling the purpose, or indeed that either is; but that is not the point. The point of the example was that both sets were self-consistent, and that since at least one of the sets cannot have maximum validity, it is possible for a set of marks to fulfil the condition of Marking-Consistency, and yet be invalid. The condition of Marking-Consistency, while *necessary*, is therefore not *sufficient* for maximum validity. Other conditions must therefore be sought.

Mark-Relevance

Since an examination's results are valid to the extent to which they are in accord with the examination's purpose (p. 4), and since these results are measures of performance, an examination's results will be lowered in validity to the extent that they are not measures *of* the performances the examination's purpose requires.

However, validity will be lowered on this account not merely because we have laid our measuring-rods alongside irrelevant performances, but only in so far as the set of marks obtained by measuring irrelevant performances fails to *correspond* with the set which would have been obtained by measuring the required performances. As was shown in the previous section, if two sets of measures do correspond perfectly, obtaining the one set is tantamount to obtaining the other set, albeit in different units; and in that case the fact that we had not actually made measurements of the required performances would not lower the marks' validity, because the measures obtained by measuring what we did measure would be equivalent to, and therefore as valid as, those that would have been obtained had we actually measured the performances we were supposed to measure. (Cf. measuring temperature by measuring length–of a column of mercury.)

In fact, measures of different sorts of human performance,

though often showing some correspondence, and occasionally a quite high correspondence, are *not* found to correspond perfectly, and so maximum validity demands measurement of the actual performances the examination's purpose requires. The lower the degree of correspondence between the set of measures which would have been obtained by measuring the required performances and the set obtained by measuring not-required performances, the lower on this account validity will be.

For the long expression 'performances required by the examination's purpose' we shall substitute 'relevant performances'. For maximum validity, then, the only performances to be measured must be relevant performances. If an *ir*relevant performance is given by a candidate, it must not be marked at all. If, for instance, spelling-performances are not relevant, marks must not be awarded for good spelling nor be deducted for bad spelling, because to do so would produce results different from (not corresponding with) those which would have been obtained had only relevant performances been measured, and so would lower validity.

Even this is not enough. Even if all the performances which *are* marked are relevant, validity will be lowered if some given performance which is relevant is *not* marked, because, since the marks for different performances do not correspond perfectly, the set of marks obtained when certain relevant performances are not marked will not correspond perfectly with the *required* set of marks, namely the set of marks relating to *all* the required performances.

For maximum validity, therefore, not only must all the marked performances be relevant ones; all the given relevant performances must be marked. This twofold statement expresses another condition of validity, but it too can be made more practical if, like the condition of Marking-Consistency, it is couched in terms of the operations to be carried out in testing for its fulfilment.

If the above condition is to be met, the marker must have a practical way of checking whether any given performance is in fact relevant. In effect, he must be able to refer to a *list* of relevant performances. Any performance appearing on the list must be marked; any performance not on the list must be ignored. Except for very simple examinations the list will have to be written, and not merely 'kept in the head', and especially when several markers are involved.[5] Also, the list will have to be detailed, indicating, for instance, whether only the final answer to a calculation is to be marked, or whether marks are to be awarded for 'halfway' answers, or for an appropriate method, even if the final answer is wrong, and the like.

It might be objected that some purposes of examining do not lend themselves to the drawing up of a list of required performances, but since it is performance and nothing but performance which examinations measure, failure to specify the performances to be marked precludes criteria of marking and so fails to safeguard validity. (But see also pp. 248ff.)

With these practical points in mind we may now state more precisely the condition stated earlier: *all* the given performances, but *only* the given performances, which appear on the list of relevant performances are to be marked. We shall call this the condition of 'Mark-Relevance'.

Note that the conditions of Mark-Relevance and Marking-Consistency are distinct conditions. It would be possible to mark consistently, but to mark irrelevant performances or to omit to

mark some relevant performances; and it would be possible to mark all the relevant performances, and only relevant performances, but to mark them inconsistently. For practical purposes, however, the rules for Marking-Consistency and the rules for Mark-Relevance can be combined in the one set of rules for marking. The 'list' would specify what performances were to be marked, and the 'consistency' rules would specify how the marking was to be done.

Question-Relevance

A third condition of validity appears when we consider that one or more of the *questions* might be irrelevant—meaning that the candidates were directed to give irrelevant *performances*.

Suppose that a question is irrelevant. Then in accord with the intrinsic nature of examinations (p. 6), any given performance constituting an appropriate answer to that question would have to be awarded marks. But to award marks in this case would be to break the condition of Mark-Relevance. The impasse can be resolved only by the exclusion of irrelevant questions.

The mere exclusion of irrelevant questions is nevertheless not enough. If one or more of the (listed) *relevant* performances were not asked for, the set of marks obtained would not correspond perfectly with the set which would have been obtained had these relevant performances been asked for and marked, because (we must assume) no two sets of marks, for different sorts of performance, will correspond perfectly—which holds good no matter whether the performances are relevant or not. But since it is the whole list of performances, required by the purpose, which has to be measured, measures of only some of these will not be of maximum validity.

We are therefore faced with a twofold condition: all the asked questions must be relevant, and all the relevant questions must be asked. It is nevertheless extremely unlikely that this theoretically proper condition can be met in practice, as the following example illustrates.

An examination has this very restricted purpose: to assess candidates' performances in adding vulgar fractions, the number of fractions to be three, all fractions to be proper fractions, no numerator to exceed 9, no denominator to exceed 10, no given fraction to be reducible (like three ninths), but no bar to two or all three of the fractions being equal. The number of such three-fraction sets is 29,791 – more than any normal examination could accommodate and any normal candidate would tolerate.

In cases like this it is obvious that the examiner has to be content with a *sample* from the 'universe' of performances comprising the list. But while the contingencies of practice make sampling inevitable it is nevertheless emphasised that, for the 'imperfect correspondence' reason already referred to, sampling will necessarily reduce validity. The best that can be done, in this connection, is to draw the sample in such a way that it will be as 'representative' as possible of the list from which it is drawn.

A practical way of doing this is to regard the universe of required performances as consisting of various 'kinds' of performance, and then to ensure that each kind is represented on the question paper. In the addition of vulgar fractions, for instance, the examiner might wish to include cases in which the lowest common denominator was a denominator of one of the given fractions, cases in which it was not, cases in which the sum of the three fractions was an improper fraction (to be converted to a mixed number), and so forth. Similarly, in setting a piece of prose in a foreign language, to test the candidates' abilities to understand it, he would select a passage (or invent one) representing the kinds of performance to be assessed.

It will be apparent that except in very simple examinations the same difficulty will arise in drawing up the list of required performances in the first place. It would be impracticable, and unnecessary, to write out all the 29,791 three-fraction sets; and here also one may simply list the various *kinds* of performance required.

In place of the twofold condition stated a moment ago we may therefore make the more practical statement: the questions must be directives to performances constituting, as closely as possible, a representative sample of the list of relevant performances. To this condition we propose to give the name 'Question-Relevance'.[6]

The more 'representative' the sample of performances asked

for, the more valid (in this respect) the results will be, for the simple reason that this is what 'representative' means.[7] The practical problem, of course, is to try to *make* the sample as representative as possible. Unfortunately, the only sure way of testing its degree of representativeness would be to check the extent to which the *results* obtained from the sample corresponded with the *results* obtained from the whole universe (list). But such a test is of course impossible, for if it were not there would be no need to draw a sample in the first place. It is for this reason that we cannot express the condition of Question-Relevance in the same way as we expressed the conditions of Marking-Consistency and Mark-Relevance, namely in terms of the test to be applied to find out to what extent the condition had been fulfilled.[8] Probably the best practice is the procedure described a moment ago, namely that of drawing a sample of *kinds* of performance and trying to ensure that all the requisite kinds are included.

Balance

When the marks for the parts of an examination (its various questions, for instance) are added to produce final, composite marks for the candidates, are all the parts to 'count' equally, or should some parts weigh more heavily than others? The issue is significant for validity because, as will be shown in a later chapter, a change in the relative 'weights' assigned to the parts of an examination can and usually does alter the candidates' relative positions overall. Different systems of 'weighting' the parts of the examination will therefore produce sets of results which do not correspond perfectly one with another, and so not all the systems of weighting will produce results of maximum validity. The weights to be assigned to the various parts must therefore be determined by the examination's purpose.

How this is to be done will be considered later; all we need note now, in passing, is that allocating different maximum possible marks to the different parts will not guarantee that the required weights are assigned. For the present we state only the condition itself, namely that the contribution of the various parts of the examination to the final marks must be in accord with the examination's purpose. Following Ebel (1965) we shall call this the condition of Balance.[9]

Necessity and sufficiency

It has been argued that each of the four conditions, Marking-Consistency, Mark-Relevance, Question-Relevance, and Balance is *necessary* for maximum validity. It is now suggested that these four conditions, together, are also *sufficient* for it. This is much more difficult to prove, but in this account we shall attempt to justify the suggestion in two ways. First we shall look at the conditions themselves, to see whether they appear to be complete. Second, we shall look at some other issues commonly associated with validity, and try to show either that they are already included in the four conditions or that they scarcely apply to what are commonly accepted as examinations (in contrast with standardised tests).

First, then, assume that there has been drawn up a list of the performances or kinds of performance the examination's purpose requires – an assumption presupposed by the condition of Question-Relevance (and also Mark-Relevance). For some purposes this is far from straightforward. An examination with the purpose of predicting performance in a subsequent examination will necessitate a list of performances whose measures will be found to *correspond* closely with the subsequent measures – an example illustrating so-called 'criterion-related validity', which is discussed in the next chapter. It may have to be discovered, to some extent by trial and error, just what performances will satisfy that correspondence criterion; that is to say, just what performances *are* in fact required; but we quote the example now merely to illustrate how wide the meaning of 'required performances' is. And when we say that we are assuming that the list of *required* performances has been drawn up, we intend to include cases of that kind.

Assume now that there has been selected, from the list of required performances, a sample which is as representative as possible. Assume, that is, that the condition of Question-Relevance has been fulfilled.

Next, assume that the condition of Mark-Relevance is fulfilled: marks are awarded or deducted *only* for relevant performances, and *all* the given performances which are relevant are marked. The marking could of course be relevant but inconsistent; so assume now that the condition of Marking-Consistency also is met.

At first sight it might seem that proper marking is not safeguarded merely by these two conditions–Mark-Relevance and Marking-Consistency; and in part this is true. It might be argued that although the marking is relevant, and consistent, yet the marks awarded are not necessarily the 'right' marks. Might not the examiner have awarded (say) only one mark for a certain point when he should have awarded two marks? As has been noted already, however, so long as the *same* system of units is used throughout the one series of measurements, it does not matter what units are used, so long as the system is applied consistently. In this respect the argument is analogous to objecting that heights 'ought' to be measured in inches, and that it is not 'right' to measure them in centimetres. However, if these measures are to be *combined* with measures of other performances it could be argued that too many marks were being awarded to some performances at the expense of others. This point, it is true, is *not* covered by the conditions of Mark-Relevance and Marking-Consistency, but it *is* covered by the condition of Balance–which refers to the relative 'weights' to be given to the various performances–whether these constitute the whole answers to questions or are parts of such answers, and so forth.

Finally, assume that the condition of Balance is fulfilled, so that marks are combined with the weights the examination's purpose requires.

Though not a formal proof, the preceding account suggests that if all four conditions are fulfilled no other condition is necessary, and therefore that these four conditions together are sufficient for maximum possible validity. Even so, we now look briefly at some other issues commonly associated with the same aim. (Since these are not essential to the main theme of the text, readers unfamiliar with them may prefer to go straight to the next chapter.)

Objectivity

'Objective marking' means that an examiner would award the same marks to the scripts on re-marking them, or that different examiners, presented with the same set of scripts, would award the same marks. But this is covered by the 'rules' presupposed by the condition of Marking-Consistency (p. 10).[10] Somewhat similarly, objectivity in setting questions means that different examiners, or the same examiner on a second draw, would select the same or an equivalent set of questions. But this is covered, and more than covered, by the condition of Question-Relevance, for that condition ensures not only that all the examiners' selections of questions would be equivalent but also that they would be relevant.

Split-half reliability

This refers to the results of comparing the candidates' scores on one half of a test with their scores on the other half, and noting the degree of correspondence. The validity of the test is judged to be lowered, in this respect, to the extent that the correspondence is poor–for example, if candidates who scored high on the even-numbered questions obtained scores scattered at random for the odd-numbered questions. This measuring of correspondence is obviously appropriate if the purpose of the test is to assess the candidates in respect of some single 'ability', for if the scores on the two halves of the test do not correspond very well, the two halves of the test cannot be measuring the same thing. But an examination does not *necessarily* have such a purpose, even if many standardised tests do. For example, an examination could have the purpose (discussed later) of assessing how well students were progressing in a course of instruction. The relevant performances, here, would be the performances in which the students were being instructed, and the results of the examination would be valid to the extent that the examiner observed also the conditions of Mark-Relevance, Marking-Consistency, and Balance. If the performances comprising the *course* were themselves such that half of them did not correspond with another half, validity would not be lowered by the finding that the correspondence *was* low. Even if it were argued that the performances included in a course *should* exhibit some correspondence, on the ground that otherwise the 'course' would be no more than a heterogeneous assortment of items, that argument would be irrelevant to the validity of the *examination*. In practice, however, the use of a 'split-half' procedure often does produce moderately good degrees of correspondence, even when one has not tried to 'match' the performances for which the candidates are asked. In such cases it may well be that the examination is measuring some 'ability' – even if it is no more than the 'ability' to work or to attend classes; but if the purpose of the examination does not presuppose a high degree of correspondence, its actual discovery, though of considerable interest, is nevertheless gratuitous.

We have discussed this issue at some length, not only in order to show that high half-by-half correspondence is not a necessary condition of validity for all examinations, but also to illustrate again the point that an examination's validity depends upon its *purpose*, and that the means appropriate to one purpose are not necessarily appropriate to another. But what of examinations in which the purpose *does* presuppose a high correspondence of this kind? This is a pertinent question, for all we have argued is that the purposes of examining do not *necessarily* presuppose it. If, then, an examination's purpose does presuppose it, are our four conditions of validity adequate? We think they are, for the following reason.

If a 'split-half' analysis of the results produced a low correspondence between the halves, despite the marking's being relevant and consistent, and the requisite balance's being given to the parts of the examination, the inference would be that some of the performances which had been asked for were inappropriate, and that these would have to be replaced by other performances. In other words, there would be something wrong with the 'list' of performances asked for, namely that some of the performances included in it were not relevant to the examination's purpose. But this is, in effect, a judgment in terms of the condition of Question-Relevance. As we mentioned before (p. 18), the meaning of 'required performances' is very wide: they may have to be such as to correspond with some other, criterion, performances – as in the purpose of Prediction; of the present case we might say that there is a sort of 'internal criterion', any half of the performances being the criterion with which the other half has to correspond.[11] Perhaps we should note that a high degree of 'split-half' correspondence does not of itself indicate *what* single ability is being measured. That question would require reference to some criterion external to the examination itself. We have been concerned here only with the issue of whether there need be any correspondence at all, and if so, whether that demand is covered by the conditions of validity already described. We have tried to show that it is so covered.

Intra-examinee variability

Sometimes referred to also as 'individual variance', or 'function fluctuation', the point here is that each candidate's performance may vary from one occasion to another, and that this sort of inconsistency, or instability of performance, may affect the examination's validity.

Suppose, for instance, that instead of an examination's being held today it had been held yesterday, and that it could be demonstrated that the scores which would have been obtained yesterday were different from those obtained today–different to the extent that they did not correspond very well. Then *both* sets of results could not be of maximum validity, for if one set were perfectly valid, another (non-corresponding) set could not be.

What that illustration is intended to make explicit is that even when the set of questions is fixed, and the system of marking is relevant and consistent, and a prescribed way of combining marks (Balance) is adhered to, the results *can* fall short in validity solely on account of the variability of the candidates' performances from one occasion to another. The question relevant to the present discussion, then, is whether this possibility requires a condition of validity additional to the four conditions already described.

In order to show that the possibility is already covered by the set of conditions already described, and by the condition of Question-Relevance in particular, we must recall that if an examination's results are not perfectly valid they are so judged on account of their not completely fulfilling the examination's purpose. That judgment would hold good no matter for what reason the purpose was not fulfilled. Specifically, if one of the reasons for low validity is instability of candidate-performance, then one of the grounds on which the results of measuring unstable performances would be judged to be of imperfect validity would have to be that measures of unstable performances do not completely fulfil the examination's purpose. Accordingly, if performance-measures *are* to be in full accord with the examination's purpose, they must *not* be measures of unstable performances. But the only way in which an examination can properly produce such measures is for it to refrain from *asking* for performances in which the candidates are unstable–over some stipulated period of time. That is to say, the examination must ask for performances which *are* stable–for the reason just given, namely that unless such performances are measured the examination's purpose will not be completely fulfilled. But this is, in effect, to conform to the condition of Question-Relevance–which demands that the performances asked for must be relevant to the purpose of the examination.

As we have already hinted, however, there may not be any performances which remain stable for any length of time. It may be that every human performance is liable to fluctuation; and even if stable performances could be discovered, they might well be alien to the examination's purpose in other respects: they might be quite irrelevant to the objectives of a course of instruction, or have no predictive value, and so forth. If this is so, the condition of Question-Relevance will never be completely fulfilled. (We noted earlier another reason, namely the need to draw a *sample* of questions.) This may well be regrettable, but the practical implication would seem to be, not that examiners should exercise regret, but rather that they should realise that no examination is likely to be perfectly valid, and that they should therefore exercise caution in applying examination results.

The main purpose of this sub-section has been to show that *if* candidates' performances vary from one occasion to another, and lower the examination's validity, this condition is already covered by the condition of Question-Relevance. But how can it be discovered to what extent this variability occurs–if it occurs at all? This question is of some importance, because the smaller the variability the greater in this respect will be the examination's validity, and the greater will be the confidence with which results can be applied. To answer this question we now consider two other issues commonly raised in connection with estimates of validity. As we shall see, however, the question is not an easy one.

Test-retest reliability

This name refers to the applying of the same test, to the same group of candidates, on two occasions, the reliability of the test being indicated by the degree of correspondence between the two sets of results.

By itself, a low degree of correspondence does not indicate intra-examinee variability–because the low correspondence could have arisen in other ways: the marking might have changed from the one occasion to the other, or the marks might have been combined in different proportions. If, however, these latter inconsistencies have been eliminated, imperfect correspondence between the two sets of results does not necessarily indicate the kind of intra-examinee variability described in the preceding section. The issue there, it will be recalled, was that the results might have been different had the examination been held at another time *instead*; whereas the issue now is that the results may be different if the examination is held at another time *as well*. The two cases are by no means the same; and it could be pointed out that the results on the second of the two actual occasions might well have been otherwise had the candidates not already taken the same examination before. As Ebel (1965) notes, in a somewhat critical comment on the test-retest procedure, the second set of scores may be affected by the candidates' recollections of the first testing; and they may even have discussed the questions in the meantime. Admittedly, one would not expect to find this sort of effect if the interval between the two testings were a long one–the recollections would have faded, and so on; but in a long interval one would not expect constancy either–in the kinds of performance with which examinations are usually concerned. One would expect the students to have learned more, and not necessarily all of them to the same extent.

The conclusion would seem to be, then, that if the test-retest procedure produces a very *high* degree of correspondence over a short period of time, there is no reason to suppose any significant variation in each candidate's performance, and therefore no reason to suppose that validity is lowered significantly in this respect. And yet, if there is a quite *moderate* degree of correspondence, this is no reason to suppose there *has* been any significant variation, for the low correspondence could be attributed, in part at least, to the effects of the previous testing.

In order to get round that latter possibility, another sort of procedure is sometimes used. It is described in the following subsection.

Alternate-form reliability

This refers to the procedure of using, on the second occasion, not exactly the same test but another test equivalent to the first. Even here there may be some effects from the previous testing, because equivalent tests are somewhat similar, but the effects are likely to be less. The use of the alternate form nevertheless raises another problem: How do we know that the two forms of test are in fact 'equivalent'? If the correspondence between the two sets of results is not very high, the low correspondence might be attributable to intra-examinee variability, but it might be attributable instead, or in addition, to the two forms asking for different performances.

Here also a very high degree of correspondence might reasonably be interpreted to mean that there was very little variation in each candidate *and* that the two forms of test were virtually equivalent; and yet, if the correspondence were rather low, we should not be able to deduce, with confidence, that the sorts of performance asked for in the first test were subject to performance-fluctuation; the deduction might be, equally properly, that the two forms of test were not equivalent after all.

Just in case the discussions of test-retest reliability and alternate-form reliability may have distracted attention from the main argument, we should emphasise that the *basic* issue concerning us at present is not what happens when the same test, or an allegedly equivalent test, is used on a subsequent occasion, but rather the validity of a *single* examination. The procedures referred to by 'test-retest' and 'alternate-form' are but means of estimating how valid a single examination is. And, as we have suggested, the information they provide may not always be very useful. If the correspondence, in either case, turns out to be very *high*, we may infer that the performances asked for in the initial test are *not liable* to much variation; but if the correspondence is somewhat *low*, we cannot confidently infer that the performances *are liable* to much variation. For the present it is enough to suggest that even if intra-examinee variability does lower validity, the condition of Question-Relevance would seem (as we have just argued) to embrace the possibility.

Discrimination

This refers to the extent to which the scores for one item (such as a question) correspond with the results of the examination as a whole. It will probably be apparent, however, that this is a special case of the 'split' procedure–special, in that it is not split-half, or 'split 50/50%', but (say) 'split 99/1%', and that the comments made about the split-half procedure apply here also.

Precision

Though the issue is not customarily referred to by this term, we intend it to refer to the extent to which an examination 'separates out' the candidates, distinguishes them one from another. In this sense, an examination in which nearly all the candidates scored the same mark would have very low precision; one in which each candidate had a mark peculiar to himself (no marks being shared) would have high precision. If, then, an examination's purpose required high precision, its validity would be lowered to the extent that precision was low. But this does not require an additional condition of validity, for it is already covered by the 'list of required performances' presupposed by the condition of Question-Relevance. If high precision is required, the *performances* asked for must be such that their measures will constitute highly precise results. One might achieve this by asking a very large *number* of questions–each question probably calling for a quite small performance or sub-performance. In whatever way the condition might be fulfilled, however, the condition itself is already covered by the conditions already described.

Difficulty

Some purposes require that the questions must be of a certain degree (or of certain degrees) of difficulty, but this means that the *performances* required must be of a certain kind–perhaps such that only about ten per cent of the candidates will be able to cope, and so this case too is already covered.

We cannot pretend to have taken into account all possible issues customarily associated with validity, but the above discussion of a fairly wide selection of issues would seem to suggest that the four conditions described in this chapter are, together, both necessary and sufficient for maximum validity. The practical problem is, of course, how to fulfil these conditions. This problem is tackled in later chapters, the chapters dealing with technique. Between this chapter and these, however, we must look at something else. This chapter has described four conditions which are 'general', in the sense that they must be met if *any* examination is to fulfil its purpose. But one might expect that the *ways* in which these conditions would have to be met (that is, the *techniques* of examining) would vary somewhat from one purpose to another. Before we look at techniques, therefore, we should consider what purposes examinations are likely to be asked to fulfil. We do this in the next chapter.

3 Purposes of examining

'Classes' of purpose

Descriptions of purposes of examining have the aim of indicating what techniques will be necessary to fulfil the conditions of validity for each purpose–the techniques for one purpose not necessarily being the same as those for another. If, however, purposes were so envisaged that every examination could be said to have a purpose peculiar to itself, the descriptions of technique would be so numerous as to be unmanageable. But specific purposes can be classified–in such a way that all the purposes within one class can be served by similar techniques. Classification of purposes will therefore reduce the number of techniques to be described.

If we are to have one set of techniques for each class of purpose, the smaller the number of classes we form the fewer the sets of techniques we shall need to describe; but at the same time the wider and more heterogeneous each class will be, and so the less precise will be our descriptions of techniques for it. Conversely, the more precisely each set of techniques has to be described, the larger must be the number of classes of purpose and the number of technique-descriptions required. Since neither of these extremes is to be recommended, we adopt an intermediate position. First we shall distinguish two very broad classes of purpose, referred to here as 'content purposes' and 'criterion purposes'–the choice of names being explained in a moment. But since each of these two broad classes will require a variety of techniques, we shall then subdivide them. These subdivisions can be extrapolated to whatever further divisions may be required.

Content purposes and criterion purposes

Some purposes of examining are expressed solely in terms of the performances to be measured–such as to measure the candidates' spelling. Since these performances constitute the 'content' of the examination (and for another reason to be mentioned), these purposes will be called 'content purposes'. Of course, every examination has the purpose of producing measures of performance, but the point here is that some purposes of examining are expressed *only* in terms of the *performances*, and nothing is specified about the measures of them.

In contrast, some purposes express a use to which the produced measures are to be applied–such as to select or to predict. Their actual usefulness may depend, however, upon the extent to which the measures satisfy some *criterion* the intended use presupposes. If, for instance, half the candidates scored nothing, it would be impossible to select the bottom ten per cent of them– a purpose presupposing a 'precision' criterion. If the measures were to be used to predict subsequent academic success, they would be useful to the extent that they corresponded with the academic measures they were to predict. That purpose presupposes a criterion consisting of these later marks. In general, in so far as the purpose expressed in terms of the measures' use necessitates the production of measures to meet some criterion (and for another reason to be mentioned), such a purpose will be referred to as a 'criterion purpose'.

Of course, some alleged 'uses' of examination marks may not presuppose criteria at all. If the candidates' marks are 'used' only in their being entered on filing cards–which scarcely constitutes a 'use' at all–a criterion is not involved; which is why we were cautious enough to say that certain purposes would be called 'criterion purposes' *in so far as* they presupposed some criterion.

The two classes of purposes, however, are not mutually exclusive, for many examinations will have to fulfil both. Measures of performance cannot be used until they have been obtained, and they can be obtained only by means of an examination with a specified performance-content. Fulfilment of a criterion purpose therefore presupposes the prior fulfilment of a content purpose. Conversely, it would be pointless to measure performances if the measures were not to be used in some way– though, as we noted, some alleged 'uses' may not presuppose criteria. (Presumably one might argue that if a use does not pre-suppose some criterion it is not much of a use!) Many examin-ations will nevertheless have to fulfil both a content and a criterion purpose.

The distinction has a bearing on validity, because results which were highly valid for a stated content purpose (such as to measure candidates' adding of vulgar fractions) might have low validity for a criterion purpose (such as to predict performance in calculus). In fact, this classification is already implicit in current testing-theory, which distinguishes *content validity* from *criterion-related validity*.* Our terms, 'content *purpose*' and 'criterion *purpose*' may be novel, but in addition to the reasons already given, the concepts they signify were assigned these names in order to make explicit the links with content and criterion-related *validity*. Content validity is validity for a content purpose; criterion-related validity is validity for a criterion purpose. We should say that 'content validity' and 'criterion-related validity' are not customarily defined in this way, but our reference to content purposes and criterion purposes would seem to focus attention on, and make less ambiguous what the two 'validity' terms mean.

In particular, we need not suppose that there are two different sorts of validity, as such. 'Validity' was defined (p. 4) as the extent to which an examination's results are in accord with its purpose, and that definition still stands. The distinction relates to different classes of *purpose* in respect of which validity (one and the same validity) has to be judged; and as is now shown, the distinction has two practical implications.

The first relates to the 'universe' (list) of performances to be sampled. For maximum content validity the examiner is free to specify whatever universe he chooses. For example, he might wish to measure the performances comprising the content of a certain course of study. These performances would constitute the universe, and no matter how poorly their measures predicted some subsequent performances, or no matter how imprecise the distri-bution of marks turned out to be, in this respect the results of the examination would be valid to the extent that the questions

* See the APA Bulletin (1966), and Gronlund (1968a).

called for a representative sample of course-performances–no matter what these performances might be.*

If, however, the specified performances were such that nearly all the candidates scored full marks, the results which were (suppose) highly valid for the content purpose would be of very low validity for a purpose requiring discrimination among the best candidates. For such a purpose the universe would have to contain performances producing much more precise measures. But since (in our example) such performances were not part of the study, the two purposes would be in conflict. The main point of the example, however, is that for maximum *criterion-related* validity the examiner is *not* free to choose the universe of performances as he wishes; it must comprise the performances implied by the criterion.

The second practical implication of the distinction between content and criterion purposes relates to the role of the *measures* the examination produces. As we have just seen, criterion purposes impose restrictions on the constitution of the universe of performances to be sampled, such as that the performances must produce measures of a certain degree of precision. But whether the measures produced by the examination *do* have the necessary degree of precision can be discovered only by inspection of the measures themselves–by observing the extent to which marks are shared in the crucial areas. Likewise, the validity of an allegedly predictive examination can be tested only by inspection of the measures it produces, in order to discover whether they do in fact correspond closely enough with the measures to be predicted. In general, in order to assess the *validity* of an examination with a criterion purpose the examiner must analyse the actual measures, the marks, the examination has produced. In contrast, when the examination has only a content purpose, inspection of the mere marks produced tells us nothing at all about the examination's validity, for the simple reason that a purely content purpose specifies no criterion the measures have to meet, and so there is nothing by which the measures, the marks themselves, can be

---

* According to Ebel (1965), content validity is concerned with the adequacy of sampling of a specified universe of content. To underline our point we might say '*any* specified universe of content'.

judged even if we choose to analyse them. Since the inspection of marks gives no indication of whether the relevant performances have been measured, the validity of an examination with a content purpose must be tested by inspection of its content, not of its marks.[12]

Content purposes

It would be possible to divide the broad class of Content Purposes into smaller classes characterised by 'subject'–such as English, Mathematics, French, and so forth; but such a system of classification would not be very profitable, because essentially the same techniques (setting questions, marking answers, and so on) apply to all subjects. Another possible system classifies in terms of the 'mental processes' called for–such as Understanding, Comprehending, Recalling, Recognising, Applying, Organising, Analysing, Synthesising, Evaluating.* That system would seem to be more profitable, in that the recalling of facts (for instance) is common to many different subjects. Likewise, in so far as there is a unique process of Understanding, it may be required no matter what the subject is. For these reasons we shall refer to such classes throughout later chapters, as when we devote a section to testing for understanding by means of multiple-choice questions. For another reason given in a much later chapter (p. 245), however, we believe that the 'mental process' system of classification has quite serious limitations, and that once the examiner has grasped the basic principles of examining he need not be unduly concerned to find *any* system of classifying content purposes. So long as he has specified unambiguously the particular performances the examination's purpose requires, he can set his questions, mark the answers, combine marks where necessary, and so forth, in accordance with the basic conditions of validity.

Criterion purposes, however, are in a different case, and these are considered in more detail in the following section.

---

* For detailed accounts of classifications of this kind see, for example, Bloom (1956) and Mager (1962).

Criterion purposes

The broad class of Criterion Purposes also is divisible into smaller classes, and the following short list would seem to cover most of the classes of use to which examination results are applied.*

To ascertain whether a specified standard has been reached.
To select a given number of candidates.
To test the efficiency of the teaching.
To indicate to the student how he is progressing.
To evaluate each candidate's particular merit.
To predict each candidate's subsequent performance.

Examinations may of course have purposes other than those just listed. One very useful function of examinations is to discover the extent to which a course's objectives are being achieved, but as a previous example illustrated (p. 30ff.), this is a *content* purpose, not a criterion one. Since an examination measures performance, and nothing but performance, it will measure the extent to which a course's objectives are being achieved only in so far as these objectives have been expressed in terms of performance. The 'list' of required performances will therefore be comprised of the performances which are the course's objectives, and the questions will be directives to give a representative sample of them. Of course, there would be little point in obtaining measures of the extent to which a course's objectives were being achieved unless these measures were subsequently to be used in one way or another—that is, for a *criterion* purpose; but the purpose of measuring the extent is *itself* a *content* purpose, and so does not appear in our list.

Other possible purposes have been omitted for other reasons. Examinations are sometimes used as incentives to study, and there can be no doubt that this function is often fulfilled. Strictly, however, the incentive is provided (when provided at all) not by the examination as such but an examination in prospect, and the *subsequent* use of examinations as incentives will depend to a large extent on the motivational effects of the previous *results*. Candidates whose results are poor, however, may be

* For comparison see, for instance, Vernon (1941) and Morris (1961).

motivated to give up; and some candidates whose results are good may be motivated to take it easy thereafter. To overcome difficulties of this kind the intrinsic rules of examining would almost certainly have to be broken, so that an examination specifically *designed* as an incentive would not properly be an examination at all. In an account concerned with the maximising of examinations' validity, therefore, the purpose of providing an incentive cannot be included. This does not mean, of course, that examinations never serve as incentives at all.

For a similar reason, the purpose of Diagnosis has been omitted also. An examination with a wide range of very precise questions can certainly discover candidates' particular weaknesses, but an examination designed to discover not only *what* mistakes were made but also *how* or *why* they were made is another matter, and a discussion of the *design* of an examination with these latter purposes would be beyond the intentions of the present account. If, however, we are content to discover *what* performances are lacking in a candidate's repertoire, that purpose can be fulfilled by *any* examination which reaches a high degree of fulfilment of the condition of Question-Relevance–that is, uses a highly representative sample of performances. We omit it from the list of criterion purposes, however, because no external criterion is involved.

It cannot be pretended that the above short list is exhaustive, but it seems likely that other criterion purposes *may* be fitted into it, either by changing their names or by combining two or more of the purposes listed, and *some* other suggested purposes will almost certainly turn out to be particular cases falling within one of the listed classes. The purpose of allocating candidates to certain categories or 'bands', for instance, is an instance of the purpose of ascertaining whether a specified standard has been reached–as noted in the next section. We now consider briefly each of the purposes listed, noting their implications for technique.

To ascertain whether a specified standard has been reached

This purpose embraces all examinations in which candidates have to be 'passed' or 'failed', or in which Merits, Distinctions, and the like are to be awarded, or in which candidates are to be allocated to certain categories, bands, and so on, because all these presuppose that some specified standard has to be reached.

As will be shown later, standards can be seen as of two kinds. The standard may be derived from the measures actually obtained, as when all candidates in the bottom ten per cent of the group are rejected. Such evaluation is known as 'norm-referenced'. In contrast, the standard may be independent of the obtained measures–what is sometimes called an 'absolute' standard, and here the evaluation is 'criterion-referenced'. That distinction will be exploited in later chapters. All we need note now is that in either case the candidate's mark will have to be *compared* with the standard, no matter what the standard may be, and that this has a practical application.

For one thing, the candidates' marks must *be* comparable with the standard, in the sense described in Chapter Two (p. 8). In addition, the results of the examination must be as *precise* as the standard presupposes. If the standard were whatever mark cut off the top ten per cent of candidates, the results must be precise enough to allow the top ten per cent to be cut off. That standard could not be used if half the candidates scored the same top mark. Again, if the standard were to be 60 per cent, meaning 60 and not either 59 or 61 per cent, the results would have to be precise enough to allow of that distinction's being made. It would not matter, of course, if a great deal of mark-sharing occurred well below or well above 60 per cent, or (referring to our first example) if the bottom 75 per cent of candidates were indistinguishable one from another. Strictly, then, the same degree of precision may not be required throughout the whole range of results; it will be enough to have the requisite degree of precision in the area around the standard. As will appear later, however, it is no easy matter to design an examination so as to get high precision only at some predetermined place; and some examinations may involve several different standards– as when candidates have to be allocated to several 'bands'; and so in practice it is sometimes simpler to strive for maximum precision for the results in general.

This purpose, then, presupposes a *precision* criterion–not necessarily the maximum possible precision, but precision at *least* as fine as the criterion implies. The techniques to be used for this purpose must therefore be such as to produce it.

To select a given number of candidates

This purpose also presupposes a precision criterion, for the simple reason that it implies the fulfilment of the purpose we have just been discussing. To select is, in fact, to separate out groups of candidates who have been distinguished by being at or above, and below, some specified standard. To select the top 10 per cent of candidates is but a simple practical consequence of having first discovered that top 10 per cent by reference to the mark ('standard') cutting them off from the remaining 90 per cent. Similarly for selecting candidates who score 60 per cent or more. In connection with this present purpose, a point already made is sometimes expressed in another way. If more than the number of candidates (at the top) to be selected score the same top mark, the examination is said to have a too low 'ceiling'. Selecting the top

candidate of 8 would be impossible if 3 candidates scored the maximum possible mark. A different set of question might have allowed these high-level candidates to stretch themselves so as to reveal differences in their statures. Of course, these 3 top candidates might well turn out to be equal no matter how finely we measured them; but it is up to the examiner to find out—by designing an examination with the maximum possible precision. Here again, however, high precision is needed only in the area around the standard on which selection is based.

    Essentially the same point holds good for selection (if that is the right word) at the *lower* end of the scale of ability–perhaps for demotion, extra tuition, or the like. In this case it would not matter if many candidates hit the ceiling, so long as the results were sufficiently precise in the area round the standard. This requirement would not be met if too many weak candidates found the questions so heavy that they could not lift any marks at all. For this aspect of selection, therefore, the techniques of

examining would have to produce, at the lower end of the scale, results at least as precise as the standard presupposed.

Many examinations must, of course, select at both ends, and in that case precision would be required at both ends, though it would not matter if many of the candidates near the middle shared the same marks.

To test the efficiency of the teaching

This purpose usually implies that an examination has to be taken, not by the teachers themselves, but by their students—what the students have learned being used as an indication of their teacher's efficiency. The purpose can refer, of course, not only to teachers as such but also to teaching materials, teaching methods, devices, and so on, such as programmed learning or the Initial Teaching Alphabet.

Even with this wide connotation, however, this purpose may mean two different things. The teaching, whether by a teacher or by some kind of apparatus, might be said to be 'efficient' if the examination showed that the candidates (or some specified percentage of them) had reached some specified standard. In this case, the purpose of testing the efficiency of the teaching is an instance of the purpose we first discussed. To test efficiency of teaching by reference to an arbitrary standard could nevertheless be unrealistic: there would be little practical value in finding that a certain method of teaching failed to produce results up to the specified standard if, in fact, all other known methods were even worse. Nor would it be sensible to recommend a teaching device on the ground that the results were above the standard if, in fact, other known devices produced results which were even better. For that reason the testing of the efficiency of teaching customarily involves the *comparison* of one mode of teaching (or perhaps one teacher) with another. For example, the effects of programmed learning would be compared with the effects of more traditional practices.

This more realistic procedure nevertheless calls for a carefully designed experiment. Obviously, one cannot try out the competing instructional methods on the same pupils, because it would be impossible to find out what they might have learned from either by itself. But if different groups of pupils are to be used, it would have to be ensured that these groups were of comparable ability to start with; and one would require to use also a third group who were not taught by either method, or were not taught at all–a so-called 'control group'. This is, of course, but the sketchiest outline of the experiment which would be required to fulfil the purpose; but it will be clear that it would involve procedures going far beyond what is customarily called an 'examination', and that an adequate account would go far beyond the scope of this book. We shall therefore exclude this purpose from our subsequent discussions. All we need note is that the examinations which form *part* of the experiment will have to conform to the conditions of validity which apply to all examinations.

To indicate to the student how he is progressing

No matter the particular form in which a student's progress is to be indicated, *any* indication of progress must involve a standard of some sort with which his performance can be compared. It might be a predetermined mark, such as 60 per cent; it might be a standard presupposing comparison with other students ('He is doing very well; he was the best student of his year!'); or it might be the student's own mark in a previous examination. This purpose therefore does not introduce a new criterion, but presupposes whatever degree of *precision* the standard in question implies.

To evaluate each candidate's particular merit

There are occasions when one wishes to know not merely that a candidate has done 'quite well', or was 'rather below average', or gave a 'poor performance', but *exactly* how good he was. In the extreme case each candidate would have a measure shared by no one else. Just what 'merit' means will be discussed in a later chapter, but the inclusion of the word 'particular' in the statement of this purpose is intended to imply the need of 'exactness' of measurement. If, then, the ideal is that *each* candidate should have his *unique* measure, the sharing of marks will have to be at a minimum, and so precision will have to be at a maximum. In this case it will not be sufficient to have high precision at only some parts of the scale of ability, as for other purposes we have already considered; here we shall need maximum precision throughout the whole range, and so the techniques will have to be designed accordingly.

To predict each candidate's subsequent performance

Although only a few examinations may be set with the explicit purpose of prediction, some of the purposes already mentioned presuppose it. For example, while the assigning of candidates to different categories is of course based upon their performances in the present examination, yet if these categories are made the basis of selection for higher education or employment it is assumed that candidates in the higher categories will continue to be superior.

Whether the purpose of prediction is implicit or explicit, however, the design of a predictive examination raises technical problems taking it beyond the intended scope of the present account, and so this purpose will not be discussed further.

This chapter has described the main classes of purpose examinations are likely to be asked to fulfil. The succeeding chapters describe techniques these different purposes require. We begin with techniques for criterion purposes, because while content purposes have to be *fulfilled* before criterion purposes, it would be shortsighted to *describe* techniques which would be adequate for an examination's content purpose but might have to be changed to be adequate for its ulterior criterion purpose. Further, of the techniques required for criterion purposes the first to be described will be techniques of analysing the examination's results–for two reasons. First, since criterion purposes demand that the measures produced should have a form in accord with some criterion (such as precision), the techniques of setting questions, marking answers, and so on, must be designed to produce measures having the requisite form, and so the examiner must know, at the outset, what form is required. That is to say, his designing of the techniques which come early in the business of examining must be based upon his foreknowledge of what is required at the end. Second, and in accord with the same basic principle, if certain criterion purposes are to be fulfilled, certain characteristics of the results will have to be made use of, and so here again the examiner must be familiar with the crucial characteristics examination results display. The next chapter, therefore, is concerned with the analysis of examination results so as to make explicit what the basic characteristics of results are.

4   Characteristics of examination results

The frequency distribution

Examination results cannot be analysed if each candidate's mark is entered only on his own script; the marks must be organised in some way, and customarily they are gathered together in a 'frequency distribution'–or 'distribution' for short–which is essentially a table showing how many candidates obtained each mark. It is compiled as follows. (Consult Table 1.)

First, the examiner enters in a column all possible marks in descending order of magnitude, entering each mark only once. Thus, if the maximum possible mark were 20, and the minimum possible were 0, he would enter 20 at the top of the column, then 19, then 18, and so on, as in the left-hand column of Table I. (If he already knew what was the highest *obtained* mark, and the lowest *obtained* mark, in our example 19 and 6 respectively, he could omit the marks of 20, 5, 4, 3, 2, 1, and 0, for these will not be used anyway.)

Second, opposite each mark in the 'Marks' column which he has just made he enters a tally for each candidate who scored that mark. The scripts need not be pre-arranged for this. If the script which happened to be at the top of the bundle showed the mark 14, the examiner would enter a tally opposite 14, and continue until every candidate had his tally entered. For convenience it is customary for each fifth tally to be drawn across the preceding four, to make a 'gate', so that each 'gate' is five tallies. When this is done the examiner will have a lay-out as in Table I. The column of tallies is headed 'frequency' because it shows the frequency (number of candidates) with which each mark was obtained.

Finally, in a third column may be entered an Arabic figure corresponding with the number of tallies for each mark. This also is shown in Table I. The sum of the numbers in that column (or the total number of tallies) should of course be the number of scripts, and it is sensible to check that this is so, for with large numbers of scripts it is easy to omit one or more, or to enter the same candidate's mark twice.

TABLE I

Marks		Frequency
20		
19	/	1
18	//	2
17	///	3
16	//	2
15	⟍⟍	5
14	⟍⟍ //	7
13	////	4
12	⟍⟍ /	6
11	///	3
10	////	4
9	//	2
8		
7	//	2
6	/	1
5		
4		
3		
2		
1		
0		
Total		42

If the marks are in the form of letters instead of figures, the Marks column will have letters (such as A, B, C, D, etc.) but the general procedure is the same.

A distribution of the kind just described contains a great

deal of information, but since it may not be obvious that it does we must now consider what information can be abstracted from it. In other words, what characteristics do distributions of marks reveal? In what respects may one frequency distribution differ from another? Three basic characteristics are now described– Central Tendency, Scatter and Shape.

Central tendency–mean, median and mode

For many purposes it is necessary to know how 'high' the marks of the candidates are–not the marks of individual candidates but the marks of the group as a whole. If a group of candidates is given the same examination after a period of time to find out whether they have progressed, we should need to know whether the marks in general were now higher. Or we might wish to know whether the boys, in general, had done better than the girls. And so on. In cases like these we need a measure of the 'highness' of the group's marks, though as these same examples illustrate, we need not quibble about 'How high is high?', because in practice the matter is one of *comparison*: what is needed is a comparison of measures of 'highness', obtained from two frequency distributions.

Consider the two distributions shown in Tables II and III below. Table II is essentially the same as Table I, though now we have made use of the conventional symbol for a mark, namely X, and the conventional symbol for frequency, namely f. The columns previously headed 'Marks' and 'Frequency', therefore, are now headed 'X' and 'f'. We have also added a fourth column, headed 'fX', which will be explained in a moment.

Even a quick glance at the tallies indicates that the marks in Table II are, in general, higher than the marks in Table III. True, *some* of the marks in Table II are *lower* than *some* of the marks in Table III, but it is clear that, overall, the marks of Table II are higher. But exactly how *much* higher?

Since the aim here is to compare, not individual marks, but the two groups of marks, the marks as a whole, we could add all the marks in Table II, add all the marks in Table III, and compare the two totals. To find these totals, however, we do not simply add 19 and 18 and 17, and so on, because some of these marks were obtained more than once. We should have to add 19 and two 18's, three 17's, two 16's, and so on. It is to simplify this

	TABLE II				TABLE III		
X		f	fX	X		f	fX
20				20			
19	I	1	19	19			
18	II	2	36	18			
17	III	3	51	17			
16	II	2	32	16			
15	THL	5	75	15	I	1	15
14	THL II	7	98	14	I	1	14
13	IIII	4	52	13	II	2	26
12	THL I	6	72	12			
11	III	3	33	11	III	3	33
10	IIII	4	40	10	III	3	30
9	II	2	18	9	IIII	4	36
8				8	III	3	24
7	II	2	14	7	THL I	6	42
6	I	1	6	6	II	2	12
5				5	IIII	4	20
4				4	THL	5	20
3				3	THL II	7	21
2				2			
1				1	I	1	1
0				0			
		42	546			42	294
	$\therefore M = 13$				$\therefore M = 7$		

addition that the fourth column, the fX column, has been included. Each entry in the fX column is the product of X and the corresponding frequency. Since seven candidates scored 14, for instance, the total has to include not 14, but seven 14's, and so opposite the mark of 14 there appears, in the fX column, the figure 98. The grand total of marks in a distribution, therefore, is the total of the fX column. As the Tables show, these totals are respectively 546 and 294. As was to be expected from our observation of the two tally-patterns, the total in Table II is the higher.

Now in our particular example it was legitimate to compare the two totals in this way because each distribution had the same number of candidates, namely forty-two. But, of course, the total of the marks in a distribution depends not only upon the magnitudes of the marks themselves but also upon the number of marks there are; and if one distribution had more candidates than another, the comparison of totals to indicate overall *highness* of the marks would be misleading. We should have to eliminate from the difference in totals whatever difference was accounted for by the difference in the numbers of candidates; and this we could do by dividing each total by the number of candidates contributing to it. If we do this with the totals in our example we arrive at the figures of 13 and 7, instead of 546 and 294.

The number arrived at by dividing the total by the number of candidates is, of course, that familiar quantity the 'average', but we introduced it in this particular way to indicate *why* it is appropriate to compare averages when we want to compare highness overall.

The term 'average' is nevertheless ambiguous, as will be noted in a moment, and strictly we ought to refer to the quantity we have been talking about as the Arithmetic Mean. For convenience, however, we shall refer to it simply as the Mean – because we shall not be using any other sort of Mean.

Now although it was not introduced as such, the Mean is in fact the 'centre of gravity' of the marks, as the marks of Table II can illustrate. Imagine a seesaw thirteen units long, the mark of 6 at one end and the mark 19 at the other, these being the extreme marks of the distribution, and that the candidates were piled up at the marks they obtained. Then by applying the Law of Moments we find that the seesaw would balance on the mark of 13 – what we found was the Mean of the distribution.

When the overall magnitude of the marks of a group is represented by its Mean, then, it is being represented by what is,

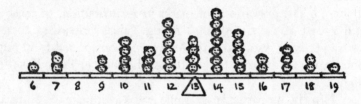

in effect, the 'centre' of the distribution. This concept of the 'centre' of a distribution can nevertheless be exploited in another way, for there is another sort of centre, called the Median, which is not the centre of *gravity* of the marks, but the central *mark*. In illustration of the difference consider Table IV. In this example the number of candidates (N) is 25, the sum of the fX column is 425, and so the Mean (M) is 17.

The middle *mark*, however, is not 17. Altogether there are twenty-five marks, and so when these are arranged, as they are in a frequency distribution, in descending order of magnitude, the middle mark will be the thirteenth mark from the bottom of the list. If, now, we count up to the thirteenth mark, using the frequency column, we find that the thirteenth mark from the bottom is one of the four marks of 18. The middle mark is therefore 18, and so the mark of 18 is the Median in this case.

In this example the Mean and Median have somewhat different values, 17 and 18 respectively. This should not be taken to suggest, however, that the Median is no more than a rough estimate of the Mean. The Mean is the better known measure, but the Median is a perfectly respectable measure existing in its own right, and (as we shall see) on occasion is more useful than the Mean. Sometimes (when the distribution is symmetrical) the Mean and Median will have the same numerical value; sometimes (when the distribution is asymmetrical) they will be different.

The simplest way to find the value of the Median is to add 1 to the number of candidates (in our example 25+1), divide by 2 (in this case giving 13), count up that number of tallies, and note the value of the corresponding mark. If the number of candidates is an even number, say 42, then N+1 divided by 2 will of course have a '$\frac{1}{2}$', in this case $21\frac{1}{2}$. In such cases the Median will be the value of the mark (an imaginary mark) halfway between the

21st and 22nd mark from the bottom of the list. Very often, however, marks will be shared at and around the middle, and the *two* middle marks are likely to be the same, and so the need to interpolate may not arise.[13]

TABLE IV

X		f	fX
20	̷H̷L̷ /	6	120
19	̷H̷L̷ /	6	114
18	////	4	72
17	//	2	34
16	/	1	16
15	/	1	15
14			
13	/	1	13
12	/	1	12
11			
10	//	2	20
9	/	1	9
8			
7			
6			
5			
4			
3			
2			
1			
0			

$$25 \quad 425$$
$$. M = 17$$

The two measures, Mean and Median, are customarily regarded as measures of a distribution's 'central tendency'. A third measure, the Mode, belongs to the same class. It is the most fashionable mark in the distribution–that is, the mark with the highest frequency. Thus, in the distribution in Table II (p. 44) the Mode is 14; in Table III it is 3. The Mode is a less useful measure than the Mean or Median, but we shall refer to it from time to time.

Scatter, spread or dispersion

Although the 'average' (Mean or Median) is probably the best known characteristic of a distribution of marks, there is another characteristic which in many respects is at least as important.

This second characteristic is the extent to which the marks of a distribution are spread out. In some distributions the marks are closely clustered together, often with a good deal of sharing of marks; in other distributions the marks are 'thinned out', the marks in general having low frequencies. This characteristic is known as Scatter, Spread or Dispersion. Since these three terms are synonymous it does not matter which one we use.

In illustration consider the distributions in Tables V and VI below. Note that the two distributions have equal Means, namely 11. Also, both distributions are symmetrical, and in each case the Mean has the same value as the Median and the Mode. Distribution VI, however, patently has a wider spread of marks, though the *number* of marks is 42 in each case.

Just as it is necessary to have a measure of Central Tendency, such as the Mean or Median, it is necessary also to have a measure of Scatter, and three such measures are now described.

The range

An obvious aspect of Distribution VI's patently greater scatter is that its top mark and its bottom mark are farther apart than are the top and bottom marks in Distribution V. We might therefore quantify their scatters by noting the difference between the highest and lowest marks in each distribution. The figure for Distribution V would then be 6 (from 14−8), and for Distribution VI would be 16 (from 19−3). This measure, namely the difference between the highest and the lowest mark, is known as the Range. It will be clear that this difference in Ranges, namely 16 as compared with 6, is of such a magnitude as to reflect a difference in scatter apparent from observation of the tally-patterns. But how accurately does it do so?

The characteristics we are interested in here are characteristics of a distribution as a *whole*; and a serious objection to the Range as

TABLE V			TABLE VI	
X	f		X	f
20			20	
19			19	I
18			18	
17			17	
16			16	II
15			15	II
14	II		14	II
13	III		13	IIII
12	ЖН III		12	ЖН I
11	ЖН ЖН ЖН I		11	ЖН III
10	ЖН III		10	ЖН I
9	III		9	IIII
8	II		8	II
7			7	II
6			6	II
5			5	
4			4	
3			3	I
2			2	
1			1	
0			0	

a measure of scatter is that it may vary considerably without much change in the scatter of the marks in general, or may remain very much the same even when there is a clear increase or decrease in the scatter of the marks as a whole. Consider again Distribution V. If one of the two top candidates (at 14) had obtained not 14 but 19, and if one of the two bottom candidates (at 8) had obtained not 8 but 3, the Range would have been 16, not 6, and Distributions V and VI would then have had the same measure of scatter, despite Distribution V's obviously having, overall, a much smaller spread of marks. Likewise, looking now at Distribution VI, the Range would remain at 16 even if all but the two extreme candidates shared the same mark of 11.

The standard deviation

Unlike the Range, the Standard Deviation has a value based upon *all* the marks of the distribution. It is customarily symbolised by its initial letters, SD, or by the small Greek letter σ (sigma). It is widely used as a measure of scatter in the standardising of tests and in large-scale examinations, and is invaluable in educational research. Its calculation is nevertheless onerous and time-consuming, and while time and labour will be saved by the use of a calculating machine or computer it is doubtful if most examinations require such a refined measure. For this reason we have relegated it to the Appendix. The *principles* of examining can be described quite adequately without it, and the reader who requires such a fine measure is referred to p. 260. For most examinations what is required is a compromise between the simple but inaccurate measure provided by the Range and the refined but complex measure provided by the Standard Deviation, and such a measure is described in the next section.

The interquartile range

As we noted, the Standard Deviation is a better measure than the Range because the SD involves *all* the marks. But the basic objection to the Range as a measure of scatter is not simply that it involves only two marks but rather that changes in these two marks are not necessarily concomitant with changes in the marks as a whole. The advantage of the SD, then, lies not only in its involving *more* measures, but also in the fact that *by* involving all the measures it is less dependent upon mark changes which are not *representative* of changes in the marks in general. Much of the objection to the Range could be overcome, therefore, not by our using more than two marks, but by our using two marks which were such that changes in them would reflect a *general* change in the distribution's scatter. That requirement would be more likely to be met if we used two marks which were further into the main body of marks. Each of these two marks, being hemmed in by other marks, would be less likely to rise or fall if the marks around it did not, and less likely to remain the same if the marks around it altered. Two marks of this sort are the Lower and Upper Quartiles, and the difference between them, known as the Interquartile Range, is often used as a measure of scatter.

The Quartiles belong to the same statistical 'family' as the Median, and are defined in the same sort of way.[14] When the marks are arranged in descending order, the Lower or First Quartile is the mark *one* quarter of the way *up* the list. It is customarily symbolised as Q_1. The Upper or Third Quartile is the mark *three* quarters of the way *up*, and is symbolised as Q_3. Note that the Quartiles, like the Median, are *marks*. In illustration consider Table VII.

Table VII shows a distribution of 79 marks. To find Q_1, the mark one quarter of the way up, add 1 to 79 and take one quarter of the sum, in this case 20; then count up to the 20th mark from the bottom. In the example the 20th mark up is one of the three marks of 83, and so $Q_1 = 83$.

To find Q_3, the mark three quarters of the way up, add 1 to 79 and take three quarters of the sum, in this example 60; then count up to the 60th mark from the bottom. In the example the 60th mark from the bottom is 92, and so $Q_3 = 92$.

(The Median, it will be recalled, is found by adding 1 to the number of marks and dividing by 2, then noting which mark is that number of marks from the bottom. In this example that mark is the 40th mark up, which is one of the marks of 89, and so here the Median is 89.)

Table VII has a type of column not mentioned before. To simplify and check the finding of the Median and Quartiles (and some other measures described later) it is useful to have a 'cumulative frequency' column. The figure in that column, opposite a mark, shows the number of candidates at *and* below that mark.

TABLE VII

X		f	Cum. f
95	I	1	79
94	IIII	4	78
93	THL I	6	74
. Q_3 = 92	THL THL	10	68
91	THL III	8	58
90	THL III	8	50
∴ Median = 89	IIII	4	42
88	II	2	38
87	IIII	4	36
86	THL	5	32
85	III	3	27
84	II	2	24
∴ Q_1 = 83	III	3	22
82	II	2	19
81	I	1	17
80	II	2	16
79	III	3	14
78	I	1	11
77	II	2	10
76	III	3	8
75	I	1	5
74	I	1	4
73	II	2	3
72	I	1	1

$$N = 79$$

Interquartile Range $= 92 - 83 = 9$

Thus, the marks of 89 and less were obtained by 42 candidates. And, of course, the marks of 95 and less (that is, *all* the marks) were obtained by 79 (all) candidates. (This column is of course derived from the frequency column by successive additions.) If we wanted to know how many candidates scored less than 81, the required number appears opposite 80, namely 16. If we wanted to know below which mark 10 per cent of the candidates fell.

that is, the mark below which 8 candidates fell, we can note that 8 candidates scored 76 or less.

For simplicity of illustration we chose an example in which we arrived at a whole number when we took one quarter, or three quarters, of the number of candidates plus one; but when the number of candidates plus one is not a multiple of 4 (such as $80 + 1 = 81$), the number to which we have to count in the frequency (or cumulative frequency) column will not be a whole number. Thus, in the case of 80 candidates the Lower Quartile would be the value of the mark which was $20\frac{1}{4}$th from the bottom of the list. There is, of course, no such mark; and while we could interpolate, it is usually adequate to take as the Quartile the nearest actual mark.

Now as the distribution increases in scatter, the two Quartiles will move farther and farther apart; and so the difference between the values of the two Quartiles will increase. That is, the Inter-quartile Range will increase as the marks in general increase their spread, and so may be used as a measure of it.

'Shape' – symmetry and skewness

The third characteristic of a distribution may be referred to as its 'shape'. Why this term is appropriate can be seen by our looking at Table VIII below, which shows three different tally-patterns. In Distribution D_1 the marks are 'piled up' at the centre, and thin out towards the ends; in D_2 they are piled up at the top end, and thin out at the lower end in a long 'tail'; in D_3 the marks are piled up at the lower end, and thin out in a long tail at the upper end. (This characteristic *can* be observed by reference to the figures in a frequency column, but if the tallies are tidily entered the 'shape' of the distribution is more easily seen.)

The distribution D_1 is virtually symmetrical. Distributions D_2 and D_3 would be said to be 'skewed'. If the *tail* is at the *higher* end, with clustering at the other end, the distribution is said to be 'positively skewed'; if the tail is at the lower end, with clustering at the other end, the distribution is said to be 'negatively skewed'. (More precisely, if the distribution has a tail, it is positively skewed when the tail is above the Mode, negatively skewed

TABLE VIII

X	D$_1$	D$_2$	D$_3$
20	/	卌 卌 //	/
19	//	卌 卌	
18	/	卌	/
17	///	////	/
16	卌 ////	///	
15	卌 卌 /	/	//
14	卌		/
13	///	/	/
12	//	/	/
11	/	/	/
10	//		///
9	/	/	卌
8	/	/	卌
7		/	卌
6			卌 //
5		/	卌 ///

$$N = 42 \qquad N = 42 \qquad N = 42$$

when the tail is below the Mode.) For our purposes here, *measures* of skewness will not be needed; it will be enough to note that distributions may be symmetrical, or very nearly so, or be positively or negatively skewed.

The 'precision' of examination results

One of our reasons for analysing examination results was that the characteristics (central tendency, scatter and shape) revealed by analysis would have to be made use of in fulfilling certain criterion purposes. How they are used is described in the chapters which follow. The other reason was that certain criterion purposes demanded that the results should conform to certain conditions. In particular, all the criterion purposes we proposed to discuss required that the measures should have a degree of precision—

maximum precision overall or high precision in certain areas. We now consider how precision is manifested.

The simplest, and in many ways the most useful way of assessing the precision of the results is by inspection of the frequency distribution itself. See Table IX below.

TABLE IX

X	f(A)	f(B)
20		I
19		
18		I
17		I
16	I	II
15	III	II
14	卌	II
13	卌 卌	卌
12	卌 III	卌
11	卌 II	IIII
10	I	III
9		II
8	I	I
7		II
6		II
5		II
4		I

$$N = 36 \quad N = 36$$

Since 'precision' refers to the extent to which marks are shared, the marks of Distribution A are obviously much less precise, overall, than the marks of Distribution B. If, then, the purposes of the examinations called for the maximum overall precision, and the two examinations were equally valid in other respects, Examination B would be more valid than Examination A. Even Examination B, however, does not manifest the *maximum* precision, because that would require that each candidate had a mark peculiar to himself: no mark would have a frequency greater than 1. Then how could the precision of either examination be increased?

One solution is to increase the number of questions, but while this *can* increase the results' precision it might well be neither necessary nor sufficient. That statement of the solution is too simple. If the additional questions were so difficult that no one could answer them, the maximum possible mark would rise but the distribution of obtained marks would remain exactly the same as before, and so precision would be unaltered. And if the additional questions were so easy that everyone got them right, every candidate's mark would rise by the same amount, so that the whole pattern of tallies would rise upwards, but *en bloc*, and the amount of mark-sharing would be identical to what it was before these questions were added. The addition of other questions, therefore, may not be *sufficient* to increase precision. Further, if the additional questions were very, but not impossibly difficult, so that only *some* of the *best* candidates could tackle them, precision would be increased only a very little–at the upper end of the distribution. (In this case nearly all the marks would remain as they were, but *some* of the best candidates, who initially shared a mark, would score a higher mark, and so the distribution would thin out a little at the upper end.) Likewise, if very easy questions were added, so that only a few of the poorest candidates would not be able to answer them, precision would increase only a little– at the lower end of the distribution. (In that case, all but the marks of the very poorest candidates would rise, *en bloc*, leaving the degree of precision unaltered in the major part of the distribution; but *some* of the poorest candidates, who previously shared a mark, would gain a higher mark, thus thinning out the marks at the lower end.) If, then, the solution is to add more questions, the maximum effect is likely to be achieved if the questions added are of *moderate* difficulty. (One could, of course, add some easy questions and some difficult ones, to increase precision at both ends; but the maximum *overall* effect is likely to be achieved by the addition of questions of a 50 per cent level of difficulty. See Ebel 1965.)

Just as the addition of other questions may not be *sufficient* for increased precision, so also it may not be *necessary*. One might obtain greater precision by more refined *marking*. For example, even if the answer were to consist of only a very short calculation it might be possible to award 'half a mark' for certain aspects of the calculation despite the calculation's being wrong overall. One might award a 'half mark' if the candidate cited the correct century for an historical event, even if he did not know the exact date; or if he used the appropriate Spanish word, even if its tense were wrong; and so forth. This sort of procedure could increase the precision of the results, in that some candidates would gain half marks here and there while others would not, or would not gain so many, so that (for instance) instead of ten candidates sharing the mark of 43, some would still score 43, some would score $43\frac{1}{2}$, and some (by the accumulation of half marks over several questions) might score even more. And this could apply, of course, throughout the whole range of marks, except for candidates whose marks were already very high. In general, instead of a distribution having a Marks column consisting of whole numbers there would be a distribution involving marks descending by $\frac{1}{2}$. Not only would there be about twice the number of marks *available*; it is extremely likely that a great many of these available marks would also be *obtained*; and so the degree of mark-sharing would be reduced.

In resorting to the latter procedure, however, one would have to conform to the condition of Mark-Relevance. In striving after increased precision there is always the danger of awarding marks for performances which are not relevant to the examination's purpose. But conversely, if these 'part-performances' (awarded half marks) *are* relevant, it will be not only permissible but obligatory to award marks for them. And it is of no technical significance whether the mark to be awarded to each 'small' performance is to be $\frac{1}{2}$, or $\frac{1}{4}$, or 1, so long as these performances are specified (on the 'list') at the outset, rules of marking are established, and the examiner adheres to them throughout. The pattern of the resulting distribution will be exactly the same no matter whether the 'unit' of measurement is $\frac{1}{4}$, $\frac{1}{2}$, 1, or anything else.

Once this point is taken it becomes apparent that, so far as increase in precision is concerned, the procedure of adding more questions and the procedure of marking in a more refined way have exactly the same technical function, namely of increasing the number of *unit-performances*, for it is upon the number of unit-performances that the examination's precision depends. This general statement has to be qualified, however, by the proviso already noted, that it would be pointless to include performances which everyone, or no one, could accomplish; ideally they would be of moderate difficulty if the overall precision of the results is to be as great as possible.

There are limits, of course, to which the examination's precision can be increased in this way. The question paper could be so long that it would become as much a test of the candidates' stamina as of their ability. And the subdivision of performances into smaller units could become so refined as to be absurd. Any increase in precision of this overall kind must be limited by its practicality,* but it is nevertheless likely that many examinations could increase in overall precision without breaching these limits, particularly by increasing the number of unit-performances required.

As we noted, however, some purposes do not demand high precision throughout the whole range; and while the overall precision may not be altered it may be increased at certain parts of the distribution. See Table X below.

Compare Distributions P and Q. We might envisage 'overall precision' as the *average* frequency. If so, Distributions P and Q, having the same number (100) of candidates, have the same overall precision, namely 4·8. But Distribution P clearly has higher precision in the upper half than has the upper half of Distribution Q; though Distribution P's lower half will of course be *less* precise. For any given overall precision, then, we might design the examination so as to maximise precision at one end or the other, depending upon where the examination's purpose required that it should be. For example, instead of having all the questions of moderate degree of difficulty, we could use rather more difficult questions, which would tend to depress the mode and thin out the marks at the upper end; or we could use less difficult questions, or a larger proportion of less difficult questions,

* See Gronlund (1965).

so raising the mode and thinning out the marks at the lower end. The former procedure would be appropriate for selection at the upper end, the latter appropriate for selection at the lower end.

TABLE X

X	f(P)	f(Q)
20	I	I
19		II
18	I	III
17	I	卌
16	I	卌
15		卌
14	I	卌 I
13	II	卌 II
12	I	卌 I
11	III	卌 III
10	IIII	卌 卌
9	卌 I	卌 IIII
8	卌 I	卌 III
7	卌 II	卌
6	卌	IIII
5	卌 III	卌
4	卌 IIII	IIII
3	卌 卌	II
2	卌 卌 II	II
1	卌 卌 III	II
0	卌 IIII	I
	N = 100	*N = 100*

This raises, of course, the practical problem of how the examiner is to know how difficult the questions he has set will in fact turn out to be. Strictly, he cannot know; he can but wait and see—which is no help at all. But from his experience of certain types of candidates, and certain kinds of question, he can make a reasonably good estimate. How this can be done is postponed until a later chapter.

Finally, and briefly, how does precision relate to the three characteristics of central tendency, scatter and shape? In general, the precision of the distribution of marks will be indicated by their standard deviation–or interquartile range. That is to say, in general the greater the *spread* of marks the greater will be their precision–for any given number of candidates. There are nevertheless some provisos. First, if the Marks column shows 'half marks', the increase in precision their use is likely to give will not be reflected by measures of scatter. If the degrees of precision of two distributions of marks are to be compared in terms of their scatters, this will be most clearly done if unit-performances in each are assessed as 1. Second, if for some reason each unit-performance were awarded the mark of 2, the scatter would be twice as great as it would have been had the measure been 1, and the greater standard deviation (or other measure of scatter) would give a false impression. (Because the frequencies of all the odd-number marks, such as 19, would be zero, and the precision would be the same if all the marks were divided by 2.) Third, though related to the first two points, it is sometimes desirable to multiply all the marks by some constant–as in converting them to percentage marks (or in 'scaling' – see pp. 92ff.); but while such multiplication will increase the measure of scatter, the amount of mark-sharing will not alter at all. As for 'differential precision', this will be indicated by the distribution's *shape*. Positive skew will indicate greater precision at the upper end, negative skew will indicate greater precision at the lower end. We need not elaborate on these relationships, however, for as was suggested at the beginning of this section, probably the best way of assessing precision is by inspection of the frequency distribution itself. Such inspection, without detailed reference to scatter and shape, will usually tell us all we need to know.

The main function of this chapter was to describe the three basic characteristics of an examination's results. It also indicated how the form of the distribution of marks could be used to assess the examination's degree of precision, and suggested how precision might be increased. Another reason for analysing results in this way, however, was that some criterion purposes require the actual use of these basic characteristics. In order to assess the merit of a candidate's mark, for instance, we must refer to the central tendency of the marks, and also to their scatter. That this is so, and how these characteristics are used, is shown in the next chapter, which is concerned with the purpose of evaluating candidates' merits.

A mark by itself is meaningless

In this chapter we shall assume that the candidates' marks have already been produced. The problem, then, is to discover not the numerical value of a candidate's mark but how good it is–its 'merit'. And, associated with that problem, how is the merit of any given mark to be reported?

There are two basically different answers to the question of how good a mark is. In this chapter, and the next two, we shall deal with one of these answers; the other answer will be discussed in Chapters Eight and Nine. There is nevertheless one fundamental principle common to both.

The principle is that a mark, by itself, does not indicate merit at all: the merit of any given mark, such as 63, varies with circumstances. We begin by illustrating and justifying that principle, and then making explicit what these varying circumstances are, and how they have to be taken into account.

Although the meaning of the word 'merit' is not commonly made explicit, its common usage seems to lead to general agreement on the following. The mark of 63, when the maximum possible mark is 100, does not necessarily have the same merit when the maximum possible mark is 150. The mark of 63 does not necessarily have the same merit in examinations identical except for the length of time allowed. And the merit of 63 in a very easy examination is not necessarily the same as the merit of 63 in a very difficult examination.

In general, the common concept of Merit would seem to be such that one and the same mark, such as 63, may be said to have different merits in different circumstances. If so, then a mark *by itself* (that is, without reference to circumstances) does not indicate its own degree of merit. In particular, simply by knowing that a candidate's mark is 63 we cannot say how good or how bad it is: in respect of *merit*, a mark by itself has no meaning at all.

'Merit' implies comparison

A fundamental and universal principle of all evaluation is that the thing to be evaluated has to be *compared* with something else which thereby serves as a *standard*. No doubt this is obvious, but in many everyday judgments the point is often forgotten, and the standard of comparison is not made explicit. Indeed, in some instances it might seem very odd if it were. The result of a

comparison will nevertheless depend upon what the standard of comparison is; and in evaluating the merit of a mark it will be necessary to make explicit what the standard of comparison has to be. Thus, in the previous section we suggested that 63 out of 100 might not have the same merit as 63 out of 150. This implies comparison, and so is in general accord with the basic principle: but it implies also that the standard is the maximum possible mark. In contrast, a mark might be judged to be very good in that it was the highest mark in the class. This also implies comparison, but now the standard of comparison consists of the marks the other candidates actually obtained. And if 63 in an easy examination is judged to be less meritorious than 63 in a difficult examination, here again comparison is implied, but the standard is the examination's degree of difficulty. Accordingly, while all the examples quoted illustrate the general principle that merit implies comparison, and so support the statement that a mark by itself cannot indicate merit, it does not follow that any one of these necessarily indicates the *particular* standard appropriate for the evaluation of merit. Many different things might serve as standards of comparison, but what basis of comparison will serve as a standard for the evaluation of *merit*? As we shall see, the answer depends very much on what we take 'merit' to mean.

There is nevertheless another principle which limits the choice of standard–the principle that like must be compared with like. (In judging how tall someone is, we compare his height with some other height–not with weight or income.) For the evaluation of a mark, therefore, the mark must be compared with some other mark or marks. We can be more precise. In establishing the condition of Marking-Consistency we noted (p. 8) that the marks within one series must be comparable one with another, and that unless a set of rules for marking was established it was unlikely that comparability would be achieved. We can have no reason to suppose, then, that marks within one series of measurements will be comparable with marks in some different series.[15] For example, the rules for marking an examination in English composition obviously cannot be the same as the rules for marking an examination in Inorganic Chemistry, and so we have no right to take for granted that 63 in the former is equal to, or greater than, or less than, 63 in the latter. The two marks are not necessarily comparable at all. Nor can we compare the percentage values of the two marks, because the maximum possible mark in the one examination is not necessarily comparable with the maximum possible mark in the other. The evaluation of a mark requires not only that it must be compared with some other mark or marks, but also that the mark or marks with which it is compared must belong to the same series; that is (usually) to the same examination.

There is still room for choice. The principle just cited would be satisfied by the use of the maximum possible mark, or the average mark, or some other candidate's mark, for instance, because all these are marks within the one examination. The problem, then, is to decide which of these marks, or others, within the examination in which the candidate in question obtained his mark, is to be the basis of comparison.

That problem is taken up in the succeeding sections. We conclude this section with a pertinent comment. Probably because comparisons are so often implicit, the explicit statement that merit implies comparison is sometimes translated as 'merit is only relative'–which is, of course, partly true. The derogatory use of 'only' is nevertheless suspect, because if merit *is* relative (as comparison presupposes), it must be relative *to something*; and so merit is not as free-floating as the half-truth suggests, because any judgment has to be anchored on some standard, namely the 'something' with which the comparison is made. Somewhat similarly, the expression 'absolute judgment' may be misleading in so far as it suggests that comparison need not be involved at all. *Every* judgment necessitates a standard of reference, and so the problem is not *whether* a basis of comparison is needed but *what* the standard of comparison is to be. This problem is now examined, several possible standards being discussed in turn.

The maximum possible mark as standard

Use of the maximum possible mark as standard implies that the merit of a mark is determined when it is compared with the maximum possible mark, which in turn implies that (say) 63 out of 100 has the same merit in all examinations. But has it?

The answer depends upon what 'merit' means–a point to which we shall have to return again; but it would seem to be widely agreed that 63 per cent in a very easy examination may not be as good as 63 per cent in a very difficult one. Or, more emphatically, that if the examination were difficult enough, 63 per cent would be a very good mark; if the examination were easy enough, 63 per cent would be a very poor mark. On this view the merit of a given percentage mark is not constant, but depends (*inter alia*, perhaps) upon the examination's degree of difficulty. At any rate, this view indicates that the merit of a given mark is *not* determined by comparison with the maximum possible mark, and therefore that the maximum possible mark is an inappropriate standard for the evaluation of a mark's merit.

It does not follow, however, that the maximum possible mark is *never* an appropriate standard. All that has been suggested is that it is an inappropriate standard for the evaluation of *merit*;

it might well be appropriate for judgments of other kinds (see pp. 122, 221).

The above view has nevertheless had a positive aspect too. It implies that a mark's merit depends upon the examination's degree of difficulty, and therefore that degree of difficulty is itself a possible standard of comparison. This is, perhaps, an unusual view, but since it is presupposed by the common view quoted above, it deserves examination; and as we shall see, it is not as odd as it might first seem.

The examination's degree of difficulty as standard

An examination's degree of difficulty may be attributable to several things–the nature of the questions, the severity or leniency of the marking, the time allowed, and so on. But if difficulty is to be used as a standard it must be assessed; and while difficulty may be *attributable* to several things it is generally accepted that it is *assessable* only by reference to the marks actually obtained. If the same group of candidates takes both Examination I and Examination II, obtaining significantly lower percentage marks in Examination I, it would be said that Examination I was the more difficult for them. If difficulty were to be used as a standard, then, it would consist of the magnitudes of the marks actually obtained in the examination. There are nevertheless two provisos.

First, a purely semantic point: if it is only by reference to the marks actually obtained that difficulty can be assessed, it would be tautologous to say that the marks were low *because* the examination was difficult. We should have to discover what caused the *difficulty*–or the marks to be low, for it is the same thing.

The second proviso is more practical. Since an examination's degree of difficulty is assessable only by reference to obtained marks, the assessed difficulty will be its difficulty for whatever group of candidates obtained these marks. For a different group of candidates, Examination II might have been more difficult than Examination I. There is nothing extraordinarily restrictive about this, for it would be silly to say that an examination was difficult but was not difficult *for* anyone. True, Examination I might be the more difficult for hundreds of candidate-groups, but that would not make its difficulty 'absolute'; it would but extend the size of the group *for* which it was the more difficult of the two. It is therefore pointless to ask whether an examination was 'really' difficult; but on the other hand, any reference to an examination's degree of difficulty should specify the nature of the candidate-group on which the judgment of difficulty has been based.

To return to the main argument. As an examination's difficulty increases, the merit of any given (numerically constant) mark rises. But at the same time the marks in general fall. As the examination's difficulty increases, however, any numerically constant mark, such as 63, will raise its *position* among the obtained marks. As the degree of difficulty increases, then, *two* things rise together: the *merit* of any given mark and that mark's *standing* in the distribution. Any given mark's standing in the distribution is therefore concomitant with its merit, and so may be used to indicate it.

This conclusion in respect of merit is in accord with the common meaning of other evaluative terms, like 'heaviness', and 'tallness'. A 'tall' man is one whose height is outstanding among his fellow men. This may not be immediately obvious. Told that someone is 78 inches high, do we not know at once that he is tall? Probably so, but only in so far as we already know the general run of height-measures for men and can compare 78

inches with them. The point is clear when we are given a measure and are unfamiliar with the general run of measures to which it belongs, such as the birth weights of elephants or the life spans of vampire bats.

Scores on intelligence and attainment tests are evaluated in the same way, namely by reference to their standings among the scores actually obtained.

Evaluation of this kind has been called 'norm-referenced',* norms being scores which summarise and so represent *obtained* scores. If some article were judged to be expensive on the ground that it cost much more than other available articles of the same kind, that evaluation would be norm-referenced, as would also that a family of twelve is 'large' nowadays.

While this section began, then, with the not uncommon view that a mark's merit depends upon the examination's degree of difficulty, it now appears that what that view implies is norm-reference–a procedure widely adopted in evaluation elsewhere. It may be, of course, that not everyone would wish to use the term 'merit' to denote the result of such reference. It could be argued, no doubt, that 'merit' should involve some 'absolute' standard also; and that even to be the top candidate among a hundred candidates may not be so meritorious if the group as a whole did not reach some predetermined criterion. But that is a purely verbal argument. The essence of the matter is that comparison of a mark with the general run of marks does tell us *something* about that mark's value; and comparison of the mark with other criteria tells us something too. Our only reason for choosing the term 'merit' to indicate the result of norm-referenced evaluation is that the term seems to be widely used in this way. At any rate, all we are concerned with now is that one way of evaluating a mark is to compare it with the other obtained marks; and to avoid unnecessary verbal arguments we shall henceforth speak of the mark's 'standing'. What else it may be called is of no practical importance.

As yet, however, we have given no hint as to how a mark's standing is to be indicated. This is taken up in the following sections.

* See, for instance, Popham and Husek (1969) and Ward (1970).

The mean or median as standard

Marks are often evaluated by reference to the 'average'–as being 'well above average', 'about average', and so on. Such evaluation is of course norm-referenced, because the average (whether Mean or Median) is based upon *obtained* marks. (If the term 'average' does *not* refer to marks actually obtained at one time or another it has no useful meaning.) But how well does comparison with the average indicate a mark's standing?

If a candidate's mark is 63 when the average is 58, then of course the mark is 'above average'; but that is all that comparison with the average reveals. Certainly, 63 is 5 above the average of 58, but how 'good' is it to be 5 above? More precisely, is 5 a lot or a little? How high is the mark's *standing* above the average? If at least a quarter of the marks exceeded 74, and at least a quarter of them fell below 35, the mark of 63 would have one standing; but if most of the marks lay between 55 and 61, 63 would have a higher standing. In the former case 5 above the average of 58 is only a little–in comparison with the many larger deviations upwards from that average. In the latter case, to be 5 above the average is quite exceptional, for most of the marks above the average deviate from it by less than 5. In general, the *standing* of a mark, even when it is a known distance from the average, depends upon the *scatter* of the distribution. Comparison with the average, then, is inadequate for more than the roughest indication of a mark's standing: all we could say for sure would be that the mark was above or below (or at) the average.

If, then, the average were to be made the standard, it would have to be supplemented by further information, namely information about the marks' scatter. As will be shown in a later section of this chapter, this is of course quite practicable; but before we consider such a procedure we consider a relatively simple method of evaluating a mark's standing, a method which eliminates the need to quote either average *or* scatter.

'Standing' in terms of rank

A simple and not uncommon way of indicating a mark's standing is to quote its rank–3rd, 19th, 83rd, and so on. But since 19th in a group of 20 cannot be assumed to have the same meaning as 19th in a group of 90, the number of candidates should be quoted too. Also, since to be 19th in a group of postgraduate students may not be the same as to be 19th in a group of schoolboys, one should quote not only the number in the group but also its nature.

This particular method of indicating a candidate's standing has one great advantage over many other methods. Not only is everyone likely to understand it; no one is likely to *mis*understand it. The naïve reader of a report may assume that 81 per cent is necessarily a high mark, 32 per cent necessarily a low one; but as we have already seen, examinations differ in difficulty, and so 81 per cent may not always be very high, 32 per cent not always very low. Quotation of the candidates' ranks prevents such misinterpretation by bypassing the question of differential difficulty. Also, while a report could be issued in terms of the candidate's numerical mark, the Mean, and some indication of scatter, some readers of the reports might fail to take scatter into account—a point made explicit later in this chapter. Here again a Rank form of indication of standing eliminates the need to explain what more complex reports mean.

A few points nevertheless deserve mention. Whether these are to be regarded as disadvantages depends upon the advantages and disadvantages of other procedures; but for the moment we merely make explicit the points themselves.

First, in most examinations ranks will be shared; and when this occurs one has to adopt some convention and adhere to it. Consider the example shown. The candidate with the mark of 19 is, of course, 1st.

$$X \quad 19 \quad 18 \quad 17 \quad 16 \quad 15$$
$$f \quad 1 \quad \quad 3 \quad 1 \quad 1$$

But what rank is to be awarded to each of the candidates sharing the next lower mark, namely 17? Obviously they must have the *same* rank, for they are indistinguishable. If, however, we call all three 'Equal 2nd', the next candidate (at 16) cannot be called '3rd', because there are four candidates above him. He must be called '5th'. This may be perfectly reasonable, but it could suggest that there is a greater difference (in merit) between equal 2nd and

5th than there is between 1st and equal 2nd–which might not be so. Alternatively, we might share the three ranks of 2nd, 3rd, and 4th among the three equal candidates, and *say* that they shared these ranks, or perhaps call them all 3rd. But these procedures could meet objections too. We have no occasion here to recommend one method of assigning ranks in preference to any other. The point is simply that *some* convention has to be adopted, and adhered to. Which convention is adopted will have to depend upon the use to be made of the ranks assigned.

A second point is that unit rank-differences may not always reflect unit mark-differences. Consider this second example.

$$X \quad 82 \quad 81 \quad 80 \quad 79 \quad 78 \quad 77 \quad 76 \quad 75 \quad 74 \quad 73$$
$$f \quad 1 \quad\quad\quad\quad\quad\quad\quad\quad\quad\quad\quad\quad\quad\quad\quad\quad\quad\quad\quad 1 \quad 1$$

The appropriate ranks, here, are obviously 1st, 2nd, and 3rd, for no mark is shared; but these rankings ignore the fact that, in terms of *marks*, the top candidate is much farther above the second than the second is above the third. This is not necessarily of any practical importance–as in selecting the top so many candidates. Also, it could be argued that mark-units are not necessarily equal one to another anyway (see Note 1). Even so, there *could* be cases in which obvious superiority (as in our example?) should be given credit, and ranks do not give it.

Third, when the number of candidates is large the computing of ranks does take time–time additional to the awarding of marks in the first place. (Ranks have to be assigned to marks by reference to the frequency distribution, and then each candidate's mark has to be assigned the rank so entered in the distribution.)

Fourth, when the results of two examinations are being combined, one cannot add a candidate's two ranks of 2nd and 8th (for instance) and say that, overall, he was 5th (the 'average' of 2nd and 8th). If the number of candidates were large, that candidate might well be *first* in terms of his total *mark*. If, however, ranks were added in this way (2+8), and then all the sums of ranks were *re*-ranked, so that the smallest sum of ranks were called 1st, this would be a quite different matter.[16] But this, of course, is irrelevant to the use of ranks to indicate standing within a single examination.

Fifth, ranks are not very useful for *comparing* a candidate's standings in several examinations if the number of candidates varies very much from one examination to another. One cannot easily compare 14th out of 51 (candidates) with 34th out of 85. This point is not entirely irrelevant to assessment in a single examination, because the indication of merit in one examination is likely to be used as a basis of comparison with merit in some other examination.

Despite the possible disadvantages just referred to, the method of indicating standing by means of ranks has much to recommend it, and might well be exploited much more than it is. Many school reports do of course quote the pupil's rank; but perhaps because it is believed that ranks alone are inadequate they often quote also other pieces of information which are virtually useless. For example, to quote the pupil's numerical mark alongside his rank adds nothing whatsoever to the reader's knowledge of the mark's standing. Neither does quotation of the candidate's mark and the class average–in addition to his rank. As we have seen, comparison of a mark with the average indicates only whether the mark is above or below the average, whereas a rank (and the number of candidates) gives a much more precise assessment.

'Standing' in terms of grade

Exemplary of grades are the letters A, B, C, D, E, or their Greek equivalents, or the numbers I, II, III, IV, V. Sometimes answers are *marked* in terms of grades, but here we are concerned with grades as means of indicating standing, even when numerical marks are available.

It will be apparent that indications of standing in terms of grade will be less precise than indications in terms of rank, for it is unlikely that the number of available grades will be nearly as large as the number of candidates (or that the number of candidates will be as few as the number of available grades). It is not uncommon for examinations to use no more than five or six grades, and so the grades will be much more widely shared than ranks are. For some purposes, therefore, indication of standing in terms of grades will be insufficiently precise, and for these purposes some other procedure will be required. It could be, of course, that while the examination's purpose is to *assess* as precisely as possible each candidate's standing (merit?), yet the examiner may not be obliged to *report* the results with as much precision as they have for him.

In illustration of the main points consider a system involving five grades called A, B, C, D, and E.

The first point to be made is that since grades are to be used (in this context) to indicate *standings*, it would be absurd to have grades which one did not use. If (we assume) A is better than B, which is better than C, and so on, Grade E will do no more than refer to the candidates with the lowest standings. It would therefore betray gross misunderstanding of this function of grades to

say that no candidate was good enough to get 'A', or that none was bad enough to get 'E'. (Grade letters *could* of course be used with other functions, as when 'F' is intended to indicate that a candidate has failed; but these are not their functions in the present case.)

Second, although candidates are likely to take for granted that A is better than B, B better than C, and so forth, the quotation of a mere grade letter conveys very little information about standing. For example, if only 2 per cent of the candidates were awarded A, and the next 15 per cent of them were awarded B, Grade B in this system would be better than Grade B in a system where A accounted for the top 20 per cent. (Because in the latter system *no* Grade B candidate would be in the top 20 per cent, whereas in the former system *every* Grade B candidate is within the top 17 per cent). A report of standing in terms of grades should therefore quote not only the candidate's own grade but also the percentage (or number) of candidates in each of all the grades, such as (purely as an example): A – top 10 per cent; B – next 20 per cent; C – next 40 per cent; D – next 20 per cent; E – lowest 10 per cent. Note that a candidate awarded any one grade cannot discover his *precise* standing, as he can when his standing is quoted as a rank; but we shall come back to this point in a moment.

Third, the percentage of candidates to be allocated to each grade is quite arbitrary, as is also the number of grades to be used. The percentage frequencies chosen would be, of course, in keeping with any subsequent use to which the grades were to be applied. For example, if the lowest 5 per cent were to be rejected, there would be little point in having 10 per cent in the lowest grade. And if the examiner were interested only in the top 10 to 15 per cent, and in the bottom 10 to 15 per cent, and the candidates had no need to know how they stood within these limits, three grades would probably be enough. To underline this point: there can be no question of how good one has to be to get an 'A', how poor to get an 'E'. The matter is one for decision, not discovery; and as we have just said, the decision must rest upon the grades' subsequent use.

A major advantage of a grade report is its ease of preparation. Suppose, for instance, that Grade A is to contain the top 10 per cent of 153 candidates. One would therefore count down 15 in the frequency column, note the corresponding numerical mark, and then award Grade A to all candidates scoring that mark or higher. Similarly for the other grades.

Note that a report of a candidate's standing in terms of grade is not enhanced by quotation of his mark also, or of the maximum possible mark, or of the marks bounding the grades, or of the average. In a grade report the maximum indication of standing is already given by quotation of the candidate's own grade, the number or percentage of candidates in each grade, and the nature of the candidate-group.

For many purposes the use of five or six grades is likely to be sufficiently precise. (If a candidate did wish more precise information, the examiner might choose to give it to him.) However, a report in terms of grades has one basic disadvantage. Grades cannot be added or averaged; and in so far as indications of candidates' standings may have to be used in combination with similar indications from other examinations, the use of grades is inappropriate. In such cases numerical marks are necessary. As we noted earlier, however, a numerical mark by itself does not indicate standing at all, and so a report including a numerical mark must provide other information also. In a moment we shall consider what this additional information should be, but first we should look at a very practical point.

As we have just observed, grades cannot be added or averaged; but as will be demonstrated in a later chapter, the naïve addition of numerical marks can be, and often is, quite improper too. So also may be the naïve *comparison* of numerical marks. In so far as the examiner may have to issue indications of *standing* ('merit'?) to those who are unfamiliar with the necessary provisos, then, he may wish to consider seriously whether he should issue numerical marks at all. One suspects that examiners may issue numerical marks, not out of any reasoned belief that they constitute the most efficient kind of report, but simply because reports are traditionally issued in this way. If, then, numerical marks may be misused by a report's reader, why issue them at all? If, for instance, a report already quotes the candidate's rank, why quote his numerical mark too? As we saw, it adds nothing to anyone's knowledge of the candidate's standing, so why quote it and risk misinterpretation?

On the other hand, there are occasions when the substance of a report may have to be used by other examiners. At the end of a session a teacher may have to combine marks issued by teachers other than himself; a form teacher or counsellor may have to compare marks in different subjects. It is with such possibilities in mind that we now describe a form of report which does quote the candidate's numerical mark and other information also, so that the value of the mark can be known.

'Standing' in terms of median and quartiles

At the beginning of this chapter it was argued that a mark by itself does not indicate its standing at all; and in the section dealing with the average as standard it was shown that comparison of a mark with the average gave only the very roughest indication of standing–namely whether the mark was above or below (or at) the average. As was illustrated, we need also information about the distribution's scatter. The form of report now described allows of the scatter's being taken into account.

In this kind of report there is quoted the candidate's numerical mark, the Median, and the two Quartiles. Here is an example:

$$Q_3 = 71$$
$$\text{Median} = 61$$
$$Q_1 = 53$$
$$\text{Tom's mark} = 85$$

It can be seen at once that Tom's mark is in the top quarter of the distribution (being above the mark of 71 obtained by the candidate three quarters of the way up the list). Now if this were all that this sort of report could show it would be no better than a grade report using four grades each of which contained 25 per cent of the candidates. But it does show more than this.

Tom's mark of 85 is 14 above Q_3. By itself this difference of 14 means very little; but reference to the values of the Quartiles show that a range of 18 marks encloses about half the group. ('About' half the group, because each of the Quartiles may be shared.) In comparison with the middle half (about) of the group, therefore, Tom's mark is quite outstanding–exceeding the Upper Quartile by nearly as much as Q_3 exceeds Q_1. (And, of course, only about a quarter of the candidates are above Q_3 anyway.) One might note also that Tom is 14 above Q_3, whereas Q_3 exceeds the Median by only 10.

Now it is true that from the information supplied in this report we cannot determine Tom's *rank*. He might be 1st. On the other hand, it is conceivable (if unlikely) that there was no mark between 71 (the Upper Quartile) and Tom's mark of 85, and that nearly one quarter of the candidates excelled him. But one could place too much importance on this point. In discussing ranks we noted that Rank reports ignore differential mark–differences between successive ranks; so that even if this extreme case occurred we could say that, in comparison with the great *majority* of candidates, Tom was still quite outstanding, and that the candidates who beat him were outstanding to a remarkable degree. In comparison with the *main group* of candidates, Tom's performance in this case would be better than in a case where he was 1st, but scored only 76, if the Median and Quartiles remained the same. And since 'standing' is a matter of relation to the distribution as a whole, the fact that we do not know a candidate's rank is not crucial.

To illustrate further this kind of report consider a different examination in which Dick scores the same numerical mark, 85, as Tom scored in our first example.

$$Q_3 = 71$$
$$\text{Median} = 50$$
$$Q_1 = 22$$
$$\text{Dick's mark} = 85$$

Dick's mark too is in the top quarter, exceeding Q_3 by 14, the same as Tom. But in the present case the mark of 85 is not nearly so 'high', in relation to the main body of marks, because now almost 50 marks enclose about the middle half of the group, and 14 compared with 49 is not nearly as good as 14 compared with 18.

One further example. Harry also scores 85, but the Median and Quartiles are as follows.

$$Q_3 = 83$$
$$\text{Median} = 59$$
$$Q_1 = 37$$

Here 85 exceeds Q_3 by 2, which is very little in comparison with the interquartile range of 46 which contains about half the group, and so Harry is at 'about the Upper Quartile'.

Marks at other positions in the distribution would be be interpreted in the same way–by comparing them with the main body of marks. Thus, 63 (in this example) is just above the Median, 35 is at about the Lower Quartile, 89 is a little (only a 'little' in comparison with the scatter of the main body of marks) above the Upper Quartile, 15 is well down into the bottom quarter.

An advantage of this way of indicating merit (in addition to the advantages of using numerical marks) is that when the groups in two examinations are of different size, comparison of a candidate's merits is more meaningful than by means of ranks. (The comparison of standings is the subject of the next chapter.) On the other hand, an obvious objection to reports of this kind is that many of their readers would not understand them, a point to which we shall return at the end of this chapter. For the moment we may nevertheless note a technical objection, namely that such reports are rather coarse, in that they provide only three reference points—the Median and the two Quartiles. A finer type of report is described in the next section.

'Standing' in terms of percentiles

Just as the marks which are the Median and Quartiles divide the distribution into quarters, the marks constituting 'percentiles' divide the group into hundredths. Thus, the 10th percentile of a distribution is the mark which is ten hundredths of the way up the distribution,[17] the 25th percentile is simply another name for the Lower Quartile, the 50th percentile is another name for the Median, and so on.

There is of course no obligation to quote *every* percentile; for many examinations five will be enough—probably the 10th, 25th, 50th, 75th, and 90th, thus providing two reference points additional to the Median and Quartiles. For example:

> 90th percentile: 95
> 75th percentile: 81
> 50th percentile: 61
> 25th percentile: 38
> 10th percentile: 11

John's mark = 89

A candidate's mark can now be 'placed' with greater precision. If only the Median and Quartiles were quoted, all we should know would be that John's mark was in the top quarter, and that in comparison with the middle half of the group he was not *very* outstanding. Now we can see that his mark is exceeded by at least 10 per cent of the group.

Note that the quotation of these five percentiles is similar to the issuing of a six-grade report, the grades containing about 10, 15, 25, 25, 15, and 10 per cent of the candidates. Quotation of the candidate's numerical mark and the values of the five percentiles, however, allows a better estimate of how the candidate stands within his grade. Also, their quotation gives an indication of the distribution's shape. In our example, for instance, there are 14 marks between the 75th and 90th percentiles, but 27 marks between the 10th and 25th percentiles: the distribution appears to be negatively skewed, having a tail at the lower end. Thus, a distance of 8 below Q_1 does not have the same value as a distance of 8 above Q_3, because the scatters in the top and bottom quarters are not the same. Or the 'badness' of being 30 below the average (Median) is not as great as the 'goodness' of being 30 above the average, because the marks above the average are not so spread out.

How 'good' is a particular standing?

Even when the concept of Standing has been fully grasped, it is not uncommon for someone to ask how 'good' a certain standing is. ('Yes, I know that Tom is at the Upper Quartile, but how *good* is that?') There are several possible replies.

Basic to all of them is the point made earlier, that whether it be norm-referenced or criterion-referenced, evaluation of a mark necessarily takes the form of comparing it with some standard, and that standard has to be some mark or set of marks in the same series as the mark to be evaluated. As was also said before, in so evaluating a mark we may choose to say we are evaluating its 'merit' or its 'goodness' or something of the kind; but the hard fact of the matter is that all the examination's results entitle us to do is determine how the mark stands in relation to the standard adopted: the mark is so much above or so much below whatever standard is being used. We emphasise that this applies not only to the evaluation of a mark in terms of its standing in the group, but to *all* evaluation, norm-referenced or otherwise. If, then, we choose to say that a certain mark is 'very good', or 'rather poor', and the like, either we are using these expressions as no more than alternative ways of indicating how the mark stands in relation to the chosen standard, or we are introducing comment for which the examination's results provide no justification – because all the results entitle us to infer is how the mark stands in relation to a mark or marks pertinent to the examination itself. If we are to give a proper (not improper) reply to the question, therefore, all we can do is indicate how the mark stands in relation to some standard.

If, then, the questioner accepts the relevance of norm-referenced evaluation (as he seems to be doing), the reply is simple, namely that in reporting to him that the mark is at Q_3 we *have* told him how good it is, because (if norm-referenced evaluation is accepted) the mark's being at Q_3 *is* its degree of goodness, and there is nothing else to be told.

Terms like 'good', 'poor', 'merit', and 'standing' too, nevertheless tend to be emotively tinged, charged with praise and blame. But examination results as such do not indicate what attitude is to be expressed towards candidates with particular standings. All an examination can do is indicate what the various standings are – in relation to whatever standard has been chosen; and in this account we shall restrict the discussion to what examinations can legitimately be expected to do.

Further, the questioner may be rejecting norm-reference and asking for evaluation by reference to a standard other than the group. Criterion-reference will be discussed later, but we may note that if this *is* what the questioner intends he is likely to get a more satisfying answer if he specifies what standard he has in mind.

Finally, although the question may be accepting norm-reference, it may nevertheless be suggesting that a high (or low) standing in a group is not so very good (or bad) if the group itself is not very good (or bad). This issue is taken up in the next section. The point of *this* section is that when it is asked how 'good' a mark is, the only proper answer is to indicate how the mark stands in relation to some standard, and to state what that standard is.

How 'good' is the group?

Evaluation of a mark in terms of its standing in the group is sometimes criticised on the ground that one ought to take into account the goodness of the group itself. High standing, it would be said, is not very good if the group itself is a poor one; low standing is not very bad if the group is a good one. The criticism deserves investigation.

THE TEACHER SAYS I'M THE BEST OF A BAD LOT!

As has been emphasised, terms like 'good' and 'poor', if they are to have proper relevance to examination results at all, can be no more than indications of how a mark stands in comparison with some chosen standard. To say that a group is 'poor', then, must mean that its marks compare unfavourably with the standard adopted, whether the standard be a norm (or set of norms) or something else. Since criterion-referenced evaluation will be discussed in a later chapter, for the moment we shall consider only norm-referenced evaluation. That is to say, what does it mean to say, in terms of norm-reference, that a group is 'good' or 'poor'?

Since like must be compared with like, to say that a group is 'good' must mean that its marks stand high in relation to the marks of another *group*, or set of groups, in the *same examination*. If, for instance, eight classes sat the same examination, and Tom's class had, in general, the lowest marks of the eight, it would be proper to say that Tom's class was a 'poor' one. If a class were second top class (perhaps by reference to the classes' Medians), it could be said to be a quite 'good' class. And if Tom were at Q_3 in the poorest class, it is very probable indeed that he would not have been as high as Q_3 in one of the better classes. Two points should nevertheless be made explicit.

First, all the classes (or whatever the 'groups' are) must have taken the same examination, for otherwise the marks will not be comparable. Accordingly, if the group said to be 'poor' (or 'good') were the *only* group which took (or ever had taken) the examination in question, or an examination known to be equivalent to it, any reference to that group's merit would be purely speculative, because there would be no basis of comparison. Obviously, an examination cannot provide information about groups which have not sat it.

Second, if another group or set of groups did take the same examination, there is no need to hypothesise about the merit of the group in question, for we can find out exactly what its standing was. We could compare their various Means or Medians. But even this would not necessarily provide an adequate answer. It is at least conceivable that the mark at the Upper Quartile in a poor group (having a relatively low Median) could be at least as high a numerical mark as the Upper Quartile in a relatively good group (with a relatively high Median). More realistic than the discovery of where Tom would have stood *had* he been in some other group would be the discovery of where he actually stood in the whole group of candidates who took the examination.

Doubtless it might still be objected that the *whole* group might not be very good (or not be very poor), but as was noted above, this objection is quite unrealistic in that it cannot be put to the test. The most that any examination can do, in respect of the evaluation of a candidate's mark, is indicate how it stands in relation to the standard. In particular, if we adopt norm-referenced evaluation, all that can be said in this respect is that the mark had such and such a standing in the marks of the group which actually sat the examination. How the *group* fared we cannot say, and it would be futile to expect the examination to tell us. Unless, of course, we adopt criterion-referenced evaluation; but as will be seen in a later chapter, this too has its natural limitations.

Choosing a method of reporting standing

Since neither a mark nor a percentage mark, by itself, indicates standing at all, and the inclusion of the average gives only a very rough indication, we shall not consider as possibilities reports quoting only the candidate's mark (percentage or otherwise) or quoting his mark and the average. Since the Median and Quartiles are Percentiles (the 25th, 50th, and 75th), this leaves a choice from three methods: Ranks, Grades and Percentiles.

No one of these is absolutely better than either of the others, for each has its advantages and disadvantages, and so the method to be adopted will have to depend upon the intention with which the report is issued. Three criteria would nevertheless seem to be worth bearing in mind: the degree of Precision required, the Comprehensibility of the report for its intended reader, and the Labour involved in preparing it.

A Rank form of report (quoting the candidate's rank and the size and nature of the group) is likely to be understood, and not misunderstood, by almost everyone. It has a quite high degree of precision (for ranks will be shared only when the marks themselves are shared—and no form of report can do other than accept this), being much more precise than a report in terms of grades, though it cannot indicate very outstanding performance at either end of the distribution. On the other hand, if the number of candidates is large the calculation of each candidate's rank does take a considerable time–much longer than the other two forms of report require. Also, if the substance of the report is to be used to compare the candidate's performances in different subjects, a Rank report makes this difficult if different numbers of candidates take the different examinations. And, of course, ranks cannot be added. This kind of report would seem to be most appropriate if the number of candidates is not very large (say not more than 50), and the substance of the report is not to be made the basis of comparison or combination.

A Grade report (quoting the candidate's own grade and the number or percentage of candidates in each grade, and the nature of the group) is also unlikely to be misunderstood. It takes less time to prepare than does a Rank report, but is much less precise. Grades cannot be combined, and can be used for comparison (of a candidate's merits in different examinations) only in so far as the pattern of percentage frequencies remains the same over the different examinations–though there is no reason why this should not occur. Further, comparison in terms of grades does not reveal improvement or deterioration *within* a grade. A Grade report would seem to be most appropriate if the number of candidates is large, and if precise position within a grade is of no great significance, and if the substance of the report is not to be used for combination or fine comparison.

A report in terms of Percentiles (quoting the candidate's numerical mark and, say, the 10th, 25th, 50th, 75th and 90th percentiles, and the size and nature of the group) is the easiest report to prepare: it is quicker to find the values of these five percentiles than to establish every candidate's rank, and no slower than the allocation to grades; and each report carries the candidate's already known mark and the *same* information about the percentiles. It is more precise than a Grade report, and at least comparable in precision with a Rank report. On the other hand, some readers of the report may find it incomprehensible. And while the report contains not only the candidate's numerical mark but also the percentiles, reference to which allows of a good assessment of standing, it only *allows* of this and does not guarantee it.

Some readers of the report could ignore the percentiles quoted and make a judgment based solely on the mark itself. Further, as will be discussed in detail in the next chapter, some readers might draw direct comparisons between the candidate's marks in different subjects when this is quite unjustifiable; and some readers might add marks, when this too could be improper–for reasons given in a later chapter. Probably this kind of report is most appropriate when the intended readers of the report are already acquainted with what it means or are prepared to learn. It is particularly useful if intended for teachers and others who have to perform calculations or base their advice on the report's content.

Even if one of these methods of indicating standing is found to be adequate (for there is no method which is at once simple to prepare, simple to understand, and completely accurate), the indication may nevertheless seem to 'hang in the air', a piece of information waiting for a buyer. The appearance would seem to be justified, for while many examinations do have the explicit purpose of discovering each candidate's merit, yet knowledge of a candidate's merit (or standing) is of very little use unless one wishes to exploit it in one way or another; and one very common use of indications of merit is *comparison*. In particular, if the candidates take examinations in several subjects, it is often necessary to find out which is each candidate's 'best' subject, so that he can be advised as to which subjects he should continue to study, which require greater study, and so on. That is to say, his merits in different subjects have to be compared. This issue is the subject-matter of the next chapter, but we conclude the present chapter with one brief comment.

All our discussion in this chapter has presupposed that the marks themselves are valid, and in particular that they are *precise* enough for an indication of standing to have a valuable meaning. If all the candidates share no more than a few successive marks (such as 53, 54, 55, and 56), the differences among the candidates will be so slight that even to say someone is equal first will mean very little. *How* mark-sharing can be minimised will be discussed in the chapters dealing with the setting of questions and the marking of answers, but we note this point now merely to reinforce a point made earlier, namely that the criterion purpose of ascertaining each candidate's particular merit presupposes a wide spread of marks. The subject-matter of this present chapter will have provided exemplification of that point.

6 Comparing a candidate's standings in different examinations

'Merit' and 'Standing'

The problem discussed in this chapter might be described as the problem of finding out, from the results of examinations in several subjects, which was a candidate's best subject, which was his poorest, and so on. In other words, in which subject did he show his greatest merit, least merit, and so forth? As we previously observed, however, there could be disagreement about the meanings of 'merit', 'good', 'best', and the like; and so in the chapter heading we have avoided ambiguity by using the term 'standing', to make it quite clear that we are still concerned with norm-referenced evaluation.

The comparison of standings

Since the standing (or merit) of a mark is not indicated by the mark itself, whether it be a percentage mark or otherwise, comparison of a candidate's standings in several examinations cannot be properly effected by comparing his marks. Suppose, for instance, that Tom scored as follows:

> English 67 per cent, History 67 per cent,
> Mathematics 72 per cent, French 51 per cent.

A naïve comparison of these percentage marks would be quite improper because their *standings* are not quoted. For all we know, Tom's standing in French (his lowest *percentage* mark) might have been his highest, Mathematics his lowest.

Were direct comparisons of this kind made in many other human situations they would certainly seem odd, even absurd. If Jones were 62 inches tall, and had a waist measurement of 50 inches, it would certainly be inappropriate to say that he was taller than he was fat. Complicated as they might seem, comparisons

across different human dimensions have to be comparisons of *standings*. Yet in examinations it is not uncommon to find the direct comparing of marks when there is no reason at all to suppose that they are in fact comparable, no reason to suppose that equal numbers represent equal standings in different examinations.

Comparison of standings, then, must be the comparison of whatever are used to *indicate* standings. In the previous chapter three modes of indication were suggested–by means of Ranks, Grades and Percentiles. We noted, however, that comparison of ranks became complicated when the number of candidates was not the same in the different examinations, and that comparison in terms of grades was somewhat rough in that it ignored rise or fall within a grade. The most efficient form of comparison would seem to be effected by means of numerical marks and percentiles. What this involves is now described.

Here is a summary of the results of four examinations, the candidate's four marks being quoted below.

Subject:	English	History	Mathematics	French
Q_3:	60	58	73	49
Median:	53	42	53	40
Q_1:	46	25	33	30
Tom's mark:	67	67	72	51

It is now apparent that while Tom is above the Median in every subject, it is only in Mathematics that his mark is below Q_3, and so in these examinations Mathematics is his poorest subject– or at any rate, this is the subject in which he has his lowest standing.

Compare now his English and History standings. He has the

same *mark* (67) in both, though he is 14 above the English Median and 25 above the History Median. But these 'deviations' from the Median are not comparable, in the sense that they do not indicate the subject of his higher *standing*. In fact, Tom's deviation of 14 above the English Median is the same as that subject's Interquartile Range, whereas his deviation of 25 above the History Median is *less* that that subject's Interquartile Range, namely 33. Apparently, then, he has the higher standing in English–*not*, it is emphasised, because the English average is higher, but because of the relationship between his deviation from the average and the *scatter*.

As for his standing in French, he is 11 above the French Median; but the Interquartile Range is 19, and 11 compares less favourably with 19 than does 14 with 14, or does 25 with 33. French, therefore, is the subject in which he has his third highest standing. His subject-standings, in descending order of merit, therefore, are English, History, French and Mathematics.

As a further illustration consider the candidate Dick, who scored 50 in each subject. French is the only subject in which he exceeds Q_3, and so it is in French that he has his highest standing. Of the remaining three subjects, History is the only one in which he is above the Median, and so it is his 'second best' subject. In both English and Mathematics he is 3 below the Median, but the two 'threes' do not have the same value. In English, 3 below the Median places him *about* half way (in terms of marks) between the Median and Q_1, whereas in Mathematics 3 below the Median is *much* nearer the Median than to Q_1. His 'order of subjects', therefore, is French, History, Mathematics and English.

Finer comparisons, if required, can of course be made if there are quoted not only the Median and Quartiles but also the 10th and 90th percentiles, but the principles are essentially the same.

Standings in different groups

Once the principles involved in the comparison of a candidate's standings are clear, it is likely to be realised that in a great many instances the *groups* in which he has the various standings will be different groups. For example, Tom's fellow-candidates in Mathematics may not be the same as his fellow-candidates in French. This, however, is no bar to proper comparison, so long as one makes clear what one is doing. All that is being said is that Tom's standing in the group which took French is higher than his standing in the group which took Mathematics. Not only is such a statement perfectly clear, it is also perfectly relevant to practice, for it would be beside the point to ask what standing Tom would have had in these topics if all the candidates had taken both. If some students study French, and others study Mathematics, and some of these studying the one are not studying the other, why wonder what would have happened if the facts had been otherwise? Also, in so far as competition is involved, Tom is not competing in French with candidates who are not taking French–and similarly for other subjects. Further, if Tom's performances in the examinations are to be made the basis of a *selection* of subjects for further study ('Drop Maths and specialise in English!'), the selection is not prejudiced by the fact that not all candidates took all subjects; but the implied prediction will gain in value to the extent that the groups are representative of the groups Tom will join later. His standings in the present groups nevertheless provide the only evidence there is.

To repeat: the most that can be said is that a candidate has a higher standing in the group which took this subject than in the group which took that subject. This may seem to be a restriction, but it is imposed, not by the particular method of comparison we have been describing, but by the very nature of examinations.

Groups may differ also in size. As we noted, this makes ranks an unsuitable basis of comparison, but the use of Median and Quartiles bypasses this difficulty, though it would of course be somewhat unrealistic to compare (say) Q_3 in a very large group with Q_3 in a very small one.

Finally, it might be objected that it is improper to compare a candidate's standings in different groups if some of the groups are good and some are poor; but this is essentially the same as a point replied to in the previous chapter. If reference to good and poor groups is to have any practical significance there must be evidence that a group is good or otherwise; that is to say, we must know how the group in question stands in relation to a still larger group which has taken the same examination. For example, comparison of the Medians of the groups quoted in the summary on p. 88 gives no indication at all of the groups' relative merits. These marks are not comparable, not even if the *same* group took all four examinations. To make the same point once more: all we can say is that a *candidate* stood higher in the group which took this subject than he did in the group which took that subject; about the groups themselves we can say nothing at all–unless, of course, they are parts of still larger groups, in which case it would be more sensible to quote the Median and Quartiles of the large group in each subject.

One of the main points of this chapter has been that no useful purpose is served by directly comparing a candidate's marks in different subjects, and that what have to be compared are his *standings* in them. As we have tried to show, this is not particularly difficult, but one has to know what one is doing; and it is no insult to many prospective readers of a candidate's report to suggest that they **may** *not* know what to do with the information it contains–namely to evaluate a mark by reference to Median and Quartiles. Obviously, comparison would be very much simpler if it *were* legitimate to compare numerical marks directly, so that if Tom scored 73 in English, 82 in Mathematics, 66 in French, and 87 in Latin, it could be inferred at once that 87 was better than 82, which was better than 73, which was better than 66. In fact it is possible to prepare a form of report from which such inferences are perfectly proper. It involves more work for the examiner–though computers can now do much of the work for him–but very much reduces the chances of the report's being misinterpreted. This 'predigestion' of marks, by what is called 'scaling', is described in the next chapter.

7   The scaling of marks

What is 'scaling'?

At the end of the previous chapter we noted that there is a procedure by which direct comparison of a candidate's marks *will* be at once a comparison of his standings. This procedure is known as 'scaling'. To 'scale' the marks of a distribution is to alter their numerical values without altering their standings. The original marks are called 'raw' marks, their new equivalents 'scaled' marks.

By definition, such conversion is justifiable when we are concerned only with the marks' *standings*. If, for instance, Tom's raw mark of 63 were half way between the raw Median and the raw Q_3, changing his mark to 75 would be in order if 75 were half way between the Median and Q_3 of the scaled distribution, and, of course, if the mark's standing were all we were concerned with.

It is perhaps worth observing that, so far as standings are concerned, the fact that scaling may result in some marks' rising in numerical value, and some marks' falling, is of no significance. For example:

	Raw Mark	Scaled Mark
Alf:	83	90
Bill:	73	70
Charles:	68	60

Alf's mark has risen by 7, Bill's mark has dropped by 3, and Charles' mark has dropped by 8; but all that matters is that the relative positions remain the same—as in this example they do.

Why scaling permits mark-comparison

As already shown, a mark's standing is indicated by its relation to certain measures representing the distribution to which it belongs. Typical of such measures are the 10th, 25th, 50th, 75th and 90th percentiles. Also, the same numerical mark, say 50, will not necessarily have the same standing in different distributions. For example:

	English	History
90th percentile:	64	83
75th percentile:	58	72
50th percentile:	53	63
25th percentile:	49	54
10th percentile:	44	46

In English, 50 is just above the 25th percentile, in History it is half way between the 10th and 25th. Its standing in English is higher than its standing in History. The reason that the same mark does not have the same standing in two distributions is of course that the representative percentiles do not have the same numerical values.

Conversely, however, the same numerical mark *will* have the same standing in different distributions if the numerical values of the representative percentiles *are* the same in the several distributions, because the *bases* of the comparison (of the mark with the percentiles) will be the same. Marks in different subjects, therefore, *will* be directly comparable for standings if the different subjects have the same representative percentiles.

Of course, these representative percentiles will rarely if ever have the same numerical values in different distributions, but the marks in the different distributions can be *scaled* so that the percentiles *will* have identical values and so allow of direct comparison.

How are marks scaled?

To allow of the direct comparison of marks, the different distributions must be scaled so that each of the 10th, 25th, 50th, 75th, and 90th percentiles has the same numerical value in every distribution. To what particular values should the raw marks be changed?

This is a matter, not of discovery, but of decision. We could scale the marks of one subject so that its new percentiles were the same as those of another subject, but it is usually preferable (as we shall see) to scale the marks in all the subjects to some predetermined common scale, such as:

> 90th percentile: 76
> 75th percentile: 68
> 50th percentile: 60
> 25th percentile: 52
> 10th percentile: 44

No special significance attaches to these particular numerical values, but in choosing the percentile values two points should be considered. First, it is often desirable to have percentile values which are equally spaced (as in the example, which has a constant difference of 8), because many purposes of examining are best served by a symmetrical distribution.[18] Second, scaling will often result in small marks becoming smaller, large marks becoming larger, and so we chose for the 10th percentile a value unlikely to result in some of the scaled marks' being negative, and for the 90th percentile a value unlikely to make some of the scaled marks'have values higher than 100. There is no technical objection to our having marks beyond these limits, for they are not 'percentage marks', but such marks might well cause unnecessary concern to the uninitiated. Subject to these two considerations, however, the values assigned to the representative percentiles can be anything we like. Having chosen certain values, we must of course adhere to them; and if we use the same values in successive examinations their meanings will become known. Candidates will learn that (say) 60 is an 'average' mark, and so on. This, it will be apparent, is a good reason for resorting to a common scale.

For the sake of illustration we shall adopt the common scale shown above. Then no matter what its raw value may be, the mark at the 90th percentile in the raw distribution will become the scaled mark of 76; the raw mark at the 75th percentile will become 68, and so forth. All the other raw marks must now be converted in accord with this pattern of change. For instance, the mark half way between the raw 75th and 90th percentiles will have to become 72.

Consider now the distribution shown in Table XIA below. All that would appear initially would be the completed Mark column (now called 'Raw Mark' column) and the Frequency column. The column headed 'Scaled Mark' would still be blank, awaiting the new values.

The first step is to calculate the *raw* values of the 10th, 25th, 50th, 75th and 90th percentiles. These are shown in Table XIA. These are the values which are to become the values of the Common Scale. Thus, as shown in the Table XIA, the old percentile values of 44, 48, 52, 56 and 60 become the new values 44, 52, 60, 68 and 76. (In this example it so happens that the 10th percentile has the same numerical value, namely 44, in both raw and scaled marks, but this is of no significance.) These new values are entered alongside their 'opposite numbers'–as shown in the Table.

The next step is to change the remaining marks 'accordingly'. Each mark must be assigned a new numerical value giving it the same standing in the scaled distribution as it had in the raw distribution.

Consider first the interval between the 75th and 90th percentiles. In the raw distribution the step from the 75th to the 90th percentile is from 56 to 60, a 'step-size' of 4. In the scaled distribution the corresponding step-size is 8. Within this interval, then, there is a rate of exchange of 2 for 1. Marks differing by 1 in the raw distribution will therefore have to differ by 2 in the scaled distribution–within that particular interval. The three marks lying there, namely 57, 58, 59, must therefore become 70, 72, 74.

Inspection of the remaining percentile intervals, 50th–75th, 25th–50th, and 10th–25th, shows that there also the rate of exchange is 2 for 1.

The scaled values of the marks above the 90th and below the 10th percentile must be found by extrapolation. Since the rate of exchange for the main body of marks, from the 10th to the 90th percentile, is 2 for 1, it is appropriate to use that same

TABLE XIA

Raw mark	Scaled mark	f	
65		I	
64			
63		II	
62		I	
61		II	
60 →	76	III	←90th
59		IIII	
58		III	
57		III	
56 →	68	IIII	←75th
55		III	
54		III	
53		THL I	
52 →	60	THL THL I	←50th
51		THL II	
50		IIII	
49		II	
48 →	52	III	←25th
47		IIII	
46		III	
45		III	
44 →	44	II	←10th
43		I	
42		II	
41		I	
40		II	

$N = 80$

TABLE XIB

Raw mark	Scaled mark	f	
65	86	I	
64	84		
63	82	II	
62	80	I	
61	78	II	
60 →	76	III	←90th
59	74	IIII	
58	72	III	
57	70	III	
56 →	68	IIII	←75th
55	66	III	
54	64	III	
53	62	THL I	
52 →	60	THL THL I	←50th
51	58	THL II	
50	56	IIII	
49	54	II	
48 →	52	III	←25th
47	50	IIII	
46	48	III	
45	46	III	
44 →	44	II	←10th
43	42	I	
42	40	II	
41	38	I	
40	36	II	

rate in extrapolating. Accordingly, raw 61 becomes scaled 78, raw 62 becomes scaled 80, and so on. Similarly below the 10th percentile. The complete conversion is shown in Table XIB.

Extrapolation would of course be unnecessary if the new values for the highest and lowest marks were predetermined also–or instead. Our present concern with scaling, however, relates to the comparison of standings in different distributions; and if we predetermined the scaled values of the highest and lowest marks the top candidate in each subject would be assigned the same mark whether he was very close to the next best candidates or was quite outstanding. Likewise for the lowest candidate. In contrast, if the distribution is 'pegged' no higher than the 90th and no lower than the 10th percentile (or thereabouts), differences in degree of 'outstandingness' (at either end) will be reflected in the scaled marks.

For explanation's sake the foregoing example was over-simple. We now consider a more awkward, but more probable, case–though using the same common scale. See Table XIIA below.

As before, we first calculate the numerical values of the five percentiles in the raw distribution; these are 53, 60, 65, 68 and 70. Note that these are not equally spaced. This will produce some distortion.

In the interval between the 75th and 90th percentiles the raw step-size is 2, the scaled step-size 8, producing a rate of exchange of 4 for 1. In the 50th–75th percentile interval, the rate of exchange is 8 for 3. In the 25th–50th percentile interval the rate of exchange is 8 for 5. In the 10th-25th percentile interval the rate of exchange is 8 for 7.

In this example, then, scaling has produced a distortion of the raw distribution, the rate of exchange not being uniform throughout. In some places a raw step of 1 becomes a scaled step of $2\frac{2}{3}$ (rate of exchange 8 for 3), whereas in some places a raw step of 1 becomes a scaled step of only $1\frac{1}{7}$.

The distortion has occured because the scaled distribution is symmetrical and the raw distribution is not; scaling will be perfectly accurate only when the raw and scaled distributions have the same shape. We shall return to that point after we complete the scaling itself.

TABLE XIIA

Raw mark	Scaled mark		f	
73			/	
72			///	
71			///	
70	76		////	←90th
69			////	
68	68		ℍℍ /	←75th
67			ℍℍ ///	
66			ℍℍ ℍℍ	
65	60		ℍℍ ///	←50th
64			////	
63			///	
62			////	
61			//	
60	52		///	←25th
59			//	
58			//	
57			/	
56			//	
55				
54			//	
53	44		/	←10th
52			//	
51			//	
50			/	
49			/	
48			/	

$$N = 80$$

TABLE XIIB

Raw mark	Scaled mark		f	
73	88	88	/	
72	84	84	///	
71	80	80	///	
70	76	76	////	←90th
69	72	72	////	
68	68	68	ℍℍ /	←75th
67	$65\frac{1}{3}$	65	ℍℍ ///	
66	$62\frac{2}{3}$	63	ℍℍ ℍℍ	
65	60	60	ℍℍ ///	←50th
64	$58\frac{2}{5}$	58	////	
63	$56\frac{4}{5}$	57	///	
62	$55\frac{1}{5}$	55	////	
61	$53\frac{3}{5}$	54	//	
60	52	52	///	←25th
59	$50\frac{6}{7}$	51	//	
58	$49\frac{5}{7}$	50	//	
57	$48\frac{4}{7}$	49	/	
56	$47\frac{3}{7}$	47	//	
55	$46\frac{2}{7}$	46		
54	$45\frac{1}{7}$	45	//	
53	44	44	/	←10th
52	$42\frac{6}{7}$	43	//	
51	$41\frac{5}{7}$	42	//	
50	$40\frac{4}{7}$	41	/	
49	$39\frac{3}{7}$	39	/	
48	$38\frac{2}{7}$	38	/	

Extrapolation beyond the 90th and below the 10th percentile was straightforward in our first example, because we could simply extrapolate the one rate of exchange common to all the intervals. For a reason given in a moment the most appropriate way of extrapolating above the 90th percentile is to use the rate of exchange immediately below it, in this case 4 for 1; and the best way to extrapolate below the 10th percentile is to use the rate of exchange immediately above it, in this case $1\frac{1}{7}$ for 1. These extrapolations are shown in the left-hand Scaled column of Table XIIB. The right-hand Scaled column shows the rounded-off scaled marks. (Since the initial marks were whole numbers, there is no point in using fractions for scaled marks.)

We can now look at the distortion. It is not as serious as it might seem to be. First, no matter how different the two distributions' (raw and scaled) shapes, no candidate's scaled mark can have a *rank* different from that of his raw mark. If, then, the purpose of the comparison of a candidate's standings in several examinations is satisfied by a degree of precision at the rank level, the distortion introduced by scaling will be of no consequence. Second, even if the precision is *not* judged to be fine enough, and one must take account of unequal mark differences between successive ranks, these differences *will* be taken into account *within* certain parts of the distribution. Since extrapolation above the 90th percentile was by the rate of exchange in the 75th-90th percentile interval, there is consistency within the top quarter of the distribution. Similarly for the bottom quarter, and, of course, there is consistency within each of the middle quarters. Distortion becomes a real issue, then, only in comparing a mark in one quarter of the distribution with a mark in a different quarter.

Even then, however, it will be of little or no consequence if the difference between the two *raw* marks is reasonably large. The most serious case is where we compare a mark at the bottom of one quarter with a mark at the top of the quarter immediately below. However, even in our quite distorted example, the discrepancies in these cases would seem to be very small in comparison with the total spread of the marks; and our view of this issue is that to quibble about such discrepancies is unrealistic. Scaling does not alter ranks, and if slightly different questions had been asked it is extremely likely that similarly knowledgeable candidates would have changed their ranks, even if just a little.

Ideally, of course, there would be no distortion at all; and since it will depend upon the difference in shape between the raw and scaled distributions, the examiner should try to set his questions in such a way that the raw distribution will have a shape very similar to the shape built into the scale to which the raw marks are to be converted. (How the setting of questions can influence the distribution's shape is considered in a later chapter.)

The method of scaling we have been describing is but one of several. Some examiners prefer a graphical method; and scaling can be done by reference to the Mean and Standard Deviation— a method lending itself very well to the use of a computer. The basic principles are nevertheless the same in all. We described it in the way we did because, we think, it illustrates most clearly what these principles are.

To anyone who has never scaled marks, the process may seem very complex. However, scaling is more difficult to describe than to do. And the operation becomes simpler, and probably less liable to error, if performed by two people. For instance, one person reads off the raw mark, and the other calls out the scaled mark shown in the scaling table. Also, one can have the whole operation carried out at a computing centre. Further, one has to balance the time and labour of scaling against the disadvantages of not scaling. As we have tried to show, the presentation of raw marks is open to misinterpretation. And, as will be shown in a later chapter, scaling is *necessary* when marks in different topics or different examinations are to be combined.

A common scale

Since all that matters for the comparison of marks is that the several distributions are converted to the same scale, it would be in order to convert the marks in (say) English, History and French to the scale of the Mathematics marks. But there are advantages in converting all the distributions to a predetermined, common, scale.

For one thing, we cannot be certain about what the scale of any particular subject will turn out to be; and it might turn out to be different from what we wanted: skewed, perhaps, rather than approximately symmetrical. Second, while conversion to the (say) Mathematics scale would allow of proper comparison in the present examination, it would not allow of comparison across examinations held at different times in the session. If a common scale is used at all times, a candidate's mark at the beginning of a session can be compared with his mark at the middle or end of it. Third, if one and the same scale is used at all times within the school or college, candidates and teachers will soon know it by heart, and can interpret a mark without having to consult it. That advantage is most likely, however, if the common scale is itself easy to remember. And since *any* numerical values will suffice (subject to the provisos made on p. 94), there is no reason why these values should not be 'memorable' ones. Thus, percentile values such as 40, 50, 60, 70 and 80 are preferable to the values of 37, 48, 59, 70 and 81. And, of course, the common scale could be printed on the report cards.

A final point: would not a common scale form of report lead some of its readers to infer that the *group* had done equally well in all subjects? It might, but if the marks in the different subjects were on different scales, these same readers would probably infer that the group had done better in some subjects than in others – which is equally unjustifiable (see pp. 81ff.) The general answer to criticisms of this kind must be, surely, that no form of report can guarantee that no one will misunderstand it, and that the form the report should take must depend upon the kind of person for whom it is intended. As we observed earlier, on some occasions it may not be politic to quote numerical marks at all.

8 Evaluating a mark by criterion-reference

Norm-reference and criterion-reference

In the foregoing chapters the evaluation of a candidate's mark has been regarded as a matter of comparing it with the marks obtained by the whole body of candidates, its value (or 'merit', etc.) being its standing in the distribution of obtained marks. As we briefly noted, evaluation of this kind has been called 'norm-referenced' – norms being marks summarising or otherwise representing the distribution of marks actually obtained in the examination. In evaluating a mark by reference to the 10th, 25th, 50th, 75th and 90th percentiles, for instance, we were using these percentiles as norms.

Norm-referenced evaluation is widespread. As we have seen, it is the essence of many everyday judgments, and it is also the basis of assessment by means of standardised intelligence and attainment tests. In recent years, however, there have appeared in several journals articles dealing with what has come to be called 'criterion-referenced' evaluation (or 'criterion-referenced measurement'). (For further details and an account more technical than will be given here see Popham and Husek 1969, Ward 1970, Glaser 1963.) These articles, it is emphasised, are not *anti* norm-reference, as if there were something intrinsically wrong with it; their point is, rather, that there are purposes for which norm-reference is inadequate, or inappropriate, and that some of the conventional statistical procedures pertinent to norm-reference are unsuitable for these purposes and would give a wrong impression if applied to them.

Criterion-referenced evaluation requires reference to a standard which is *not* a norm: there is no question of inter-candidate 'competition', of how one candidate compares with others. In this kind of evaluation a candidate failing to reach the standard would still have 'failed' no matter how many candidates were even worse; a candidate reaching the standard would not suffer even if he were surpassed by everyone else.

But while a negative definition of this sort may be of some value it does not specify what the standard *is*. Popham and Husek (1969), making a positive approach, say that criterion-reference has the function of ascertaining an individual's status with respect to some *performance* standard. Since they make it clear that the criterion, in criterion-referenced evaluation, is of the nature of performance, we shall use the term 'criterion' in this way too, restricting the term 'standard' to denoting the *measure* of that performance. That is, in criterion-reference the standard is the measure representing the criterion, the criterion itself being a specified performance.

Nevertheless, since the measurement of performance is the function of every examination, a norm also is a performance standard, and so the comparison of a candidate's mark with a measure representing a performance is not peculiar to criterion-reference. Admittedly, in evaluating a mark by norm-reference it is customary to refer it to the whole body of obtained marks (as when its standing is quoted); but it *could* be (and sometimes is) compared with some particular mark (such as the 50th percentile), and so this particular difference is not crucial. The essential difference lies, not in the nature of the process of referral, for in both kinds of evaluation a candidate's mark is compared with a measure of performance, but rather in the way in which the basis of comparison, the standard, is determined in the first place, as is now shown.

In this connection there are three interrelated variables: a measure's numerical value, its standing among the measures obtained, and the particular performance of which it is the measure. Within any one examination, for any particular group of candidates, these three things will vary concomitantly: the better the candidate's performance the greater the measure and the higher its standing. But although they are interdependent in this way, *predetermining* the standard by its particular standing (say 50th percentile) does not determine the performance whose measure will have that standing–because that will depend upon how the group of candidates subsequently performs in the examination, and so is not predictable. For the same reason, *predetermining* the particular performance which is to be the criterion does not determine the particular standing the criterion's measure will have. In other words, to fix the standard in terms of performance as such does not fix it in terms of standing, and to fix it in terms of standing does not fix it in terms of performance, because the 'not-fixed' parameter will vary from one candidate-group to another and cannot be predetermined for the candidate-group by whom the examination has to be taken.

For these reasons the examiner may fix the standard either in terms of standing or in terms of performance, but not in terms of both. A standard in terms of standing commits him to norm-referenced evaluation, a standard in terms of performance to criterion-referenced evaluation—not because of any difference in the reference-process but because of the way in which the standard has been set.

Which standard he uses will depend, as do all other examination procedures, upon the examination's purpose. If 'selection' means creaming off a given number or percentage of candidates, the standard will be a norm, namely the percentile corresponding with the proportion of candidates to be selected. If, on the other hand, 'selection' means accepting all those candidates reaching a certain sort of performance, the standard would be the mark which is the measure of that criterion-performance. In the former case the performance represented by the chosen percentile-measure will be irrelevant; in the latter case candidates reaching the criterion-performance would be accepted irrespective of their standings.

Which type of reference different purposes require is discussed in the next chapter. For the present we are concerned with but one purpose, namely that of evaluating a candidate's mark, indicating how 'good' his performance has been.

As we have seen, it is not only customary but also in accord with many everyday judgments to evaluate a mark by *norm-*reference, as by quoting its rank, or by comparing it with the average, or by stating its percentile position. It could be argued, however, that norm-reference does not always tell us all we want to know. For example, when someone doubts the 'goodness' of a mark even as high as the 95th percentile, saying that the group itself may not be very good, he may be doing no more than suggesting that that group will have to be compared with other groups–which would be a request for norm-reference again. But he may be suggesting that the group's performance is not good *enough*–compared with a level of performance he has in mind; and if so, the case is now one of *criterion*-reference. In this case a candidate's performance will be 'good enough' only if it is up to the level of performance to which the critic, implicitly perhaps, is referring; and a candidate's mark will have to be evaluated by its being compared with the measure of that criterion-performance (once it *is* made explicit).

It is with this kind of comparison that this chapter, and parts of the next, are concerned; but before we consider how the comparison can be made we must consider something else. A mark cannot be compared with the standard representing the criterion until the criterion itself has been set. This problem does not arise with norm-reference, because there the 'goodness' of a mark is its standing in the distribution of obtained marks, and the standard is that distribution, so that, in so far as the standard could be said to be 'set' at all, it is set by the candidate-group. In criterion-reference, however, the standard has to be set by the examiner; and where he sets it will affect the meaning of any comparison with it. To be somewhat below a 'high' standard, for instance, will not mean quite the same as to be somewhat below

a 'low' standard. In the next section, therefore, we consider the setting of the standard itself.

In leaving this discussion of the difference between norm-reference and criterion-reference we should nevertheless make one final point. Any report or comment on how a candidate or group of candidates has done in an examination must have regard to which sort of standard (norm or criterion-measure) is being used, for otherwise confusion, even absurdity, may arise if the language appropriate to the one standard is used in referring to the other.

Setting the standard for criterion-reference

Since the standard, here, is the measure of the criterion, which itself is a specified performance, the question of setting a standard is essentially the question of *what* performance is to be specified. (The criterion-performance need not be, of course, a 'unit' performance, but is likely to be a composite or set of unit-performances.)

Here again the decision must depend upon the examination's purpose–in this instance its ulterior purpose, ulterior, that is, to the immediate purpose of evaluation. In particular, it must depend upon the *consequences* of a candidate's reaching or not reaching the standard specified, such as his being admitted to or debarred from a higher course, his being required to repeat the course, or to take another examination, his being granted or refused a degree, and the like. Obviously, there would be no point in setting a standard if there were to be no such consequences, for a standard (whether norm or criterion-based) presupposes consequences of comparison with it. And whatever standard may have been set, it presupposes consequences *contingent* upon its having been reached, or not reached. In the *setting* of the standard in the first place, however, the contingency will be the other way round: the performance (criterion) which is to be represented by the standard must itself be appropriate to the consequences. For example, once the entry-standard to a higher course in a topic has *been* set, a candidate will be refused entry because he has not reached that set standard; but the standard will *be* set at this level rather than that because candidates failing to reach it will not benefit from the higher course. To express both contingencies at once: a candidate is rejected because he has not reached the standard, because that standard is appropriate to rejection. If the latter contingency did not hold there would be no justification of the former.

To repeat, the mark constituting the standard is not set in an arbitrary way, as if '50 per cent should do'. It has to be the mark which is the measure of the criterion. Neither is the criterion set arbitrarily. It has to be a performance (simple or complex) appropriate to the consequences of its being reached or not reached. When a standard is to be set, therefore, the first essential is an explicit statement of what the consequences are, because it is upon the nature of these consequences that the setting of the standard must depend.

Even within one examination there could of course be several standards, but as Popham and Husek (1969) point out, the number of standards to be set will be restricted by the number of courses of action available—what we have been calling 'the consequences'. If only a straight Admit-Reject judgment is involved, only one standard is needed; but if a distinction is to be drawn between Rejects who are to be utterly rejected and Rejects who are to be offered a further examination, two standards will be required. In general, the *maximum* number of standards required will be one less than the number of different consequences. This will be also, however, the *minimum* number of standards required, because to each consequence-choice there will have to correspond a crucial level of performance, and each of these will have to be represented by the standard which is its measure. If, then, the number of different consequences is C, the number of standards will have to be precisely $C - 1$.

How many different consequences (and therefore how many different standards) there ought to be will of course be determined by the examination's purpose, for the ulterior purpose of the examination is to discover, not what the consequences should be, but which candidates are to be subject to the consequences written into the reason for having the examination in the first place. In this connection it may be observed, in passing, that a multiplicity of standards may have certain advantages for the examinees; but it does not relieve the examiner of the obligation to set standards which are appropriate; on the contrary, his obligation will be multiplied, because it will have to be met for each of the standards set. For example, what standard will justify the examiner's failing a candidate but granting him an extended course and subsequent re-examination, but not requiring the candidate to repeat the whole course?

The general answer to questions of this sort is that when a standard has to be set the consequences contingent upon its being reached or not reached must be expressed in terms of *performance*, so that the criterion-performance can be set to match them. The complexity of this task will vary from case to case. When entry to a course, trade, or profession depends upon the candidate's possessing skills to be employed in it, the criterion will consist of that body of skills. But while in such cases it is easy enough to state the general nature of the criterion it is not always easy to specify it in particular instances, because not all trades and professions have been subjected to the necessary job-analysis. Even greater difficulty arises when there is little or no overlap of performances in the areas preceding and succeeding the examination. For example, some university and college subjects are not studied at school, and so in such cases the examination cannot consist of a sample of the performances to be studied later. The technicalities of dealing with this kind of problem will not be discussed here: it is a matter for experiment, aimed at discovering which performances, in subjects the candidates have already studied, will provide the best prediction.

Comparing a mark with the standard

In this section we shall assume that, in the light of the examination's consequences, the criterion has been established and that its measure (the standard) has been determined, and consider what is involved in the actual evaluation of a mark by reference to that standard. As we have noted, within one examination there may be several criteria, and accordingly several standards, but if so we shall assume that each of these is known, and consider what is involved in comparing a candidate's mark with any one of them.

Suppose that in a particular case there are two criteria, one represented by the mark of 50, the other by the mark of 30, and that a particular candidate scored 43. He has therefore met the lower criterion, but not the higher. And for all practical purposes, so far as that candidate is concerned, that is all that need be said. If candidates meeting the higher criterion have 'passed', candidates not meeting the higher criterion but meeting the lower have 'failed' but are allowed to resit, and candidates failing to meet the lower criterion are not allowed to resit, it does not matter that our candidate scored 43 instead of 49 or 30, for the consequences are the same. For all practical purposes the candidates in this examina-

tion fall into three bands—those at 50 and above, those from 30 to 49, and those below 30; and the consequences are identical for all candidates within the one band. Precisely where a candidate is within one band is quite *in*consequential.

It could of course be argued that a candidate who misses the standard by only 1 or 2 should *not* be subject to the same consequences as candidates who miss it by more; but the reply must be that if that argument has any justification at all, these different consequences ought to have been reflected in an additional criterion, and corresponding standard, in the first place. Our argument has been based upon the assumption that all available consequences (such as the three described above) have already been made explicit and the corresponding standards determined. Accordingly, the objection is not an objection to our argument, but refers to the inadequacy of the initial statement of consequences.

An apparently more serious objection could be that, since no examination is perfectly valid, particularly in respect of marking-consistency and sampling of questions, small divergences from the standard should be discounted. For instance (in our example) a candidate scoring 49, or even 48, might be allowed to pass. This is a fair point, but in order to effect it one should know exactly *how* inconsistent the marks are, so that one can determine exactly how far below the standard one may go. Even if we assume, however, that this can be estimated (and it seldom will be), our previous argument still holds, because to make the pass mark 48 *instead* of 50 is simply to change the standard–to set up a new *standard* to which the argument still applies. Obviously one could not then treat candidates who just missed this new standard of 48 as if they had reached the criterion, because that sort of allowance has already been made.

Moreover, the 'imperfect validity' objection cuts both ways. While re-marking or setting a different sample of questions might well have raised above 50 some of those formerly below it, it might equally well put below 50 some of those formerly above it. Although there is certainly a danger of failing some candidates who might have passed, there is also the danger of passing some who might have failed; and to reduce the latter danger one would have to raise the standard, say to 52 or 53, not lower it to 48.

In which direction, up or down, the standard should be moved will depend upon the nature of the examination's consequences. In some instances of doubt it would be reasonable to chance the candidate's passing–perhaps on the ground that he

would continue to learn on the job, and that initial imperfections would not be serious. But in other instances of doubt the consequences of inability could be so grave that no such allowances could be made.

The examiner can mimimise both these dangers, of course, by maximising the examination's validity–by reference to the conditions of Question-Relevance, Mark-Relevance, Marking-Consistency, and Balance.

Now so far it has been argued only that, in comparing a candidate's mark with the standard, in criterion-reference, it is sufficient to say that the mark was, or was not, up to a stated standard: for example, that he passed, and can now practise as a teacher, doctor or dentist; or that he failed, but can resit in September; or that he failed completely. Such statements are perfectly clear and indicate unambiguously the 'value' of the candidate's performance. It might nevertheless be objected that greater precision could be useful, and that (for instance) it would be in order to report not merely that the candidate had failed though entitled to resit, but also that his mark was 43, and was precisely 7 below the standard of 50.

To this objection there are two replies. First, if greater precision would in fact be of use, that use would constitute a 'consequence' which should have been reflected by an additional criterion. If it is of use to know that the candidate scored 43 rather than (say) 37, then somewhere between 37 and 43 there should a standard which is the measure of that additional criterion. If certain differences between marks are of any *consequence*, these consequences should be made explicit at the outset.

The second reply is that any attempt to *evaluate* the numerical difference between a candidate's mark and the standard would seem to lead inevitably to *norm*-reference. For instance, in scoring 43 a candidate has done better than *if* he had scored only 37; but that is tantamount to saying that he has done better than another candidate who *did* score 37–and that is of the nature of norm-reference, not criterion-reference. Again, if (in the same example) the standard (the measure of the criterion) were 50, it could be said that our candidate had given 86 per cent of the performances required to meet the criterion. But how *good* is it to score 86 per cent of them? Our answer has been, 'Not good enough!' And if it were pointed out that no other candidate scored even that much, this might be worth pointing out, but it would exemplify reference to a norm, not to the criterion.

Within the context of criterion-reference the discrepancy between the candidate's score (say 43) and the criterion-score (say 50) must be described, if it is to be described at all, in terms of performance. If the criterion-score were at once the maximum possible score, it would be necessary to state what performances were represented by the difference of 7–for that candidate. ('For that candidate', because some other candidate with the same score might have obtained that score in another way.) If, however, the maximum possible mark were (say) 80, there would be 37 performances the candidate had failed to give. In any case the candidate could of course be given information about the performances he failed to give, but useful as this might be it does not constitute *evaluation*.

To recapitulate: in criterion-reference the evaluation of a candidate's performance would seem to be restricted to the statement of whether he reached some specified criterion. A statement of the numerical difference between his mark and the standard might be of interest, and do no harm, but for the reasons given above can scarcely qualify as an evaluation. There is, of course, no technical objection to the use of *norm*-reference too, but this is not the point presently at issue.

Comparing a candidate's marks

It has already been argued that a candidate's mark in one examination cannot be directly compared with his mark in a different examination. If Tom scores 43 in Art and 36 in Biology, we cannot properly infer that he has done better in the former than in the latter. We can nevertheless compare his 'standings' in the two examinations, and in so far as 'good', 'merit', and so on, refer to standings, Tom's 'better' performance is in the subject in which he has the higher standing. But this is, of course, *norm*-reference. Then what of *criterion*-reference? Since we cannot properly compare his marks, what *do* we compare?

The same basic *principle* still applies, namely that we compare the candidate's mark in Examination A with the standard in Examination A, compare his mark in Examination B with the standard in Examination B, and then compare the results of these initial comparisons. In norm-reference, the standard in each case is the set of marks obtained by the group, and the result of each of the two initial comparisons is a 'standing' (such as a percentile), so that what we finally compare are two standings. In criterion-reference, the standard is the measure of the criterion, so that what we finally compare are the results of the two comparisons with these measures.

As we argued in the previous section, however, comparison of a mark with the standard (criterion-score) is restricted to the observation that the mark reached, or did not reach, the standard. The most that can be said of the final comparison, then, is that the candidate reached both criteria, or failed to reach either, or reached one but not the other. For instance, if he scored 43 in Art, the criterion being 50, and scored 36 in Biology, the criterion being 33, we might say that he did better in Biology–on the ground that he 'passed' in Biology but 'failed' in Art. Note that we cannot say that the Biology standard was 'lower' than the Art standard–for the oft-quoted reason that marks in different examinations are not comparable. Nor would it be proper to inquire whether the Biology examination was more difficult, or easier, than the Art examination–because measures of difficulty necessitate *norm*-reference (see Chapter 5). For the same reason it would be irrelevant to point out (assuming it to be true) that the candidate was top in Art and quite low in the merit list in Biology –norm-reference again. It would be improper also to allege that, by missing the criterion by 7 marks in one examination and by only 3 marks in another, the candidate had done somewhat better in the latter–because (once more) marks in different examinations cannot be assumed to be directly comparable.

Generally, if the evaluation of a candidate's marks in two examinations is restricted to criterion-reference alone, there is very little that can properly be said about the results of a comparison. We might say that he had done better in Examination P than in Examination Q (in that he passed in P and failed in Q, or in that he failed P but was allowed to resit it but was not even allowed to resit Q). But why say it? Why not just cite the facts?

The comparison of standards

Students often allege that the pass-standard in one subject, say French, is higher than the pass-standard in some other subject, say English. Critics of an educational system sometimes assert that standards are falling; more optimistic commentators argue that standards are rising. Boards of examiners are likely to want to maintain the same standard in a subject from one year to another. All these views are nevertheless the same in one important respect: they presuppose the possibility of *demonstrating* that one standard is higher than, equal to, or lower than some other standard. (If they do not presuppose such a possibility, they are of no practical significance.) Is the presupposition true?

In the previous section we noted that it cannot be said that the standard in one subject is higher than the standard in another merely because the measure constituting the former is a larger number than the measure constituting the latter–for marks in different examinations cannot be assumed to be comparable. And for that same reason we cannot assume that two standards are equal merely because both are, say, 55.

Standards cannot be compared, then, merely by our looking at their numerical values. How they *can* be compared is nevertheless indicated by the kinds of evidence commonly cited in support of assertions about them. As we should have reason to expect, the evidence tends to be of two kinds, evidence referring to norms and evidence referring to actual performance.

When students allege that the pass-standard in (say) French is higher than the pass-standard in (say) English, they are likely to point out, in support of the allegation, that a higher proportion of candidates fail in French than in English. All that this 'proves', however, is that the pass-standard in French is a higher *norm* than is the pass-standard in English–such as the 50th percentile as against the 30th. In so far as this is the only evidence submitted, saying that the pass-standard in French is the higher *means* simply that a higher proportion of candidates fail in that subject.

Likewise, if a Board of Examiners notes that 12 per cent of the 527 candidates failed in Psychology this year, whereas only $5\frac{1}{2}$ per cent failed last year, and someone comments that the standard has been raised, all we can properly infer is that the crucial *norm* has risen–from the $5\frac{1}{2}$th percentile to the 12th.

But (following up the last example) the Psychology examiner might correctly point out that there was a sense in which the standard had not risen at all, and was in fact the same as before. He had applied the same test in the two successive years, and had used the same mark as the pass mark on both occasions. (We are not suggesting that pass-fail decisions should rest on the results of only one test. We take this simple case merely to illustrate the difference between standards which are norms and standards which are measures of criterion-performances.) He can then say, correctly, that it was not the standard which rose, but it was the present year's group which was poorer.

This latter example illustrates an important point. The Psychology examiner was entitled to say that the standard was the same on the two occasions because the *same examination* was taken on both, and because within the one examination the marks *are* comparable. In particular, the pass mark of (say) 67 this year represents the same *performance* as did the pass mark of 67 last year, although the *norm*-value of that mark changed. In saying that the standard has remained the same, then, the Psychology examiner is referring, not to a norm, but to the standard representing a criterion.

In contrast, had this year's Psychology examination been concerned with different performances, the very issue of the comparison of criteria would be improper. A criterion, it will be recalled, is a specified performance (or set of performances). In establishing a criterion we have to say what the performances *are*. It would be proper, then, to say that one criterion was the same as another only if the two criteria consisted of the *same* performances; and it would be proper to say that one criterion was higher (or greater, etc.) than another only if it *contained* the performances constituting the other, and other performances also. Accordingly, if the performances in one examination are different from those in another, it will be improper to say that the one criterion is equal to, *or* lower than, *or* higher than the other; it will be improper to draw any comparison at all.

If, then, it is improper to compare criteria in two different examinations in the one subject (such as Psychology), in so far as these two examinations call for different performances, it will be apparent that it will certainly be improper to compare criteria in examinations in different subjects–in which, almost by definition of 'different subjects', the performances *will* be different.

Criterion-reference, it would seem, virtually precludes the comparison of standards; it just does not make sense to say that the (criterion-) standard in one subject or one examination is higher or lower or equal to the (criterion-) standard in another. If standards are to be compared, therefore, they must be standards in the form of norms. The only apparent exception, which strictly is not an exception, is within the one subject when the *same* examination is applied again, or when one examination contains the performances of the other.

9   Norm-reference or criterion-reference?

Is there a choice?

As we have seen, a candidate's mark may be evaluated in either of two ways – by reference to a norm or by reference to a criterion-measure – but while both types of reference are possible, the examiner does not have a free choice, for whether he is to use norm-reference or criterion-reference depends upon the (ulterior) purpose for which the evaluation is made. This was mentioned in the previous chapter by way of illustration; in this chapter we examine the issue, looking again at some of the purposes already described, in order to make explicit which type of reference is appropriate to each.

The purposes we proposed to discuss further were those of ascertaining whether a specified standard had been reached, selection, indicating student progress, and discovering the extent to which a course's objectives were being achieved. The issue is not always clearcut, however, for although the type of reference to be used in evaluating a mark must depend upon the purpose ulterior to evaluation, yet that ulterior purpose may allow the examiner a choice – even if only for the reason that its statement is insufficiently precise.

Ascertaining whether a specified standard has been reached

Strictly, this purpose is not ulterior to evaluation at all, because to ascertain whether a candidate's mark has reached a specified standard is to compare it with that standard – which is what evaluation itself is. We have nevertheless included it here, because it refers to a 'specified' standard, and because it might therefore seem that a specified standard would indicate which type of reference is required.

The obvious way to make a standard a specific one is to

quote it as a quite precise measure–for example as 50, and not as 'about 50'; but while such exactitude is highly desirable in some respects, it does not indicate whether evaluation is to be by reference to a norm or by reference to a criterion, because it is not specified whether the mark of 50 is a raw mark or a scaled mark, and this is crucial.

Consider first the case in which the prescribed standard is the *scaled* mark of 50. As we saw in Chapter Seven, a scaled mark is essentially an indicator of a particular percentile position. Reference to a scaled mark is therefore reference to a *norm*. To underline the point: if the scaled mark of 50 is a 'pass mark', to fail all candidates with scaled marks of less than 50 is to fail a predetermined number of candidates, the magnitude of the number depending upon the particular percentile position that mark has been defined to have. We are not suggesting, of course, that to fail a predetermined number of candidates is necessarily to be deplored; the example was intended only to illustrate that a standard which is a scaled mark presupposes norm-reference.

In contrast, a standard which is a prescribed *raw* mark does *not* presuppose norm-reference, because in advance of the examination's results one cannot know what the percentile value of any prescribed raw mark will be. But it does not follow that a prescribed raw mark as standard presupposes *criterion*-reference–for the reason now given.

The previous chapter emphasised that in criterion-referenced evaluation the criterion is a specified *performance*, specified in the light of the consequences of its being adopted *as* criterion, the standard being its measure. For criterion-reference, therefore, no other raw mark will serve; the standard has to be the mark which is the measure of the performance previously specified as the criterion. Nor, indeed, will any other raw mark be any sort of standard at all, for it will have no prescribed meaning, indicating neither a *specified* level of performance as such nor a *specified* percentile position.

One might of course decide that the standard should be some 'traditional' pass mark, say 50, and *then* devise a marking scheme in such a way that the previously specified criterion-performance would have that particular mark; but this does not affect the main argument, namely that for criterion-reference the standard must be the measure of the prescribed criterion.

To recapitulate: to specify a *scaled* mark as standard is to presuppose *norm*-reference; to specify a *raw* mark as standard is not necessarily to presuppose either type of reference, for a raw mark as standard never presupposes norm-reference, and presupposes criterion-reference only when (in accord with the prepared marking scheme) it is the measure of the criterion.

However, even if the specification of the standard did include notice that it was a scaled mark (presupposing norm-reference) or was the raw mark which *was* the measure of the criterion (presupposing criterion-reference), such notification would still leave open the question of which sort of reference it *ought* to have been. And to answer that question it is necessary to look to whatever purpose is ulterior to the evaluation. Otherwise expressed, while a standard *can* be specified in such a way as to make clear which type of reference is to be made, the examiner is not entitled to specify the type of reference until he has considered *why* the candidates' marks are to be evaluated.

Selection

When, as is customary, 'selection' means creaming off a prescribed number or percentage of candidates, it presupposes *norm*-reference. If the top 70 candidates are to be selected, the standard will be the mark obtained or surpassed by 70 candidates. If the top 15 per cent of candidates are to be selected, the standard will be the mark found, by inspection of the frequency distribution, to lie at the 85th percentile. In both cases the standard is determined by its having a prescribed standing among the marks actually obtained, and this is, of course, characteristic of norm-reference.

(It might seem odd to speak of 'selecting' candidates from the lower end of the list—say the poorest 10 per cent, or the 23 weakest; but whatever word might be substituted for 'selection' in this sort of case, the case would still be one of norm-reference.)

But why should the standard mark be set at one particular standing rather than at another? Why select 70 candidates rather than 80 or 43; why the top 15 per cent rather than the top 3 or 34 per cent? The answer is essentially the same as was given in Chapter Eight in connection with criterion-reference. The standard will be set at a particular percentile level (or at a mark obtained or surpassed by a prescribed number of candidates–which comes to the same thing) because that particular percentile will be appropriate to the *consequences* contingent upon a candidate's reaching or failing to reach it; that is, appropriate to what the selection is *for*.

For instance, if the number of 'places' in a college, school, or course is predetermined, say at 70, the 'consequences' are 'getting one of the 70 places' and 'not getting one of the 70 places', and so the standard must be the mark cutting off the top 70 candidates. Likewise, if there are places for a predetermined percentage of candidates, say 15 per cent of them, the standard will have to be the mark lying at the 85th percentile.

At first sight it might seem unnecessarily prolix to refer to a *mark* at all–the mark found to lie at (say) the 85th percentile. Why not just say that the top 15 per cent will be admitted? The reason is, of course, that reference to a specific mark simplifies the task of discovering *which* candidates comprise the top 15 per cent: the economical way of discovering this is to draw up a frequency distribution, note from it which mark cuts off the top 15 per cent, and then pick out all candidates scoring that mark or higher.

Our example was nevertheless intended to illustrate a more important point. We supposed that the number of places was predetermined, such as 70, or as a percentage of the total number of candidates–say the top 15 per cent. We had to suppose this, for otherwise the example would not have been an example of selection. If the number of places is not predetermined, there is no prescription of the crucial percentile; and if no particular percentile is prescribed there is no specification of a standard of the kind selection requires, and so selection, presupposing norm-reference, is impossible. Selection is the appropriate procedure only when the 'consequences' involve a predetermined number of places. Of course, for 'places' one may read 'scholarships', 'prizes', 'posts', 'promotions', and so on; the principle remains the same.

Now of a great many instances in which selection procedures are used it could be asked whether the number of places (etc.) *ought* to be predetermined. Important as this question may be, it is outside the scope of our discussion–concerned with the

evaluation of techniques for given purposes, not with the evaluation of purposes themselves. Before we leave the topic of selection, however, two final points may be made. First, there is no need to quarrel about what we have taken 'selection' to mean in this section. If it is to mean that the number of candidates to be accepted does *not* necessarily have to be predetermined, and that all candidates reaching a *criterion* will be accepted–then of course the appropriate procedure is criterion-reference. Second, even if (as we supposed here) 'selection' does presuppose a fixed number or percentage of acceptable candidates, such selection may nevertheless be coupled with criterion-reference. For instance, even if 70 places were available, not all of them might be filled; the candidates could be required also to reach a specified criterion. Conversely, some candidates might reach the criterion but not be accepted, because they were not in the top 70.

Discovering the extent to which course objectives have been met

This statement of purpose is rather general, and could mean several things. We shall consider these in turn, but first we consider what they have in common.

Since all that an examination can assess is performance, a

purpose concerned with the attainment of objectives can be fulfilled only if the objectives themselves are expressed as performances, that is, as what the students will *do* if the course is satisfactorily completed. The questions must therefore be directives to give these performances. And since no other performances are relevant to this purpose, only candidates obtaining the maximum possible mark will have met all the objectives. We now look at several different purposes of which these points are true.

First, the examination's purpose could be to discover the extent to which *each candidate* had mastered the course's objectives. The simplest way to fulfil this purpose is to award each unit-performance the mark of 1; a candidate's mark then indicates the number of performances he has mastered, and the extent to which he has mastered them is indicated by a comparison of his mark with the maximum possible mark representing the full extent. (Earlier, the maximum possible mark was rejected as a standard, but in respect of *norm*-reference. The present purpose presupposes *criterion*-reference, to which our earlier objections are irrelevant.)

If, then, a candidate scored 42 out of a possible 90, we could say he had mastered about half the course's objectives. It would be a different matter, however, to *evaluate* that extent; for as we argued earlier, evaluation which goes beyond the mere comparison of a mark with the criterion-mark presupposes *norm*-reference. Further, knowing that a candidate has mastered half the objectives is not the same as knowing what these objectives are.[19] Finally (p. 112), there is no consequential difference between a candidate who misses the standard by 48 objectives and another who misses it by 6. These three points suggest that there is not a great deal of value in fulfilling this particular purpose.

But second, the purpose might be not so much to assess the candidates *per se* as to assess the course. True, we cannot test the success of the course except by testing the students who took it, their degrees of success on the course providing a measure of the course's success with them. But there is a difference in emphasis, affecting the way in which student-success is to be assessed. If one candidate mastered only half the course's objectives, it might be said that the course had not been much of a success so far as he was concerned; but most of the other candidates might have mastered every objective, and so it might be argued that, overall, the course had been a successful one. On this view, what would be required would be a mark or set of marks representing the whole group.

One possible way of fulfilling that purpose, then, would be to provide the *average* score of the group. If the group average were 78 out of a possible 90, we should then have a measure of the extent to which the course had been successful for its students. As we saw earlier, however, to quote an average without quoting also some measure of scatter can be misleading. The average of 78 might obscure the fact that very many students had fulfilled every single objective and that a small number had fulfilled scarcely any. A better picture would be provided by quoting how many candidates achieved all the objectives, how many achieved all but one, how many all but two, and so on; that is by quoting the frequency distribution.

There is a third possible version of the purpose. Instead of our finding out the number of objectives achieved by each candidate, we could find out the number of candidates achieving each objective. Just as the extent of a candidate's success is the number of objectives he achieved, the extent of an objective's success is the number of candidates who achieved it. For instance, if a particular objective were achieved by 63 out of 140 candidates, its 'success rate' would be 45 per cent. This way of analysing the results is the basis of 'item analysis', discussed in more detail in a later chapter, but it will be apparent that it will be a very useful form of analysis when an examination is intended to discover how well the various parts of a course have gone–and therefore to indicate which parts will require greater emphasis, or more time, or a different form of presentation, and the like. In general, item analysis is particularly appropriate for the investigation of what Glaser (1963) has called 'instructional treatments'.

Useful as item analysis is, however, it could be objected that information about the success-rate of each single objective is not at the same time information about the success of the course as a whole. (This is of essentially the same form as the objection that the marks of individual candidates do not them-selves indicate how well the group has done.) We might therefore choose to calculate the *average* success-rate of the objectives; or since averages can be misleading without indications of scatter, we might quote that so many objectives had 100 per cent success, so many had 99 per cent, and so on. It is doubtful, however, if there is any practical value in knowing such a thing. Would it not be of greater value to know the success-rate of each single objective? What sort of consequences could sensibly follow the assessment of a course *as a whole*?

Which of these specific versions of the purpose of discovering the extent to which course objectives have been met is the best? Surely the version most in accord with what the examiner needs to find out – in accord with his reason for having the examination in the first place? Our opinion, however, is that some form of item analysis is likely to be the most appropriate for most purposes.

Finally, some comments about precision. For many purposes, validity is lowered to the extent that marks are shared, but for the three purposes relating to course objectives this is not necessarily so. If the questions are in fact directives to give the performances constituting the course's objectives, and if the marking is both relevant and consistent, and if every candidate scored full marks, there are no grounds for doubting the validity of the results. Similarly if every candidate scored no marks at all – and for all intermediate cases. The very purpose of assessing the extent to which objectives have been achieved *presupposes* the possibility that all were achieved, or none was achieved, and so on; and so it would be illogical and naïve to assume that for this purpose imprecision of results lowers their validity.

(A corollary deserves mention. As we commented in the Preface, in terms of the traditional concept of Reliability an examination cannot be valid if it is not reliable. Traditional measures of reliability, however, decrease with the distribution's standard deviation. In particular, if every candidate obtained the same mark (such as the maximum possible mark), the standard deviation would be zero, and according to the traditional view the results would have no validity. As we argued in the previous paragraph, however, it would be illogical to apply such an assumption to the purpose we have been discussing in this section. Indeed, as has been pointed out elsewhere (e.g. Popham and

Husek 1969), such measures of reliability–and therefore of validity–are not appropriate to *any* instance of criterion-referenced evaluation. These measures developed, of course, in the traditional context of *norm*-reference, where they are relevant; but we make this comment here to illustrate and emphasise the point that statistical measures should not be used in a purely routine way without reference to the examination's purpose. This point in turn, it will be recognised, provides a good reason for the view of validity recommended by the APA in 1966 and elaborated in our first chapter.)

It does not follow, of course, that precision can be ignored. If an examiner recognised (correctly) that precision of results is not necessary for maximum validity, but (incorrectly) were somewhat imprecise in his *marking*, he could be glossing over performances which should have received a mark and perhaps awarding marks for performances which were irrelevant. And the result could be that some candidates who, with more careful marking, would have reached the criterion, did not reach it; and conversely. In general, while imprecision of results does not necessarily lower validity, yet the marking must be such as to *allow* of maximum precision, even if it is not in fact producible. The conditions of Mark-Relevance and Marking-Consistency must still be observed.

Indicating student progress

In Chapter Three it was noted that while this purpose presupposes a standard of comparison, yet the standard might be any of several different things. It will now be apparent, however, that all possible standards will be norms or measures of a criterion. Since comparison with each of these types of standard has already been described in some detail, all we need do now is comment briefly on comparison in respect of this particular purpose.

First, it is pointless to compare a candidate's raw marks in successive examinations. There is no guarantee that the change from 43 to 61 per cent constitutes an improvement, because these marks in themselves indicate neither standings nor approximations to criteria. Direct comparison is legitimate only if the two examinations are the same examination held on successive occasions—with, of course, the same marking scheme.

If, however, 'progress' means that the candidate has raised his standing, there is no need to use the same examination twice—so long as it could be said that the two examinations were concerned with the same topic, and in so far as the same group of candidates took both. For instance, if in consequence of the first examination the candidate were demoted to a less able group, the fact that he had a higher standing in the poorer group than he previously had in the better group could scarcely be taken to indicate 'progress'.

If, on the other hand, 'progress' were to be assessed by reference to a criterion, then since different criteria are not comparable we could say a candidate was 'progressing' only in so far as he approximated more closely to the *same* criterion—which would require the use of the same examination on the two occasions.

Finally, an inquiry about a student's 'progress' might use that word in a rather loose way, as if it were asked 'how he was getting on'. That sort of question might not require the sorts of comparison we have just described, but might well be answered by our saying he was in the top quarter of the class, or so far had achieved about half the course's objectives.

The need to specify purpose

The aim of this chapter, it will be recalled, was to indicate which purposes of examining called for norm-reference, which for criterion-reference. Since conclusions based upon the one form of reference can be very different from those based upon the other, choice of the wrong form of reference can lead to conclusions which are invalid. And since validity has to be assessed in respect of the examination's purpose, plainly the examiner must begin by stating unambiguously what his purpose is. As we saw in this chapter, the statements of some purposes, even when they appear to be quite clear, are not specific enough to indicate what form of evaluation is to be used.

Further, as we tried to show, the initial determination of the norm or criterion-measure which is to serve as standard must depend upon the examination's *consequences*. A useful way of bringing the statement of a purpose down to earth, then, is to express the purpose *in terms of* the particular consequences to which the candidates will eventually be subject. For example, instead of saying simply that the purpose is to select the best 10 per cent of candidates, we could say it was to select the (say) twenty-two candidates who are best equipped to enter a certain course of study, or profession, etc. Precise statements of this sort do not, of course, make examining easier. Perhaps the contrary! But they do serve to increase the likelihood of its being more valid—by indicating not only what performances should be asked for (Question-Relevance), and how answers should be marked (Mark-Relevance), but also what *sort* of standard should be used (norm or criterion-measure) and at what *level* the appropriate standard should be set.

PART TWO

The combining of marks

10   Some basic facts of combination

Problems and facts

Frequently, a candidate's mark in a paper is a combination of his marks in several questions; his mark in an examination is a composite of his marks in several papers; his mark at the end of a session or semester is compounded of his marks in several examinations. Whatever the areas or topics in which marks are combined the problems are nevertheless the same, and it is with the problems of combination that this part of the book is concerned.

Discussion of problems will be unprofitable, however, unless based upon facts. In this chapter we look at some of the most basic facts of combination. In the next chapter we consider why marks should be combined at all, and examine the issue of validity. And in the last chapter of this part we note how the relevant facts have to be taken into account in dealing with practical problems.

Throughout, we shall refer to the mark obtained by combining a candidate's marks in various topics as his 'composite mark', to the marks so combined as the 'component marks', to the distribution of composite marks as the 'composite distribution', and to the distributions of component marks as the 'component distributions'. At first, however, for simplicity's sake, we shall consider the combination of marks in only two areas; that is, only two component distributions.

The scatter of the composite marks

There is one fundamental fact of combination which is sometimes overlooked. For each of the component topics there will be, of course, a frequency distribution to which the examiner will doubtless have made reference—in calculating an average mark, for instance, or in assessing the candidates' relative merits within the topic. But when the marks in these distributions are added, candidate by candidate, that very addition produces another distribution–namely the distribution of composite marks. Admittedly, not every examiner may actually draw up this distribution; but there are occasions when reference to it is necessary for the understanding of what a candidate's composite mark means, and so we ought to make explicit some of its characteristics. Its Mean is simply the sum of the Means of the component distributions, but as we saw earlier, the scatter of a distribution can be of fundamental importance too, and in this section we consider that characteristic.

Since the composite distribution derives from the component distributions, one might assume that its scatter would be dependent upon the scatters of the component distributions. This is true, but the composite distribution's scatter depends also upon the degree of *correspondence* between the two component distributions. This point is illustrated by the following examples, in which A and B are the components, C the composite.

	EXAMPLE I			EXAMPLE II			EXAMPLE III			EXAMPLE IV		
	A	B	C	A	B	C	A	B	C	A	B	C
Jan:	72	60	132	72	55	127	72	45	117	72	45	117
Jed:	61	55	116	61	60	121	61	55	116	61	50	111
Jim:	50	50	100	50	45	95	50	60	110	50	55	105
Joe:	39	45	84	39	50	89	39	50	89	39	60	99

The A-distribution is the same in all four examples. It has a Range of 33, and in each example the order of merit is the same too. In the B-topic, however, the order of merit changes from one example to another; but the actual marks, the *distribution*, remains the same–and have a Range of 15. In Example I the B-order is the same as the A-order; in Example II the two orders are slightly different; in Example III they are even more different; and in Example IV the B-order is the complete reversal of the A-order.

If we now look at the Range of the composite marks in

each example we see that in Example I it is the largest, namely 48–which is the sum of the components' Ranges, 33+15. In Example II the composite's Range is rather less, namely 38. In Example III it is only 28; and in Example IV it is 18–which is the difference between the components' ranges, 33–15. The point is that the composite scatter depends, not only upon the components' scatters, but also upon the extent to which their orders of merit correspond.

Of course, as we noted in an earlier chapter, the Range is not the best measure of scatter; and in any case four examples can at best illustrate a principle; they cannot prove it. Proof requires reference to a general formula.[20] The principle is that the scatter of the composite varies with the scatters of the components *and* with the degree of correspondence between the components themselves. What the component scatters do, in effect, is to determine the upper and lower limits of the composite scatter–the upper limit being the sum of the component scatters, the lower limit being their difference. In particular, given the component scatters, a high degree of correspondence between the components will produce a large composite scatter, a low degree of correspondence a small scatter.

Correlation

As the previous section illustrated, some facts of combination can be stated only by reference to 'degrees of correspondence' between distributions; that is, by our speaking of 'correspondence' in quantitative terms. When this has to be done it is convenient to do it in terms of the concept of Correlation.

The degree of correspondence between two distributions is customarily referred to as the 'correlation' between them. The actual measure of the correlation is known as a 'correlation coefficient'. To obtain such a measure in any given case we must have a formula into which we can feed the relevant data. Two formulae are in common use. One of these produces a measure of the degree of correspondence between the candidates' *ranks* in the two distributions. The other is more precise, but both produce measures (correlation coefficients) with very similar meanings, and in this account we need not examine or even quote the formulae themselves; it will be enough to look at the meanings of the measures they produce. (For the formulae see Appendix I, pp. 263-4.)

Irrespective of its particular numerical value, a correlation coefficient indicates the correspondence between the candidates' *standings* (e.g. ranks) in two distributions. Its conventional symbol is r (though the rank-order correlation coefficient is sometimes symbolised by the small Greek letter *rho*). Particular values of r, then, indicate particular degrees of correlation between (the standings in) two distributions.

The formulae which produce correlation coefficients are such that r has a maximum value of $+1 \cdot 0$, a minimum value of $-1 \cdot 0$. When each candidate has the same standing in A as he has in B, the correlation is at the maximum, namely $+1 \cdot 0$. In complete contrast, when each candidate's standing in B is the reversal of his standing in A (so that, for instance, someone who was fourth top in A was fourth bottom in B), the correlation is at a minimum, namely $-1 \cdot 0$. In other words, $r = +1 \cdot 0$ means that the two sets of standings are *perfectly similar*, and $r = -1 \cdot 0$ means that they are *utterly dissimilar*. The value of $r = 0 \cdot 0$, half way between $+1 \cdot 0$ and $-1 \cdot 0$, would be taken to mean that the (standings in) two distributions in this respect were half way between being utterly similar and utterly dissimilar–that is, that there was no sort of correspondence at all. (Note that utter dissimilarity can be envisaged as being a sort of perfect correspondence.)

Rarely, however, will r have one of these three particular values in practice. Intermediate values are to be expected, and these will have intermediate meanings. Thus a correlation of $+0 \cdot 8$ would indicate that while there was not a *perfect* positive correlation between the two variables, yet there was a quite marked *tendency* for high scorers in the one topic to score highly in the other topic also, and for low scores in the one to belong to the same candidates as had low scores in the other. A coefficient of $+0 \cdot 5$ would indicate a less marked tendency in the same direction. A correlation of $-0 \cdot 2$ would indicate that there was very little correspondence at all–but that what correspondence there was was negative; that is, that a few low scorers in A were higher scorers in B, and the like.

Three points about correlation deserve emphasis. First, correlation is about standings not marks as such. Second, because correlation coefficients can have negative as well as positive values, one cannot properly speak of one correlation's being a multiple of another; one may speak only of *differences* between them. Third, a point which is obvious once stated: correlations can be used only when the same candidates have marks in both topics, because a candidate's two standings cannot be compared if he has only one. For instance, one cannot correlate the scores of a class in German with those of a different class taking Greek.

In terms of 'correlation', then, the main points of the *preceding* section may be summarised thus: if r_{ab} is the correlation between the components A and B, then when $r_{ab} = +1\cdot0$, the composite scatter is at a maximum, namely the sum of the A and B scatters; when $r_{ab} = -1\cdot0$, the composite scatter is at a minimum, namely the difference between the A and B scatters; and for intermediate values of r_{ab} the composite scatter has values between its maximum and minimum values.

Component-composite correlations

Since the composite distribution is formed from the component distributions one would expect the candidates' standings in the composite to resemble their standings in the components. But to what extents? To what extent will the composite *correlate* with each of the components? And what determines these extents?

As before, A, B and C refer, respectively, to the two components and the composite. The symbols r_{ab}, r_{ac}, and r_{bc} refer to the correlations between A and B, between A and C, and between B and C. We include some cases unlikely to arise in practice, but they serve to throw light on the general issue.

CASE I
When $r_{ab} = +1 \cdot 0$, then both r_{ac} and r_{bc} will also be $+1 \cdot 0$.

EXAMPLE V

	A	B	C
Ron:	53	99	152
Sue:	43	90	133
Tom:	33	81	114
Una:	23	72	95
Vic:	13	63	76

Obviously, since the rank orders in A and B are the same, they must correlate *equally* with C. It may not be obvious, however, that these correlations will be $+1 \cdot 0$. That this is so is shown in Note 21.

CASE 2
When $r_{ab} = -1 \cdot 0$, and the A-scatter exceeds the B-scatter, then $r_{ac} = +1 \cdot 0$, and $r_{bc} = -1 \cdot 0$. (See formulae in Note 21.)

EXAMPLE VI

	A	B	C
Ron:	53	63	116
Sue:	43	72	115
Tom:	33	81	114
Una:	23	90	113
Vic:	13	99	112

Note that although the rank order of B is the complete reversal of A, yet the two sets of marks do not cancel each other out and give every candidate the same composite mark. In fact, the composite has a perfect positive correlation with Component A and a perfect negative correlation with Component B. Certainly, B's reversal of the order of A cuts down the inter-candidate A-differences from 10 to only 1. For instance, in A the candidates Ron and Sue differ by 10, but in the composite their marks are 116 and 115. But the *order* in C is nevertheless the same as that in A and the complete reversal of the order in B. This cannot be due to the A-marks' being larger–for they are not. It is due entirely to the A-marks' having the greater scatter–and even the addition of 100 to every B-mark would make no change. (Note that if the B inter-candidate differences were 10 and not 9, the composite marks *would* all be the same–because the scatters would then be equal.)

CASE 3

When $r_{ab} = -1 \cdot 0$, and the components have equal scatters, then all the candidates have the same composite mark–the composite distribution having no scatter at all.

EXAMPLE VII

	A	B	C
Ron:	97	14	111
Sue:	92	19	111
Tom:	87	24	111
Una:	82	29	111
Vic:	77	34	111

Here again it is the scatter of the marks, not their magnitudes, which produce the effect. The A-marks are larger than the B-marks, but this is of no significance.

CASE 4

When r_{ab} lies between $-1 \cdot 0$ and $+1 \cdot 0$, and the A-scatter exceeds the B-scatter, then r_{ac} exceeds r_{bc}, the difference increasing as the ratio of the A and B scatters increases, and/or as the value of r_{ab} decreases.

This case is not only the most likely to arise in practice; it is also the most complicated. We therefore add the following comments.

Irrespective of the marks' magnitudes, the composite will correlate more highly with the component having the larger scatter. This is important, because in practice no two distributions (unless they have been scaled for it) will have equal scatters. And the more the one component-scatter exceeds the other, the more similar the composite will be to the former, the less similar will it be to the latter.

Also, while this holds good for any value of the inter-component correlation between $-1 \cdot 0$ and $+1 \cdot 0$, yet the extent of the composite's correlation with the components depends upon the particular value the inter-component correlation has. For any given scatter ratio, the composite will correlate increasingly highly with the larger-scatter component as the inter-component correlation falls. The extreme cases have already been considered. When $r_{ab} = +1 \cdot 0$ (Case 1), the two components will correlate equally and perfectly with the composite–no matter by how *much* the one component-scatter exceeds the other. When $r_{ab} = -1 \cdot 0$ (Case 2), the component is utterly similar to the larger-scatter component and utterly dissimilar to the smaller-scatter component, no matter by how *little* the one component-scatter exceeds the other. As we have said, however, in practice virtually all cases will lie between these extremes.

We cannot provide simple illustrative examples of this case in the way we did for the others, because by mere observation of lists of marks one cannot ascertain the extent to which the rank orders differ. Calculation is necessary. A proof of the point is nevertheless provided in Note 22.

CASE 5
When the A-scatter and B-scatter are equal, then $r_{ac} = r_{bc}$, their common value decreasing with r_{ab}.

Examples of this case would not be particularly helpful either, because mere visual inspection of the three distributions (A, B and C) does not indicate the precise values of the three intercorrelations. Proof requires reference to a general formula.[23]

To summarise these somewhat technical points. First, if (as is highly unlikely) there is a perfect positive correlation between the two components, each of them will have a perfect positive correlation with the composite also. Second, if (as is highly unlikely) there is a perfect negative correlation between the two components, the composite will have a perfect positive correlation with the larger-scatter component, a perfect negative correlation with the smaller-scatter component–no matter by how little the one component's scatter exceeds the other. Third, if (as is highly unlikely) there is a perfect negative correlation between the components, and the components have equal scatters, all the composite marks will be the same. Fourth, as *is* highly likely, if the components have a correlation somewhere between perfect positive and perfect negative, the composite will correlate more highly with, be more 'influenced' by, the component with the larger scatter. And the (relatively) greater its scatter, the greater will be its influence. Also, the effect will increase as the correlation of the components decreases. Finally, if (perhaps as the result of scaling) the two components have equal scatters, they will have the same influence upon the standings in the composite.

The 'weights' of the components

Some purposes of examining will require each candidate's standing in the composite to be more influenced by his standing in one component than in the other–in the sense that his composite standing is to be more *similar* to one component standing than to the other. Some purposes will require his composite standing to be equally similar to the component standings. How can the examiner ensure that the requisite similarities are effected?

When candidates' standings in the composite are more similar to their Component A standings than to their Component B standings, Component A is customarily said to have the 'greater weight'. If the composite standings are equally similar to the two sets of component standings, the two components are said to have 'equal weight'. How, then, can the examiner ensure that the components will have the weights required?

Obviously, they will have the requisite weights only in so

far as the examiner observes the conditions determining the components' weights. What are these conditions?

We have seen already that 'similarity' can be envisaged in terms of correlation, and that the composite's correlation with a component depends upon two things, namely the components' relative scatters and their intercorrelation. It might seem, then, that the examiner can ensure the requisite weights by controlling these two conditions. But while he can control the components' scatter-ratio by scaling either or both of the component distributions, he cannot control their intercorrelation–because he cannot legitimately alter the candidates' standings in these components, and so he must accept whatever intercorrelation (r_{ab}) they have. Accordingly, the examiner cannot effect the requisite degrees of similarity between composite and each component–in so far as he envisages the issue of similarity in terms of *correlation*. To effect them he must envisage similarity in some other way.

Another way appears if, instead of concentrating on whole distributions of marks and their intercorrelations, he attends to the composite standing of each individual candidate. A candidate's composite standing then can be seen to consist of two parts. One part is a fraction of his standing in the one component, the other part a fraction of his standing in the other component.[24] When the A-component scatter and the B-component scatter are equal, these two fractions are equal also: with equal component-scatters, a candidate's standings in the components make equal contributions to his standing in the composite. Further, if the A-scatter is p times the B-scatter, the contribution of his A-standing to his composite standing is p times the contribution of his B-standing. In general, any candidate's standing in the composite consists of a fraction of his standing in one component and a fraction of his standing in the other component, the ratio of their contributions to his composite standing being the ratio of the components' scatters.

Here, then, is a view of 'similarity' which involves only the components' scatters, and does not involve their intercorrelation at all. In this sense of 'similarity', therefore, the examiner does have the necessary control over the extent to which each candidate's composite standing is 'similar' to his two component standings. The degree of similarity, in this sense, lies entirely in each composite standing's genetic consitution. In this sense, to say that a composite standing is equally similar to the two component standings is to say that it consists of *equal parts* of the two component standings. To say that the composite standing is three times as like the A-standing as it is to the B-standing is to say that it consists of three parts of the A-standing to one part of the B-standing.

On this view, then, the 'weight' of a distribution may be described as the (relative) number of times its standings are counted into the composite standings. Two points merit comment. We have to say 'relative number of times' because the effect upon the composite standings is a matter of *ratio*. Counting in the A-standings six times and the B-standings three times has the same effect as counting in the A-standing twice and the B-standings once. And since the weights (on this view) are directly proportional to the scatters, giving A a scatter (say SD) of 12 and B a scatter of 8 would have the same effect on the composite standings as would an A-scatter of 36 and a B-scatter of 24. Second, we have to say that weight *may* be described in this way, because at present there does not appear to be any universally accepted definition. This is a somewhat technical problem and will not be enlarged upon here. It is enough to say that the *issue* we have been discussing in this section is customarily discussed in terms of 'weight'. For a more detailed argument see Thyne (1966a), in which various viewpoints are summarised and the case for the above definition is given.

The practical significance of weight

As we have seen, if the components' scatters are in the ratio $p:1$, each candidate's composite standing consists of his component standings in the ratio $p:1$. In this respect, therefore, weighting treats all candidates alike; the same principle is applied to all. The application of that same principle to all will nevertheless have different effects upon different candidates. If the scatter-ratio is (say) 2:1 instead of 1:1, some candidates will benefit in the composite, some will suffer. (As we shall see, this is not a criticism; quite the contrary.) The following examples illustrate the point.

EXAMPLE VIII

A and B Scatters Equal

	A	B
Q_3:	61 (Sam)	92 (Sid)
Median:	53 (Sid) (Joe)	84 (Sam) (Jack)
Q_1:	45 (Jack)	76 (Joe)

Note that Sam and Sid are in a tit-for-tat relationship in respect of their standings in the two components: the candidate who is at Q_3 in the one component is at the Median in the other component. As the example shows, when the scatters are equal ($Q_3 - Q_1$ being 16 in both A and B), Sam and Sid have the same composite mark, namely 145, and will therefore have the same composite standing. Similarly for Joe and Jack, each of whom has a composite mark of 129. Note also that the absolute *magnitudes* of the marks is irrelevant–for the A-marks are lower than the B-marks.

EXAMPLE IX

A-Scatter exceeds B-Scatter

	A	B
Q_3:	67 (Sam)	92 (Sid)
Median:	53 (Sid) (Joe)	84 (Sam) (Jack)
Q_1:	39 (Jack)	76 (Joe)

In contrast, consider Example IX, in which the A-marks have a greater scatter than the B-marks. ($Q_3 - Q_1$ is 28 in A and 16 in B.) Here again Sam and Sid are in the same tit-for-tat relationship as before in respect of their component standings.

This time, however, Sam's composite mark is 151, whereas Sid's composite mark is only 145. Likewise, while Joe and Jack have the same component standings as before, Joe's composite mark is 129 while Jack's is only 123.

The main point illustrated here is that when A has a greater scatter than B (irrespective of the marks' magnitudes), it 'pays' more to be at Q_3 in A and at the Median in B (Sam) than to be the other way round (Sid). And one is penalised more by being at Q_1 in A and at the Median in B (Jack) than by being the other way round (Joe). In general, there is greater *pay-off*, in the composite, by being relatively *high* in the *larger-scatter* component and relatively low in the small-scatter component, than conversely; and there is greater *penalty*, in the composite, by being *low* in the *large-scatter* component and high in the small-scatter component, than conversely. In other words, there is *both* a greater pay-off for being relatively high, and a greater penalty for being relatively low, in the more heavily weighted component.

The point has practical significance. If examiners were to make explicit what they intend by saying that Topic A is to be 'more important' than Topic B, it seems almost certain that they would be saying that high A-standings should 'count for more' in the composite than should equally high standings in B; *and* that candidates with low standings in A should suffer more, in the composite, than should candidates with equally low standings in B. If a topic is *not* very important, would it not be sensible to say that relatively high scores in it should not be given very much credit *and* that relatively low scores in it should not be regarded as serious? If so, *neither* high standings *nor* low standings should have as much effect as they do in a more important topic. But this is precisely what happens when the more important topic has the greater scatter.

Furthermore, this is the *only* way in which one can have the required effects at both ends of the distribution. If, through ignorance, the examiner were to try to achieve this effect by arranging that the important topic should have relatively high marks, the other topic relatively low marks, the effect would not be achieved unless the high marks also had the greater scatter. In Example IX, for instance, the B-marks were generally higher than the A-marks, but it is the A-marks which in fact have the greater weight. Nor will the effect necessarily be obtained by his setting a higher maximum possible mark for the more important topic. A higher maximum possible mark certainly *allows* of greater scatter, but it does not *oblige* it. One sometimes sees topics 'marked out of 50' having a greater scatter than topics 'marked out of 100'.

A final point. Much of what has been said in this chapter is somewhat technical, and the prospective examiner who finds these issues of weighting, intercorrelations, and so forth rather complex might well decide that he will have nothing to do with them. As we have tried to show, however, if one component does have a greater scatter than another, it *will* have greater weight, *will* in fact have greater importance for the candidates' composite standings. This effect will be achieved whether the examiner realises it or not. He may not deliberately choose to weight the components; or he may fail to do so out of ignorance; or he may (wrongly) take for granted that if he leaves the marks alone the

various topics will make equal contributions to the total. But if he does not assign weights to the components by controlling their scatters the components will weight themselves in accordance with whatever scatters they may have. Whether ignorance of this principle serves as an excuse is beside the point; ignorance of it does not prevent it from operating.

Combining several distributions

So far, in order to avoid unnecessary complexity, we have considered the combination of only two distributions of marks, but there will be many occasions when more than two sets of marks have to be combined. The basic principles are nevertheless the same as those described in the foregoing sections of this chapter; and by way of summarising them we shall now re-state them briefly in respect of several components.

First, the scatter of the composite distribution depends upon the intercorrelations of the various components as well as upon their several scatters. In general, given the components' scatters, then the lower the intercorrelations the smaller the scatter of the composite.

Second, the extent to which the composite correlates with the components depends upon the various intercorrelations of the components themselves and also upon their relative scatters.

Third, for each and every candidate the contributions to his standing in the composite by his standings in the components are in the same proportions as are the components' scatters. If four components have scatters (say standard deviations) of 18, 12, 24 and 9, then each composite standing will consist of fractions of the standings in these four components, and in the proportions of $3:2:4:1\frac{1}{2}$. In other words, the components' several 'weights' will be proportional to their scatters.

Fourth, the components will actually have weights in proportion to their scatters irrespective of the examiner's knowledge, or ignorance, of that fact.

Throughout this chapter we have presupposed that the evaluation of marks will be by *norm*-reference. The reason for this restriction will be made apparent in the next chapter.

Why combine marks at all?

The previous chapter stated some basic facts about what happens *when* marks are combined. For some purposes, however, the combination of marks may be not only unnecessary but improper. In these cases the composite marks cannot claim to have any validity, and so it would be a waste of time to become involved in problems of correlation or weighting if the combination of marks were irrelevant. Before we look (in the next chapter) at the practical procedures necessary for proper combination we must therefore consider why marks should be combined at all.

A very general answer is that the examiner will resort to combination only when he needs an 'overall' assessment of each candidate. But that answer is too wide, because overall assessment can be made by reference to the candidate's merits in the separate topics – that is, without combination. Suppose that Tom's standings are as follows:

English:	60th %ile.	French:	55th %ile.
Science:	10th %ile.	Music:	90th %ile.
Mathematics:	15th %ile.	Art:	85th %ile.

From this information we can compare Tom's merits in the different topics and ascertain his particular strengths and weaknesses – with a view to our advising him about what topics he should continue to study. Since an overall assessment can be made, as in our example, without the combining of marks, we need a more precise answer.

The answer is straightforward when there is an external criterion with which the results of the examination are to have the maximum correlation: the marks of a composite distribution can be made to correlate more highly with an external criterion by the examiner's adopting certain weight-ratios for the components. In many school and college examinations, however, there is no external validity-criterion, and then the answer is less straightforward. Indeed, in many such examinations there is *no* reason why marks in different topics should be combined – as in the example given in the previous paragraph. Then what *is* the reason for combination?

When marks in different topics are *not* combined, a mark in any topic must be evaluated by reference to a standard within that topic – a standard we shall assume, for the present, to be a norm. For simplicity's sake let us say that a candidate reaching the standard has 'passed' in the topic. Suppose now that there is a rule that a candidate will pass *overall* only if he passes in every topic. If the marks in the topics are now combined, and that rule applies, plainly the pass mark in the composite cannot be less than the sum of the pass marks in the separate topics, because a lesser score would mean that the candidate had not reached every standard – as the rule demands. (To avoid irrelevant arguments we may assume that steps have been taken to ensure that the addition of marks in the various topics is legitimate.)

It would nevertheless be possible for a candidate to have a composite mark *higher* than the sum of the separate standards and yet have failed to reach some of them – by his doing particularly well in no more than one topic. In accordance with the rule, then, such a candidate would not pass. The example illustrates why composite marks are inadequate when that rule applies – because in order to discover whether a candidate has passed overall, we must look at his marks in the individual topics to see whether he has failed in any of them. When the rule applies, it is not *necessary* to combine marks – because the requisite information is already available within the topics. But neither is it *sufficient* to combine marks – because reference to a composite mark cannot always indicate whether the candidate has passed. (We could be sure only that candidates scoring *less* than the sum of the standards had *failed*.)

It follows that evaluation by means of composite marks is unequivocally useful only when the 'pass in every topic' rule is *not* made. But to set aside that rule is to adopt the principle commonly called 'compensation': a candidate may fail in one (or perhaps more) topics, yet still pass overall if he does well enough in the other topic or topics–well enough, that is, to reach some *composite* standard.

For the sake of illustration we made several assumptions which, strictly, the argument does not require. We assumed that candidates were to 'pass' or 'fail'; that the composite standard was derived from the component standards; and (thereby) that there *were* component standards. But even without these assumptions the argument is essentially the same. A composite standard *could* be set without reference to component standards–even if there were any; and an overall assessment might be required for the award of merit, prizes, and so forth. There still remains the point that different candidates may reach the composite standard (no matter how it has been determined in the first place) in different ways. Some candidates might have done equally well in every topic; some candidates might have done badly in some topics and very well in others, and so on; yet all of these might reach the same composite mark. But with respect to any given standing in the composite, this means that the principle of compensation is operating.

It is this principle which is the gist of the argument, and distinguishes overall assessment by means of combination from overall assessment without it. As we have tried to show, if compensation is *not* allowed, combination is neither necessary nor sufficient. But further, it would appear that compensation is the *only* thing necessarily achieved by combination–and cannot be achieved by reference to the separate topics alone.[25]

If, then, it is only in respect of compensation that the combination of marks differs from overall assessment without combination, it follows that the only purposes requiring mark-combination are those presupposing the principle of compensation. In other words, the answer to our question, 'Why combine marks at all?' is simply 'To allow of compensation!' Accordingly, and despite the ubiquitous practice of combining marks in various topics, papers, examinations, and so on, the combination of marks is quite pointless unless compensation is actually required. We have already given one example of a purpose for which compensation is irrelevant. It is not difficult to think of other purposes for which compensation, presupposed by the addition of measures for different things, would be absurd.

Compensation by weight

Even when it has been established that the examiner's purpose does require compensation, there still remains the question of whether the different topics are to be equally compensatory or are to be compensatory to different extents. For example, is a high standing in Topic A to compensate for an average standing in Topic B to the same extent as an equally high standing in B is to compensate for an average standing in A? Or should a high standing in one topic provide greater compensation than an equally high standing in the other? (Reference is made to *standings* because for the present the discussion is restricted to norm-reference.) The answers to these questions depend upon the examiner's purpose, but before we consider what his purpose might be we shall consider the technical problem of how different degrees of compensation can be effected. We begin with the case of equal compensation, remembering that within the context of norm-reference all that matters are the candidates' standings, and therefore that compensation must be compensation in respect of standings–not mere marks.

Two topics, A and B, will be equally compensatory if, and only if, any two candidates in a 'tit-for-tat' relationship in respect of standings have the *same composite* standing. See Example X.

EXAMPLE X

	A	B
83rd %ile:	74 (Tim)	66 (Ted)
71st %ile:	65 (Ted)	57 (Tim)

Tim's Total = 131 = Ted's Total

The relevant point is that Tim's being at the 83rd percentile in A compensates for his being at the 71st percentile in B to the same extent as Ted's being at the 83rd percentile in B compensates for his being at the 71st percentile in A. Of course, equal compensation does not depend upon there *being* two such 'tit-for-tat' candidates; but reference to two such candidates–even if they are imaginary–allows the conditions of equal compensation to be made clear. Also, the basic point is the same no matter what the two percentiles are. The general principle is that any two 'tit-for-tat' candidates will have the same composite standing, by virtue of having the same composite mark, only if the *mark-difference* between any two percentiles in the one distribution is the same as the mark-difference between the same two percentiles in the other distribution. And this is but another way of saying that the two topics must have the *same scatter*.[26]

If, then, the examiner's purpose requires that the two topics are to be not only compensatory but also *equally* compensatory, the composite marks will not be of maximum validity unless the two topics have equal scatters.

Consider now Example XI which illustrates a case in which the two topics are *not* equally compensatory.

EXAMPLE XI

	A	B
Percentile P:	65 (Vic)	78 (Val)
Percentile P':	53 (Val)	72 (Vic)

Vic's total = 137; Val's total = 131

In this case, Vic's being at Percentile P in A compensates for his being at Percentile P' in B to a *greater* extent than Val's being at Percentile P in B compensates for his being at Percentile P' in A. This happens, not because the A-marks are larger (for they are not), but because the A-marks have the greater scatter. In general, although two topics may be mutually compensatory, yet they are not necessarily equally compensatory. Greater compensation will be given by the topic with the larger scatter.

If, then, the examiner's purpose requires that Topic A should provide greater compensation than Topic B, the composite marks will not be of maximum validity unless Topic A's scatter is greater than that of Topic B.

It would be an imprecise purpose, however, if it required only that A's compensation be 'greater' than that of B. How *much* greater? This question has to be answered, for the following reason. Although, as Example XI illustrated (and Note 26 proved), the greater the difference between the topics' scatters the greater the difference in the two ('tit-for-tat') candidates' composite *marks*, yet it can be shown also that the greater the difference between the topics' scatters the greater will be the difference between these two candidates' composite *standings*.[27] But it is not difficult to appreciate that if, by virtue of a change in the topics' scatters, two candidates alter somewhat their positions in the composite, other candidates must change their relative positions too; and so different scatter-ratios of the components will produce somewhat different orders of merit in the composite. But not all of these different orders can be of maximum validity, for if one is, the others cannot. And so, since it would be an odd purpose indeed if several different orders of merit could fulfil it, the purpose must specify what the relative scatters are to be; that is, in terms of 'comepnsation' state by how *much* the one topic's compensation is to exceed that of the other.

If, then, a purpose requires compensation, its statement must specify whether the topics are to be equally compensatory, or if they are not to be, the precise extent to which one topic is to be more compensatory than the other.

This may well seem to be a tall order – or at least an unusual one, for examiners who speak in terms of 'compensation' do not always make explicit what the *degrees* of compensation are to be, perhaps because they take for granted that compensation is bound to be equal in both directions. As we have just seen, however, two topics will be equally, and mutually, compensatory only when they have equal scatters. Another reason may be that the *concept* of Compensation, as customarily employed, is not itself precise enough to allow of our speaking sensibly of one topic's being 'twice as compensatory' as another. If so, then we cannot lay down clearcut principles about how compensation is to be effected to different degrees. From what we *have* been able to say, however, it would seem that *if* the common concept of Compensation were extrapolated it would turn out to be very similar indeed to the concept of Weight. At any rate, the facts do suggest that the problems raised in connection with compensation are essentially the same as those customarily referred to in terms of 'weight'; and so from now on we shall speak in terms of 'weight' and not in terms of 'compensation'.

The condition of Balance

Since this chapter is concerned with the *combining* of marks in different topics we shall assume that *within* each topic the conditions of Question-Relevance, Mark-Relevance, and Marking-Consistency have been observed. Our aim now is to examine the remaining condition of validity, namely the condition of Balance. This condition, it will be recalled (p. 17), refers to the issue of whether all the parts of an examination are to 'count for the same' or some parts are to be more important than others; and if the latter, what should their relative degrees of importance be? Or, as we can now say, what should be the components' weights? What the condition of Balance says, in effect, is that the components' various weights must be in accord with the examiner's purpose if maximum validity is to be achieved.

Now as was emphasised in Chapter One, strictly it is the *results* which are assessable for validity; and since it may not be immediately apparent why the results are affected by the components' *weights*, we should give a brief explanation now. (The point has already been made in passing, but is now stated in rather greater detail.)

As noted in Chapter Ten, correlations of the composite with the components depend upon the ratios of the components' scatters. If we change the scatter-ratios, we change these correlations. But correlations refer to standings. Accordingly, since the candidates' standings in the *components* are unalterable data (in respect of combination), any change in the correlation between the composite and a component will be of necessity a change in the candidates' standings in the *composite*. To underline the point: different scatter-ratios for the components will produce different composite orders of merit. But different orders of merit cannot all be of maximum validity, for if one is the others cannot be; and so different scatter-ratios of the components will produce composite marks of different degrees of validity. Accordingly, since the scatter-ratios determine the components' weights, the results (that is, the distribution of composite marks) will vary in degree of validity with different systems of weights. In particular, only one set of weights will produce results of maximum validity. Then what does this set of weights have to be?

The answer to that question, as to any other question about validity, requires reference to the examiner's purpose. It is a relatively simple answer when there is a purpose involving an external criterion with which the results are to have the maximum possible correlation: the 'correct' system of weights is the one which produces results correlating maximally with the criterion. (The actual discovery of that system of weights requires a fairly complex experiment, which need not be discussed here.) For many examinations, however, there is no such criterion; their purposes are of the Content kind (see pp. 28, 32), and so if the results of such examinations are to be susceptible of validation, the weights to be assigned to the various topics must be specified by, or at least deducible from, the statement of the content purpose. If not, there will be nothing to choose from various possible sets of mutually incompatible results.

This demand for specification of the required weights cannot be escaped by the expedient of leaving the marks alone, for as we emphasised earlier, if the examiner does not weight the components they will weight themselves in accord with whatever scatters they happen to have. Nor can the demand be met by the examiner's initially assigning maximum possible marks in proportion to the topics' estimated degree of importance, for although a maximum possible mark of 100 permits of greater scatter than does a maximum possible mark of 50, it does not compel it. Nor, of course, can it be assumed that by leaving the marks alone, and adding them as they stand, the different topics will have *equal* weights. For one thing, the different topics will not necessarily *have* equal scatters; for another, equal weights may not be what the purpose requires anyway. However, these are essentially comments of a technical kind–and we shall be considering technical issues in the next chapter. The immediate problem is not how the specified weights are to be given, but what particular weights are to be specified in the first place.

It might nevertheless be argued that the demand can be sidestepped by our abandoning the very notion of distinct components. After all (the argument would run), one simply adds marks within one question, and sometimes even within one paper consisting of several questions, so why should we not ignore the probably arbitrary distinction between 'topics' and add the marks right across these purely conventional boundaries? Since the issue of weighting arises only when there *are* distinct topics, the problems of weighting would disappear if these academic distinctions were dispensed with.

This plausible argument merits an argued reply.

The straightforward addition of measures (marks) presupposes equivalence of their units, a presupposition holding good within a single marking scheme because a marking scheme constitutes a set of rules which lays down (among other things) what performances *are* to be counted as equivalent. There is, of course, no way in which these defined equivalences can be shown to be, in any absolute sense, 'really' equivalent. Performances which would be treated as equivalent for one purpose would not necessarily be regarded as equivalent for any other purpose. In general, the equivalence of performances is not a matter of the discovery of hidden equalities but rather a matter of declaration; and a marking scheme in this respect constitutes a Declaration of Equivalence. Admittedly, on occasion certain equivalences might strike the observer as idiosyncratic, but there is no case for our saying that a declaration is 'wrong', because in respect of content purposes there is no external criterion to which appeal can be made. The validity of the results of addition, *within a single marking scheme*, can be assessed only by reference to that marking scheme itself. If the questions have been set in accord with the condition of Question-Relevance, and the marking scheme has been devised in accord with the conditions of Mark-Relevance and Marking-Consistency, the results of adding the marks can be validated only by 'reference back' to the prescribed marking scheme in which the equivalences have been declared. But although the 'criterion' in this case is a purely internal one, it nevertheless provides a basis for the validation of the results.

To repeat the main point so far: the straightforward addition of marks is warrantable within a single marking scheme.

In many instances, however, the marks to be combined will derive from independently devised marking schemes, often because the examiner who is competent to draw up a marking scheme in one topic (say French) will not be competent to draw up a marking scheme in another topic (say Physics). When this is so, the necessary equivalences, across the whole area, will not have been established, and so there will be no way in which the validity of the results can be assessed. And while it is conceivable, it is nevertheless very unlikely that anyone could, or at least would, attempt to declare equivalences of performances in topics as different as (say) French, Physics and Art. How, for instance, would one judge that the performing of an experiment in Chemistry was to be assigned (say) 12, whereas the translating of a short prose was to be assigned the mark of (say) 10?

In such instances, likely to be very common, the results of addition are not susceptible of validation at all, and so if the results are to be validated there must be established a different sort of rule to which appeal can be made.

To that demand there would seem to be but one answer: if there are no specified relationships among the various topics' *performance*-units, one must declare relationships in terms of *standings*—that is, in terms of weights. And this, of course, takes us back to the very demand made earlier, from which we digressed in order to consider proposed escapes from it. To repeat: the specification of weight-ratios constitutes a rule, and so the results can be assessed for validity (in this respect) by reference to whether the procedures of combining marks do in fact conform

Do you suffer from
Combination Problems?
Then use Skram!

SKRAM! SKRAM! SKRAM!

No matter how complicated your problem of summation, just apply the SKRAM label and the problem will Disappear At Once!

SKRAM ADDS A NEW DIMENSION TO BIOMETRICS

So simple a child can use it

You can add absolutely anything with

SKRAM

If you are 36 years old, and 6½ feet tall, and weigh 148 pounds and have an I.Q. of 61, just call all these different measures 'SKRAM', and you can simply add them up to get your overall measure of 251½. Any other problem can be solved in exactly the same way!

Thousands of easily satisfied customers!!

(Remember the name!
SKRAM is simply the backward reading of MARKS.
It's so easy!)

SKRAM! SKRAM! SKRAM!

to it; that is, whether the components have scatters proportional to their prescribed weights.

We stress that unless the combination of marks in different areas is effected by reference either to specified performance-equivalences or to specified weight-ratios the composite marks will not be assessable for validity at all. Naïvely to combine the component marks as they stand is tantamount to regarding as valid whatever results happen to turn up. Marks are measures, just as inches, feet, yards and miles are; and the fact that in examinations measures of all kinds are commonly labelled 'marks' does not give us licence to add them without regard to what they mean.

If, then, it is not found possible to establish either performance equivalences for the various topics, or weight-ratios, there is no case for combining marks, no case for compensation, because the validity of the composite marks will not be determinable.

In many instances, however, it *will* be possible to specify the relative 'importances', that is weights, in accord with one's purpose. It could be, for example, that all the topics of a course are regarded as equally important, and therefore that each should make the same contribution to the candidates' composite marks. In this case all the topics would have to be given equal scatters. Or, if one examination were based upon the work of only one term of ten weeks, and the next examination covered the work of twenty weeks, it might be agreed that the second examination should have twice the weight of the first. As has already been emphasised, however, when there is no external criterion there can be no absolutely 'correct' system of weights. The matter is necessarily one of decision—reasoned decision no doubt, but decision none the less.

One final point. When the correlations among the component distributions are moderately high (positive), alteration of their scatters (for the purpose of giving them the specified weights) alters the composite order of merit to only a small extent (see Case 4, p. 137). It could therefore be argued that in such cases scaling is scarcely worth while—for all the difference it makes. But while the difference may be small in terms of correlation–calculated from the marks of the whole group of candidates–yet if the group is reasonably large a small change in the value of the correlation coefficient could be occasioned by *large* changes in the composite standings of a few candidates. And omission to scale the marks could have serious consequences for these few candidates; it could make all the difference between pass and fail, accept or reject, and the like. In fairness, then, the specified weights should be assigned even when the intercorrelations of the components appear to be high. (And it is simpler to weight the distributions than to calculate their correlations with a view to discovering whether weighting will have much effect!)

Mark-combination and criterion-reference

So far, we have considered mark-combination in the context of norm-reference. Now we look at mark-combination for criterion-reference–though only in order to show that when criterion-reference is required the addition of marks in different topics is irrelevant.

We should recall two points. First, a criterion is a set of specified *performances*, its statement prescribing what the candidate has to *do*; and the standard is the measure of that set of performances. Second, the criterion itself is established in the first place by reference to the consequences of its being reached or not reached.

By 'different topics', in this connection, we mean topics having separately established criteria. For instance, the criterion in French will be a set of performances in French; the criterion in Mathematics will be a set of performances in Mathematics; and these two criteria will have been established independently–in the light of the appropriate consequences.

Now if the standard for any one topic is to be determined, the marks *within* that topic will have to be susceptible of addition. The examiner will have to add the marks for the various performances constituting the criterion: say 3 for the use of the appropriate formula, say 5 for each equation correctly solved, and the like. Obviously, for each particular topic there will have to be a marking scheme (conforming to the conditions of Mark-

Relevance and Marking-Consistency), and that marking scheme, as we noted earlier, will constitute a Declaration of Equivalence of unit-performances within that topic. What we have to show is, not that the combination of marks within a topic is irrelevant, but rather that it is irrelevant to add marks across different topics.

One reason for not adding marks for criterion-reference is the same as that for not adding marks for norm-reference—namely that there may be no declared equivalences of performances in the different topics. In the case of norm-reference, however, this can be dealt with by combining marks in such a way as to give the topics specified weights; but for criterion-reference this is irrelevant, because weight is a matter of standings, with which criterion-reference is not concerned.

Even so, this is not the basic reason for refraining from combination for criterion-reference. It would be pointless to combine marks in different topics, and thereby produce composite marks, unless these composite marks were to be evaluated in some way. In particular, it would be pointless to combine marks for criterion-reference unless each candidate's composite mark were to be compared with a standard in the composite distribution, a standard representing a specified *criterion*. When, however, we bear in mind that it is the criterion which has to be established first, and that the standard is no more than the measure of that set of previously specified performances, it becomes apparent that there can be no composite standard unless there is first a composite criterion. And if there is no such standard the candidates' composite marks cannot be evaluated – by criterion-reference.

The argument hinges, then, on the question of whether there is a composite criterion – and hence a composite standard. Suppose, first, that there is a criterion within each topic – a very reasonable supposition – and also that in each topic the criterion covers *all* the performances asked for. In this case the standard in each topic is the maximum possible mark. In this case, then, there is no harm in adding up a candidate's marks; he 'fails' overall if his composite mark is less than the sum of the maximum possible marks for the various topics. But while there is no harm in doing this, it is quite pointless, because the composite mark tells us nothing we do not already know. Indeed, it is *less* useful than inspection of the separate topics, because if he fails we do not know where.

Second, however, suppose that the criterion within each topic is *not* the maximum possible performance, so that the standard in each topic is *not* the maximum possible mark. If we now combine a candidate's marks and compare his composite mark with the sum of the various standards, we thereby lose sight of the separate standards; and the fact that his composite mark exceeds that sum does not mean that he has satisfied all the criteria. He could have reached or exceeded some, but failed to reach others. To 'pass' someone whose composite mark exceeded the sum of the various topics' standards but who failed to reach one or more criteria, would therefore make nonsense of these criteria. Why set up a criterion in a topic, a criterion based upon the consequences of reaching or not reaching it, if that criterion can subsequently be set aside? (To allow of rather lower criteria for the purpose of combination does not affect the basic argument, for we should still have to ascertain whether each of these lower criteria had been reached.)

The only case in which the combination of marks in different topics would seem to have any point is the case in which there are *no* criteria within the separate topics, and the criterion consists of a set of performances drawn from all the topics together. This would mean, of course, that the 'topics' would no longer be distinguished one from another. Solving a quadratic equation in algebra might have the same criterion-referenced meaning as (say) translating a French prose or giving a brief account of the basic reasons for the Russian revolution. Not only would it be extremely difficult for the various topic-examiners to find any reasonable basis for establishing the necessary equivalences; it is difficult to conceive of purposes for which criterion-reference would be required for composite marks and *not* for marks within the topics themselves. What sorts of 'consequences' (upon which criteria have to be based) could there be which demanded a criterion for a complex mixture of school, college or university subjects but did not demand any criterion within any one subject?

It would appear, then, that the combination of marks in different topics is quite irrelevant for criterion-reference. And if so, the composite marks produced by such combination could claim no sort of validity. We are not arguing, however, that when there is a variety of topics each candidate must satisfy each criterion before 'passing' overall. It might well be that for some purposes a candidate would move on to a subsequent year without reaching one or more criteria. The argument has been, rather, that no good purpose is served by *combining* his marks.

Combination and precision

We conclude this discussion of the validity of composite marks with a point which, though important, may not be generally recognised. Suppose that a paper consists of four questions, and that the distributions of marks in these four questions have been given the appropriate weights. In each of the four distributions these scaled marks lie within the limits of o and 19. For one reason or another, however, it is decided that marks for a question need not be retained in such a precise form, and so the original (scaled) marks are converted as follows. (We use Roman numerals for the converted marks merely to avoid confusion in the example.) The new (Roman) marks are then combined. But consider two candidates, Tom and Jack, whose marks are shown below.

$$
\left.\begin{matrix}19\\18\\17\\16\end{matrix}\right\}V \quad
\left.\begin{matrix}15\\14\\13\\12\end{matrix}\right\}IV \quad
\left.\begin{matrix}11\\10\\9\\8\end{matrix}\right\}III \quad
\left.\begin{matrix}7\\6\\5\\4\end{matrix}\right\}II \quad
\left.\begin{matrix}3\\2\\1\\0\end{matrix}\right\}I
$$

	Tom		Jack	
Question 1	7	II	8	III
Question 2	7	II	4	II
Question 3	11	III	5	II
Question 4	2	I	8	III
Totals	27	VIII	25	X

The significant point is that when the original, precise, marks are combined, Tom (with 27) beats Jack (with 25); but when the less precise (Roman) marks are combined, it is Jack (with X) who beats Tom (with VIII).

Of course, this will not always happen. It happens when one candidate's precise marks tend to be 'low' within the new broad categories, and another candidate's tend to be 'high'. But it *can* happen, and even if it does not happen very often, the event may be very important indeed for the few candidates concerned.

We emphasise that the discrepancy arises (when it does arise) solely because of the 'coarsening' of the marks before combination. As our example illustrates, it cannot be attributed to inappropriate weighting, or to differences in the questions' scatters, because in our example we stated that the marks had been appropriately scaled.

The connection with validity is that the precise marks and the coarse marks have different orders of merit, and so if one set of marks is of maximum validity, the other set cannot be. (If the precise marks were *not* very valid in the first place, it would be wrong to assume that the changed order effected by coarsening the marks would necessarily improve them. It might make them worse.)

The practical implication will be apparent: in combining marks in several distributions one should always retain the precision these distributions have.[28]

Equalising the weights

For convenience we shall continue to refer to the various components as 'topics', though they could of course be questions, or papers, or separate examinations. Also, until the next section, we shall continue to assume that all the topics have been taken by all the candidates.

Since the topics' weights are proportional to their scatters (as already shown), the problem of ensuring that the topics have the requisite weights is the problem of ensuring they have the requisite scatters. We begin with the requirement for equal weights, that is, equal scatters.

An appropriate way to meet this demand is to convert the various component-distributions to a common scale (see Chapter Seven). It is appropriate for two reasons. First, a common scale ensures equal scatters–which is required. Second, if (as is likely) the results are to allow each candidate's merits in the various topics to be *compared*, conversion to a common scale provides a basis for this as well as for combination.

Conversion to a common scale, however, is not really necessary. Equal weight requires only equal *scatter*; it does not demand that the equivalent percentiles in the various components should have equal numerical values. For instance, the Medians do not have to be the same. But it is usually quicker to convert to a common scale than to check all the scatters and then, almost certainly, to adjust the scatters only. Furthermore, if the marks have already been brought to a common scale to allow of *comparison*, no extra labour is involved.

'Optional' topics with equal weight

For simplicity's sake the foregoing discussions of weight have assumed that all the candidates take all the topics. We now consider the case when this is not so.

As we have already seen, when all the candidates take all the topics, the demand for equal weights is met by the various topics' having equal scatters. As we saw also, in that case it is not necessary that equal standings in the different distributions should be represented by the same numerical mark. Equal scatters alone guarantee that any pair of 'tit-for-tat' candidates will have identical *composite* marks. What we must now show is that when not all candidates take the same topics (even when they take the same *number* of topics), equality of scatters gives no such guarantee. If, as valid comparison of composite marks requires, candidates at the same percentile level in different topics are to be regarded as equal, it is necessary for the *marks* representing identical standings to be equal too.

For simplicity of exposition we have used symmetrical distributions in the following example (to make clear that the scatters are equal), but the same basic points apply to other distributions also.

EXAMPLE XII

Scaled Marks in:	English	Mathematics	French	History
90th percentile:	77 (C1)	86 (C2)	52	90
50th percentile:	60 (C2)	69 (C1)	35	73
10th percentile:	43	52	18 (C1)	56 (C2)

All the candidates take English and Mathematics, and either French or History. Candidate C1 opted for French, Candidate C2 for History. As indicated by the difference between the 90th and 10th percentiles in each topic, all the topics have the same *scatter*; but the *magnitudes* of the marks at any given percentile are not equal.

First, by reference to 'tit-for-tat' candidates, let us re-illustrate the point that, when all the candidates take all the topics, it is sufficient that the topics should have the same scatter. English and Mathematics provide such a case. Thus, Candidate C1 has a composite mark (English+Mathematics) of 77+69, namely 146. Candidate C2, who is 'tit-for-tat' in terms of standings with Candidate C1 in these two topics, has a composite mark of 60+86, which is 146–the same as that of Candidate C1, despite the fact that the equivalent standings in the two topics have different numerical values.

But second, consider now these two candidates' composite marks for all three topics. C1 is at the 10th percentile in French, C2 at that same percentile in History. If, as is necessary, these two percentiles are to *count* as equivalent (for otherwise combination is invalid), then since C1 and C2 are already equal over English and Mathematics, their composites over the three topics should be identical. But they are not. C1 scores 146+18 = 164, whereas C2 scores 146+56 = 203. Obviously, the only way in which these two candidates can have identical composite marks is for the *numerical values* of the 10th percentiles in French and History to be the same. And likewise, of course, for any other percentile.

The same sort of discrepancy would of course arise were the compulsory topics English and History, with optional topics of Mathematics and French.

To repeat: when the components are to have equal weights, but not all candidates take the same topics, any particular standing must have the same numerical value in all the optional topics. We need not add that they must have the same scatter, because equal numerical values for the percentiles presupposes that the scatters will be equal. But the argument does assume that equal standings in different topics, even when taken by different candidates, are accepted as equivalent.

Differential weighting

In this section we shall again assume that all candidates take all topics; the 'optional' case is discussed in the following section.

When different topics are to have different weights, their scatters must be in the same proportions as the weights required – such as 1:2:3. (See p. 141.)

Here also it will be useful if the various distributions have already been converted to a common scale (to allow of comparison), because then the required weights can be given by our multiplying the marks in each distribution by the appropriate numbers. If the weights of Topics A, B, and C are to be in the proportions 1:2:3, the A-marks would be unaltered, the B-marks multiplied by 2, the C-marks multiplied by 3. Of course, this gives the required weights, not because multiplying the B and C marks makes them larger (though it does make them larger), but because by multiplying all the marks in a distribution by m we thereby multiply all the mark-*differences* by m. For instance, if $Q_1 = 48$, and $Q_3 = 64$, so that the Interquartile Range is 16, doubling all the marks would make $Q_1 = 96$, and make $Q_3 = 128$, thus giving a new Interquartile Range of 32. And, as reference to its formula (p. 260) reveals, the same happens to the Standard Deviation.

If, however, the various distributions have not already been converted to a common scale, and if comparisons across topics are not required, it would be a waste of time to convert all topics to a common scale and then perform multiplications. Here, one would convert the distributions straight away to scales having the requisite scatter-ratios. (In our example with a required weighting of 1:2:3, these latter *scales* could be set up by leaving the common scale alone for Topic A, multiplying its representative percentiles by 2 for Topic B, and by 3 for Topic C.)

A final point: although the weights to be given to the various topics must be determined by the examiner's purpose, yet when (as is likely) the correlations among the components are positive, a weight-ratio of (for instance) 8:9 would be unrealistic. Such a weighting, in these circumstances, would almost certainly produce the same standings in the composite as would a ratio of 1:1. Further, when the correlations are positive there is a practical limit to the magnitude of the proportion. For instance, to weight 8:1 would produce results extremely similar to those produced by the ratio 4:1. We are not saying, however, that differential weighting is itself unrealistic–a point already argued (p. 157). The point we have just been making is, rather, that very small differences in proportion are of no practical significance. To weight 2:1 or 3:1 is very likely to produce a composite order of merit significantly different (even if only for a few candidates) from that produced by a weighting of 1:1. But a weighting of 4:1 is unlikely to produce results differing significantly from those produced by a weighting of 3:1. We suggest, as a good working rule, that there is unlikely to be any need to go beyond a ratio of 4:1 – and even this is probably overdoing it. This would allow of the ratios 1:1, 2:1, 3:1, 4:1, 3:2, 4:3 (the ratio 4:2 being the same as 2:1), which would appear to be adequate for all practical purposes. Should it be objected that a ratio of (say) 6:1 might be demanded by the examiner's purpose, the answer is that it is difficult to imagine what sort of purpose would require 6:1 but definitely not 4:1. Purposes too must be realistic!

'Optional' topics in a differential weighing system

This matter can be dealt with very briefly, for the principle will be obvious: optional topics must be given equal weights. If this were not done, and the optional subject French were given a weight of 2 and the optional subject History a weight of 1, this would mean that a candidate choosing French would have his standing in French counted *twice* into the composite, whereas the candidates choosing History would have their standings in History counted into the composite only once. And since 'optional' customarily presupposes equivalence of the options, standings in the one option must be counted into the composite the same number of times as standings in the other. This does not mean, of course, that each option must have the weight of 1. It means only that whatever weights they have must be the same. (Indeed, it is not improbable that the examiners might decide that subjects chosen by the candidates themselves should count for *more* than compulsory subjects.) Also, for the reasons already given (p. 164), the *magnitudes* of marks at any particular percentile in different options must be equal too.

'Average-composite' marks

Sometimes composite marks are divided by the number of topics, so producing an overall average mark for each candidate. So that we can refer to such marks without confusing them with the composite marks themselves, we shall call them 'average-composite' marks. Thus, if Tom's marks in English, History, and Arithmetic were respectively 66, 54 and 39, his composite mark would be 159, his average-composite mark 159/3, namely 53.

There is no technical objection to marks of this kind, because division of all the composite marks by the same number, while reducing their magnitudes and their scatter, has no effect at all upon the candidates' standings, and so the average-composite marks have exactly the same validity as the composite marks from which they derive. Examiners who adopt this procedure, however, do not always make explicit why they are doing so. It may be simply to reduce each candidate's final mark in magnitude, and so make these final marks more manageable. Or it may be to re-produce marks of the 'same sort' as the marks in the topics. But whatever may be the reason for producing average-composite marks, one basic fact must be kept in mind.

Suppose, for simplicity's sake, that there are only three topics, that all three are to have equal weight, and that in accord with that demand all three distributions have been converted to a common scale—such as the scale shown.

90th percentile:	80
75th percentile:	70
50th percentile:	60
25th percentile:	50
10th percentile:	40

If the marks in the three topics are now combined, candidate by candidate, the composite distribution will have a scatter which is *less than* the sum of the topics' scatters. (See pp. 133, 135. We are ignoring the highly improbable case in which the inter-component correlations are all $+ 1 \cdot 0$.) In the present case, however, all three topics have the same scatter—that of the common scale; and so the composite scatter will be less than three times the common scale's scatter. If, then, the composite marks are divided by 3 (the number of topics), this will divide the composite scatter by 3, and so the average-composite marks will have a scatter less than that of the common scale.* Negatively expressed, division of the composite marks by the number of topics does *not* reproduce the common scale. The resulting average-composite marks will have the same Median as the common scale, but they will have a smaller scatter.

The implication is plain. Since any mark's merit depends not only upon the Median (or Mean) but also upon the scatter of the distribution to which it belongs, we should be mistaken in interpreting an average-composite mark as if it were a common scale mark. One example will suffice.

The common scale and the average-composite marks have the same Median – say 60 – but the latter marks have, so to speak, 'crept in' towards it. Thus, in the average-composite distribution there will be fewer candidates above 80 than in the common scale. The average-composite mark of 80 will therefore have a standing *higher* than 80 in the common scale. If, in that scale, 80 were the 90th percentile, then the average-composite 80 would be *above* the 90th percentile of the average-composite distribution. Likewise, if 40 were the 10th percentile of the common scale, the average-composite mark of 40 would be *below* the 10th percentile of the average-composite distribution.

In general, any given numerical mark *above* the Median will be a better mark in the average-composite distribution than it was in the common scale; and any given numerical mark *below* the Median will be a poorer mark in the average-composite distribution than it was in the common scale.

The extents of these discrepancies in merit depend upon the extent of the 'creeping in', which depends upon two things, namely the inter-topic correlations (see again p. 133), and the number of topics. The more topics there are, the greater the shrinkage in scatter.[29]

A possible application of these facts is worth considering. If 40 were the 10th percentile of the common scale, and the pass mark were 40 *in the average-composite* distribution, this would *not* mean that 10 per cent of candidates must fail – because the average-composite mark of 40 will have a *lower* standing in the

* Exactly the same conclusion holds good no matter how many topics there are; and a similar sort of conclusion holds good if the weights are not equal.

average-composite distribution. The percentage of candidates below it would depend upon the number of topics combined and their intercorrelations, but it would not be remarkable if, for three topics, it were at least as low as 4 per cent. Note that fixing a pass mark in the average-composite distribution does not predetermine the percentage of candidates who fail, for that depends upon something which the examiner does not control, namely the inter-topic correlations.

If, then, average-composite marks are to be a basis of assessment, with norm-reference, what is required is *not* inference from the component distributions, even when they have a common scale, but analysis of the average-composite distribution itself.

PART THREE

Setting questions and marking answers

Question-Relevance

In this final part of the book, concerned with setting questions and marking answers, we shall try to treat these two issues separately, but they are so closely related that in looking at the one we shall have to keep an eye on the other.

First we should recall that to set questions is to issue directives to the candidates to give the performances (or a sample of them) required by the examination's purpose. We suggested that a list of these should be prepared; and it is to these listed performances, and to no others, that the questions must be directives. The first essential in setting questions, therefore, is drawing up the list of performances to which the questions have to refer.

Since these performances will vary from one purpose to another, and from topic to topic, we cannot draw up 'the' required list here, but we shall illustrate the setting of questions by reference to topics discussed in this book. A very small sample, from the topic of 'Weighting', will be enough for our immediate purpose. The following performances could be among those listed:

1   State what determines the weights different topics in an examination ought to have.
2   State what determines the weights different topics in an examination actually have.
3   State what happens to the weight of a distribution of marks when all the marks are doubled, and explain why this happens.
4   Given the numerical values of the 10th, 50th and 90th percentiles of each of four distributions of marks, state which distribution will have the greatest, and which the smallest weight.

Two points to note: reference is made to *performances* – 'stating' something, 'explaining' something, and not to undefined things like 'knowing' or 'appreciating'; and No. 4 specifies not only what the candidate has to do (state and explain) but also the conditions in which he has to do it.

We now consider some of the forms questions can take.

'Open' and 'closed' questions

Questions are sometimes classified under two general heads, Open and Closed. In open questions the candidate has to *provide* the answer–by writing an essay, or a paragraph, drawing a diagram, filling in details in a map, computing, and so on. Closed questions require him to *select* an answer from several the examiner has provided.

To illustrate the difference consider Performance 2, above. In an open form the question could read,

Q1 *On what characteristic of a distribution does its weight depend?*

In contrast, a possible form of closed question could be,

Q2 *The weight of a distribution of marks depends upon*
A *Its maximum possible mark.*
B *Its standard deviation.*
C *Its validity.*
D *Its median.*

In this question all the examinee is required to do is indicate in some prescribed way the letter (A, B, C, D) corresponding to the answer he has selected.

The same Open-Closed classification can be made even for 'practical' examinations. In an open question the candidate would be required to perform the practical task himself; for instance, to operate a machine in a certain way. In a closed question he would observe one or more people operating it and would then indicate which of these was the way required.

This example illustrates two important points. Observing other people performing a task and indicating which performance was correct is not the same as performing the task correctly oneself. Thus, while both forms of question have the same subject-matter, they call for different sorts of examination performance.

In some cases the difference is so small as to be of no significance—as in Questions 1 and 2 above; but in many cases the two forms of questions are not merely different ways of directing the candidate to give the one and the same performance, because the two performances are *not* the same. In general, despite appearances to the contrary, an open question and a closed question *referring* to the same performance will not necessarily *require* one and the same performance.

The second, though related, point is that when two forms of question call for different sorts of performance, the examiner must refer to his 'list' in order to decide which form of question he must use. For instance, in connection with our recent example of operating a machine, a directive to operate the machine might seem better than a directive to observe and assess other people's operations; but if the examinee were a prospective teacher it would be reasonable to examine him not only as an operator but also as an assessor of students' attempts at operating. In general, the form of question to be used will depend upon the examination's purpose.

Since this matter is of some importance, one other example may be in order. As the use of private transport continues to increase, and more and more school pupils may be expected to own a car or motor-cycle after (?) they leave school, it could be sensible to give them some practice in using maps. In this context consider these two questions, one open and one closed. (The place is fictitious.)

Q3 *In the blank map supplied put a dot to represent the following towns, and write the first letter of the name of the town beside the dot in each case.*

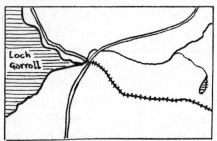

Garsburgh

Sperlie

Auchendowie

Tarroch

Wildon

Minzie

This is, of course, an open question. In contrast consider another question which, while dealing with the same subject-matter, is of the closed form.

Q4 *In the blank map supplied the dots represent towns. Each dot has a number beside it. In the column of town names insert, opposite each name, the number of the dot corresponding to it.*

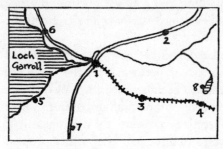

Garsburgh	....
Sperlie	....
Auchendowie	....
Tarroch	....
Wildon	....
Minzie	....

In this case, candidates who can correctly answer the open question will almost certainly be able to answer the closed one; but a candidate who can recognise the location of towns on the second map might not be able to place the dots on the first map with sufficient accuracy to be counted correct. Here again the form of question must depend upon the purpose. If, for example, the aim were to familiarise students with map *reading*, the closed form of the question might well be the more appropriate one. Also, as we shall see, closed questions have certain advantages. (The example given above is by no means novel, being adapted from one in P. B. Ballard's Book, *The New Examiner*, first published in 1923.)

Closed questions have an important advantage over most open questions, namely in being more likely to fulfil the condition of Marking-Consistency. Our last example illustrates the point. In Question 3, how far from the correct position does the centre of the candidate's dot have to be before he is marked wrong? And how large does his dot have to be before we penalise him for playing safe? Can we be sure that our leniency extends to the same degree with every candidate? And will different examiners mark with the same leniency? Again, in Question 1, many different answers might be accepted as correct, depending upon the precision (or opinion) with which 'weight' had been defined. Would 'scatter' be correct? Or would it have to be 'standard deviation'? And what of the candidate who writes 'SD', or the letter σ? If marking is to be consistent, and especially if the scripts are shared by several examiners, a decision about such issues must be made before the scripts are marked. For open questions this is not always an easy task, because candidates may think up answers the examiners had not.

This problem is less likely to arise with closed questions, because decisions about the correctness of answers can be made in advance. There is nevertheless a possible disadvantage: in striving after marking-consistency the examiner may devise questions falling short in relevance. True, if he sticks to his 'list', none of his questions will be *ir*relevant; but since it may be that not all the listed performances can be tested by closed questions, the attractiveness of such questions may lead him to bias his sample of questions in favour of performances which can be tested in this way. In particular, there is the danger of triviality, because closed questions lend themselves very well to the testing of simple recall–of definitions, technical terms, the names of people and places, and the like. Such things may well be relevant enough, but for many purposes they are likely to be less important than understanding the substance of definitions, using technical terms in a sensible way, introducing names in a context, and so forth. As we shall try to show later, closed questions *can* be devised to test comprehension, understanding, and application; but it is very much easier to devise questions testing rote-learning, and it is for this reason that a sample of closed questions may fail to be representative of the performances the purpose requires.

We nevertheless repeat a significant advantage of closed questions: they are likely to be much more effective in fulfilling the condition of Marking-Consistency.

'Subjective' and 'objective' questions

Another system of classification of questions, overlapping with the Open-Closed system, assigns questions to the two classes of 'Subjective' and 'Objective'. These terms are sometimes defined (too loosely) somewhat as follows. In subjective questions, what is to be accepted as the correct answer is a matter of opinion, whereas in objective questions opinion is not involved, the rightness or wrongness of the answer being a matter of fact.

It is not difficult to find examples fitting neatly into this simple system. Examiners may well differ in their interpretations of history, or politics (to name only two), and it is notorious that one and the same essay may be judged to be very good by one examiner, poor by another. In contrast, to the question requiring candidates to multiply 2345 by 67 there is only one correct answer. The former would therefore be regarded as 'subjective', the latter as 'objective'. But the matter as a whole is not so simple, because it is not always easy to disentangle facts from opinions (even when one is critical enough to try). Many, perhaps all, facts *are* facts, so to speak, only on certain assumptions; and it would surely be naïve to assume that all opinion could be eliminated from our questions–if for no other reason than that we could never know for sure that we had eliminated it. The most we can hope for is to reduce, to a minimum, *differences* of opinion among experts in the topic in question. It would therefore seem more sensible to regard the terms 'subjective' and 'objective', not as the names of separate classes, but rather as referring to a continuum–as with 'tall' and 'short', 'rich' and 'poor'. At the one extreme would lie questions so designed that there could be no difference of opinion about whether a candidate's answer was right or wrong; at the other extreme there would be gross disagreement. Most questions probably lie between these extremes, and it would be in accord with the view just expressed to speak of 'degrees' of objectivity (or subjectivity), some questions being more objective than others.

Since the matter is essentially one of agreement (or disagreement), the only sure way of testing for the objectivity of one's questions is to submit them first for the consideration of other people who are at least as well qualified as oneself. Of course, one cannot consult all possible examiners, but that is no argument for failing to consult any at all. It will be obvious that we are not suggesting that a little group of examiners should 'gang up' and make arbitrary decisions. The team's function is to design *questions* in such a way that difference of opinion about candidates' answers will be reduced to a minimum.

I SAID I WAS RIGHT. THE EXAMINERS SAID I WAS WRONG. I WAS OUTVOTED!

This is easier said than done. As we commented in the previous section, examinees may give answers the examiners had not thought of. For this reason, attempts to increase objectivity tend to produce questions of the closed type, or open questions calling for very short answers. It will be apparent why closed questions are appropriate. Since the *examiner* provides the correct answer and wrong answers, from which the candidates have to select, agreement about what is a right and what is a wrong answer can be reached (by discussion with other examiners) before the candidates take the examination.

Although the terms 'subjective' and 'objective' have been introduced in this chapter, strictly they do not define questions in terms of ther intrinsic characteristics. The terms do not indicate the form questions are to take. Rather, they refer to the kind of *marking* the questions allow. As we have noted, however, 'objective' questions are likely to be closed rather than open; or, if they are open, to require short answers. The latter point is taken up in the next section.

'Short-answer' and 'long-answer' questions

Here again the epithet applies, strictly, not to the intrinsic nature of questions but to the nature of the answers to them, but it is possible to infer what the questions' characteristics must be.

Obviously, if a question is to be given only a short answer the question must either ask expressly for a short answer ('Answer each of the following questions in a phrase or short sentence', and the like) or be so constructed that a long answer would be unacceptable. For example,

> *Define the term 'correlation'.*

clearly asks for a short reply. In contrast,

> *What is 'correlation'?*

does not, because it would be appropriate to reply by giving not merely a definition but also an account of the function of correlation in educational research, examples of the meanings of various values of correlation coefficients, and so forth. Likewise, the question,

> *What is the 'scaling' of marks?*

allows of a much longer answer than does the question,

> *When a distribution of marks is 'scaled', it is legitimate to alter some but not all of its characteristics. What must NOT be altered?*

This last example illustrates a relevant point, namely that in order to oblige candidates to give a short *answer*, the *question* may have to be longer than is required for long answers. Sometimes the question has to direct the candiate not only about what he *is* to do but also about what he is *not* to do. For example,

> *One reason for scaling marks to a common scale is to give the different distributions equal weights. Give another reason.*

A 'ban' of this kind on certain answers is particularly useful when the examiner knows that almost every candidate will be able to give 'easy' answers. They add little or nothing to the precision of the results, and so there is little point in requiring candidates to give them, and no profit in the examiner's wasting his time reading them. (Of course, some candidates may still give them, but the nature of the question justifies their getting no marks for them.)

From what has been said it will be apparent that short-answer questions are not devices for forcing candidates to write briefly what they might otherwise write at length. Short-answer questions *ask* for less than do other questions. A set of short-answer questions subdivides the required performances, so that (say) twenty such questions might ask for no more than might be covered by one 'long-answer' question–'Give an account of . . .'.

We should therefore draw attention to a related practical point. As we noted, a short-answer *question* may be considerably *longer* than an essay-type question, and there have to be *more* questions of the short-answer type. A paper consisting entirely of short-answer questions may therefore be very much larger than the papers required in more 'conventional' examinations. Even a question paper allowing no more than an hour's writing might well run to several pages, and so candidates ought to be prepared, beforehand, for an examination of this kind if they are not to be floored by the paper's mere appearance.

Short-answer questions have four major advantages. First, they allow of more objective marking. In marking essay-type answers the examiner may have to wade through a great deal of verbiage to find crucial points–and he might miss some; or he might award a mark twice for the same point, for candidates do tend to repeat themselves. In dealing with short answers, on the other hand, the examiner can compare each answer with the required answer in a systematic way, because the order of answers is the same for every candidate. Perhaps we should note that we are not claiming that all short answers can be marked with extreme objectivity; the point is only that their marking will usually be much *more* objective than the marking of long answers. That advantage is nevertheless an important one.

The second major advantage of short-answer questions is that they can be exploited in the interest of the condition of Question-Relevance. This condition, it will be recalled, requires not only that all the performances asked for must be on the 'list' of required performances but also that they should constitute a representative sample of them. A paper consisting of short-answer questions can be devised to meet that latter demand because it can contain a very large number of questions, and so can require performances from a great many pockets of the topic. Note, however, that such a paper does not *necessarily* provide better sampling. It does not do so automatically; but the examiner who is sensitive to the need of good sampling *can* exploit a short-answer paper for that purpose.

Very much the same point can be made, less technically, in

terms of 'fairness'. Jack and Jill have each done about half the work required-but not the same half. Jack has covered topics A, B, C and D; Jill has covered C, D, E and F. But a paper with only a small number of questions might ask only for topics A, C and G. If so, Jack will do better than Jill, despite the fact that the two candidates share the same level of knowledge (or ignorance). Jack could be said to have been 'lucky'. But while luck enters in some degree into all examinations, the greater the degree the less valid will be the results. Short-answer questions, by being more searching-because there can be more of them-could therefore be said to be 'fairer'.

A third advantage of short-answer questions is that a paper consisting of them is likely to produce results of greater precision-that is, with less sharing of marks, largely because so many single performances can be asked for. True, a long-answer question, of the essay-type, certainly *allows* a candidate to give a great many unit-performances. But a short-answer paper with a great many questions *directs* him to give them; and where it is not crucial that candidates have to recall the host of things relevant to a general question, a short-answer paper is preferable in this respect.

Fourth, by means of item analysis (see later-p. 225) an examiner can determine the difficulty of each question for a particular category of candidates-such as candidates taking a certain sort of course. He can then exploit the information to devise subsequent papers in such a way that they are likely to produce distributions of the requisite *shape*. For example, a paper with a high proportion of very difficult questions is likely to produce a positively skewed distribution; that is, with many candidates getting very low marks, and only a few candidates getting high marks. With a high proportion of very easy questions, the paper is likely to produce a negatively skewed distribution. And if nearly all the questions are of average difficulty, the resulting distribution is likely to be approximately symmetrical. Item analysis becomes feasible, however, only if there is a large number of items (questions), and so a paper with a large number of short-answer questions allows of control of the shape the distribution will have-not because the answers are short, but because there were many of them.

A final point about short-answer questions. A paper directing the candidates to give specific short performances does not have to take the form of a large number of separately numbered, ostensibly independent, questions. Indeed, in many cases the short performances *will* constitute a family of related performances; and in such cases it would be not only legitimate but sensible to design a question with constituent parts. Here is an example.

There are occasions when marks have to be 'scaled'.
a) *What is meant by the 'scaling' of marks? In your answer state what aspects of the marks may properly be altered, and what aspects may not.*
b) *State briefly two reasons for converting the marks in two subjects to a common scale.*
c) *Convert the following set of marks so that it will have a Mean of 60 and a Standard Deviation of 12. (Round off each scaled mark to the nearest whole number.)*

55, 67, 41, 63, 62, 58, 64, 59, 47, 70, 65,
60, 63, 61, 62, 72, 59, 50, 61, 62, 63, 66.

Because short-answer questions are probably less well known than essay questions, we have taken some time to describe their advantages. But, of course, there are occasions when short-answer questions will not suffice, and long answers will be required. For example, if (as we hinted a moment ago) part of the test is to find out whether candidates can *recall*, without prompting, all the facts relevant to some issue, short-answer questions would beg the very issue – by telling them what sorts of facts had to be recalled. Again, if the examiner needs to assess candidates' abilities to *organise* information, to lay out facts in a systematic way, for instance, to express themselves clearly, and so forth, longer answers will be required. (The issue of answer-length is raised again later – p. 238.)

Which type of question to use?

Advantages and disadvantages of the various types of question have already been noted, and the types themselves will be described in greater detail in the following chapter, but a summary at this stage may be useful.

First of all, the three classifications we have been describing (Open-Closed, Subjective-Objective, Short-Long Answer) overlap to a considerable extent. Closed questions are likely to be at the same time more objective than open questions, and they are also likely to call for short answers. But open questions, if they require short answers, can be very objective too. But they are not necessarily so. Consider again an example used before. There will be no doubt about the correctness of the answer to 2345×67; but unless there is a very detailed marking scheme (which, of course, there ought to be anyway), examiners could disagree about what mark was to be given for various wrong answers.

At first sight there might seem to be no doubt at all about the desirability of *objective* questions–in so far as this means that the marking will be highly consistent and relevant. But questions allowing of highly consistent and relevant marking tend to be short–or even closed as well; and (as we illustrated in the previous section) not all performances are assessable in this way. Plainly, the only way to discover how well candidates can write essays is to oblige them to write essays! However, there must be a great many instances in which essay questions are used when the fundamental purpose is *not* that of assessing essay-writing, but could be more accurately fulfilled in some other way. Also, as will be suggested in the following chapters, while assessment of understanding may be part of the examination's purpose, it does not follow that the best way of assessing it is to get candidates to write out long explanations. As we keep emphasising, reference must always be made to the examination's purpose: there is no absolutely best type of question; the best type is the one which best fulfils the purpose in hand.

Even so, one has to be familiar with the details of the various types before one can make a decision; and in the following chapters we examine a variety of types of question in detail. We suggest that an examination of these types, and consideration of their respective advantages and disadvantages, may suggest to the reader that no matter what kinds of question he has been accustomed to use, there may be a still better way.

Basic characteristics

In illustration of the basic characteristics of a multiple-choice question* consider the following example.

---

1   The term 'first quartile' refers to the

   A Marks of the candidates in the bottom quarter of the order of merit.

   B Marks of the candidates in the top quarter of the order of merit.

   C Mark of the candidate one quarter of the way up the order of merit.

   D Mark of the candidate one quarter of the way down the order of merit.

                                           (C)

The question's introductory statement is the 'stem'. The succeeding statements, labelled A, B, C and D in our example, are the 'responses', or the 'options' (or, sometimes, the 'alternatives' even if there are more than two.) The candidate has to choose the correct response. The responses which are not correct are sometimes called 'distractors'. (The right response-letter, in the corner of each of our examples, has been inserted, of course, purely for the sake of the present reader.)

Some details of the lay-out of a multiple-choice question will vary from writer to writer. For example, some would insist that only the last option should end with a full stop, that none of the options should begin with a capital unless the option

---

* Multiple-choice questions are frequently referred to, not as 'questions', but as 'items'.

begins a sentence, and so on. Points like these, we think, are trivial. There are more important issues to argue about.

In our illustrative example, above, there is only one correct response, though later we shall consider the possibility of there being more than one. Also, our example has four options, though (presumably) there could be any number greater than one. But this point too is raised again later.

We now look, in turn, at a multiple-choice question's two basic parts – the stem and the set of options.

The stem

Since a question has to be a directive, to the candidates, to give a certain performance, it is reasonable to suggest that the specifically directive part of the question should be built into its introductory part, namely the stem. (Critics of question-writers are wont to be disparaging about some questions on the ground that their stems are 'non-directive'.)

The question we used in illustration would seem to be adequate in this respect, for in effect it asks for a definition of 'first quartile'. An example of a non-directive stem will be given in a moment.

When the stem is highly directive, the candidate may indeed be able to *provide* (recall) the required response just as in an open question. Once again, our first example would seem to be of this kind. But as we shall see, by no means all questions, even good ones, lend themselves to recall alone.

This next example is intended to illustrate a non-directive stem.

---

2 The Maximum Possible Mark

A Determines the distribution's weight.
B Should not constitute a 'ceiling'.
C Should be reached by all average candidates.
D If obtained, indicates that the candidate's knowledge of the topic is complete.

(?)

This question is deplorable on several counts, but all we need note at present is that its stem gives no directive at all. (Unless we are naïve enough to imagine that 'This question is about the maximum possible mark' constitutes a directive.) The candidate can have no idea what he is supposed to do until he has read all the options, and even then he has every right to be in doubt.

Another possible weakness of a stem is not just that it may fail to direct the candidate to the required performance but that it is *mis*directive, setting the candidates off on a false trail:

---

3   The validity of an examination is

   A   Lowered by inconsistent marking.
   B   Dependent upon . . . etc.
   C   Likely to be raised if . . . etc.
   D   etc.

Although the stem, here, does not ask specifically for a definition of 'validity', it certainly suggests that a definition is what will be required; whereas the responses (which we have not troubled to complete) refer to the conditions *governing* validity. If the intention *were* to test the candidates' ability to identify a particular condition of validity, the stem should have made this clear, and might have read:

---

4   Which of the following will lower an examination's validity?

   A   Inconsistent marking.
   B   etc.
   C   etc.

A similar weakness is demonstrated by the next example.

> **5** The validity of an examination will be lowered by
>
> **A** Awarding marks for answers which, though irrelevant to the questions, do indicate that the candidate knows something about the topic.
> **B** Adhering strictly to a prepared marking scheme.
> **C** Adapting the leniency of the marking to the ability of the candidate.
> **D** Setting questions irrelevant to the examination's purpose.
>
> Which of the above statements is not true?
> **(B)**

This question may be misleading because candidates are likely to be accustomed to selecting a *correct* response, and in this case do not know they have to select a false response until they have read the whole question. There is no very strong objection to requiring candidates to select a false response, but such a requirement is best imposed in the *stem*, perhaps as follows:

Of the following statements about what may lower an examination's validity, three are true and one is false. Which one is false?

One could of course recast the whole question by switching the contents of stem and responses and forming *four* questions, each new question asking about the effect, on validity, of a particular condition. (Or set four True-False questions–p. 229.)

A moment ago we suggested that there was no strong objection to asking the candidate to select a false statement, but to a related point objections can be raised: the inclusion of 'negative' statements–containing the word 'not'. These tend to be confusing, and may well be tests of the candidate's ability to unravel the language of the question rather than to deal with its substance. (Interpretation of the question can be a legitimate task, but that is not the issue here.) For example:

The maximum possible mark does not provide a useful standard of judgment because . . .

Such a stem would probably be intended to discover whether candidates could identify a reason why the maximum possible mark does not provide a useful standard of judgment. But it *could* be taken to be saying that the maximum possible mark *does* provide a useful standard—but not because of . . . . In this example, admittedly, the trouble is caused by the word 'because' as well as by the word 'not', and it would be possible to avoid this particular ambiguity by rewriting the stem without removing the negative:

The maximum possible mark does not provide a useful standard of judgment. One reason is that . . .

However, the responses in such a question are almost certain to contain negatives too, and the ambiguity arising from the double negative is notorious.

In general, stems are likely to serve their directive function more efficiently if expressed positively. Of course, there may be occasions when the inclusion of a negative is obliged by the very nature of the performance required. If so, the negative should be emphasised—by italics, or underlining, or capitals.

Finally, unless the purpose of the question is to test the candidate's understanding of it, a stem expressed in simple language is usually to be preferred.

It is one thing, however, to be knowledgeable about the

basic principles of writing stems, and even to recognise their application in examples provided, but quite another thing to produce good stems oneself. The best way to learn to write stems, and indeed multiple-choice questions generally, is to construct them with the guidance and criticism of someone who has already acquired the skill.

The correct response

Since different questions will require different content for their correct responses, any basic principle governing the construction of a correct response will have to be concerned not with its content but with its function.

That function is indicated succinctly by the term 'response' itself. The performance the examination's purpose requires the candidate to give consists not merely in his thinking and selecting the correct option, but in his doing so *in response to* the substance of the stem. For example:

---

6 The weight of a distribution is determined by its

   A Mean.
   B Difficulty.
   C Standard Deviation.
   D Maximum Possible Mark.

(C)

Here the correct response is 'Standard Deviation', but it is correct, of course, only in respect of this particular stem. With a different stem, the response 'Standard Deviation' could have been wrong. The candidate performs correctly only when, in response to the gist of the stem, he selects the required statement, and it is in serving *as* a response to the gist of the stem that the option fulfils its proper function.

We can now state more precisely the function of the stem. Since the candidate has to offer the correct option in response to the gist of the stem, the stem itself must provide him with the 'cue' for his doing so, in the theatrical sense in which a cue directs the performer towards, or triggers off, the required performance. (The term 'cue' has a very similar significance in some theories of learning.*)

The required performance, then, embraces not the mere picking of the correct option, nor the reading of the stem, but the two together. The stem must provide the cue for the candidate's selecting the right option in response to that cue. Of course, the candidate will not give the required response to the cue if he has not *learned* to do so. But that is the point. The test consists of our giving him the appropriate cue and discovering whether he responds in the required way.

This two-part, cue-response, way of envisaging performance is both pertinent and profitable. First, consider its relevance to the testing of what is generally referred to as 'knowledge'. In illustration consider the item of knowledge expressed by the statement,

The mode is the most frequently obtained mark.

This might be tested by the question, 'What is the mode?', but it could also be tested by 'What name is given to the most frequently obtained mark?' A candidate might of course be able to answer both questions correctly, but what is given as the cue in the one question is required as response in the other, and a candidate who was able to answer one question might not be able to answer the other question. Given the term 'mode', he might recall what it meant; but given the description, 'most frequently obtained mark', he might not recall its conventional name. Or, of course, the converse. 'Association' is not necessarily two-way. One part of an item of knowledge, given as cue, may elicit another part as response; but that other part, given as cue, may not elicit the former part. In testing whether a candidate 'knows' something, the examiner must therefore decide which part of the item of knowledge is to be the cue, which the response. And if the candidate's knowledge is to be thoroughly tested, both forms of question will be necessary.

* e.g. Miller and Dollard (1945) say that cues determine when the learner will respond, and which response he will make. And in Thyne (1966a) the same term is exploited further.

At first sight the point may seem irrelevant to multiple-choice questions, because they do not necessitate *recall*; the correct response is explicitly stated among the options. But it does apply, as Questions 7 and 8 illustrate. These are, respectively, closed versions of the open questions, 'What is the Mode?' and 'What name is given to the most frequently obtained mark?'

---

7 The Mode is the

   A Highest mark actually obtained.
   B Most frequently obtained mark.
   C Number of candidates obtaining the average mark.
   D Number of questions all candidates answer correctly.

                                               (B)

---

8 The most frequently obtained mark is known as the

   A Median.
   B Mean.
   C Mode.
   D Measure.

                                               (C)

Here again, the candidate who 'knows' what the mode is could answer correctly no matter which form the question took. For him, interchange of cue and response makes no difference. But a candidate who did not know could correctly answer Question 8 if he did know the meanings of Median and Mode, and that 'Measure' is too general a term. (We are assuming that questions are set to test what the candidate knows, not whether he can arrive at the correct answer by elimination.)

Of course, the sort of possibility we are considering might arise irrespective of which part of the statement was made the stem and which part the correct response. But one form rather than the other usually lends itself better to preventing it. For instance, it would be difficult, in Question 8, to substitute realistic responses in place of 'Median' and 'Mean'—the terms we assumed the candidate might know. (Indeed, the response 'Measure' is no more than a stopgap.) In Question 7, in contrast, there is no customary term for the content of any wrong response, and it is much less likely that the correct response would be 'selected' merely by rejection of the others.

This point relates closely to another point made in a subsequent section, namely with the need to make the wrong responses 'plausible'; the present point is simply that even in multiple-choice questions the possibility of interchanging cue and response deserves consideration.

The cue-response way of envisaging performance is relevant in another way, with reference to questions calling for understanding and not mere recall. In such questions, although the stem must contain the cue, yet it is not made obvious; only those candidates who have the requisite understanding will be able to pick out the gist of the stem, namely the cue, and so be able to give the correct response. The candidate has to 'see into the question', as it were, and his giving the correct response is a criterion that he has 'seen' what is necessary. This issue nevertheless deserves more detailed discussion, and is taken up again in a later section of this chapter.

Two other comments about the correct response. First, there is always the danger that the correct response may be correct only in certain circumstances. If so (and the probability is higher than is often realised), either these circumstances should be stated or the question should be framed in such a way that they are irrelevant. On the other hand, to hedge the stem with a list of provisos is likely to floor the weaker candidates and perhaps mislead the best—who may become unduly cautious themselves. Second, some questions may ask for the 'best' response—which might seem to presuppose that *all* the responses could be correct. Questions taking this particular form are sometimes referred to as 'best answer' questions, but the term 'correct response' is still appropriate because, provided the stem has given the necessary cue, only the 'best answer' is the correct one.

This section has presupposed that there is only one correct

response. In the next section we consider the possibility of there being more than one.

More than one correct response

In illustration consider the following example:

> 9 A distribution's degree of scatter is indicated by its
>
> A Standard Deviation.
> B Maximum Possible Mark.
> C Interquartile Range.
> D Median
>
> (A, C)

In offering such a question the examiner would have to make it clear to the candidates that there might *be* more than one correct response; if he did not, and such a question appeared amid others having only one correct response, the candidate could be puzzled and think the examiner had made a mistake. Accordingly, either the rubric for a set of questions would have to give that indication, or the stem of the question would have to do so. In the latter case the stem of Question 9 might read, instead, 'Which of the following provide(s) a measure of a distribution's scatter?'

However, to a multiple-choice question with more than one correct response there is one very serious objection: it is difficult to devise a satisfactory way of marking it. (Gronlund 1965 goes so far as to say there is *no* satisfactory way.)

For Question 9 there are two correct responses, A and C, and so a candidate who chooses these two has answered the question correctly. But do we award him the mark of 2 (because he has chosen the two correct options) or the mark of 1 (because it is these two responses together which constitue *the* correct answer)?

If we award him 2, to be consistent we should award 1 to a candidate who chooses Response A only, or Response C only. Then what of a candidate who chooses A (correct) and B (incorrect)? Does he get 1? Or do we subtract a mark for his wrong response, so that he gets 0? If we do, he gets the same mark–of 0–as a candidate who chooses all four options. Yet it would be reasonable to argue that the candidate who chooses only A and B knows more than the candidate who picks all four. The former has indicated that he knows that D is *not* a measure of scatter.

On the other hand, if we award the mark of 1 for the (correct) double response A and C, it might be argued that this is unfair to the candidate who answered A, or C, and left the other options alone. (Awarding $\frac{1}{2}$ is no solution, for this raises exactly the same arguments.)

Our own view is that *if* we must use multiple-choice questions with more than one correct response, the mark of 1 should be awarded only for *the* correct answer–in the above case for A and C together. Further, we think it appropriate in most cases to state, in the stem, how many right responses there are. (For instance, 'Which *two* of the following . . .?'.)

However, there are many very good arguments against that point of view–which illustrates our initial point that it is difficult to devise a satisfactory way of marking (satisfactory, that is, for a *team* of examiners). Our conclusion is the same as Gronlund's (1965), namely that such questions should be avoided. Then how can the subject-matter be examined?

There are four broad solutions. First, the (prospective) multiple-choice question can be broken down into several True-False questions, though there is no need to write out each in full. If we did, in connection with Question 9, the substance of its stem would have to be written out each time. Instead, we could use the 'cluster type' presentation. Thus:

10	A distribution's degree of scatter is indicated by its		
	Standard Deviation.	T	F
	Maximum Possible Mark.	T	F
	Interquartile Range.	T	F
	Median.	T	F

That is to say, Question 10 is in effect four questions, to be marked as such. However, as we shall see later, True–False questions have disadvantages too.

Second, it may be possible, when all but one of the original question's responses are incorrect, to introduce a negative into the stem: 'Which one of the following is NOT . . .?'. But this has two possible weaknesses. As noted on p. 189, it is usually advisable to avoid negatives, for they tend to confuse the candidates. And simply to change from positive to negative may completely change the focus of the question. Our desire to find out whether the candidate knows that such-and-such *is* true is not likely to be satisfied by our discovering that he knows that something *else* is *not* true.

A third suggestion, therefore, is that the examiner should re-examine what he wants to measure, and, if need be, set several questions, each with one correct response, instead of only one question with several correct responses. For instance (and still with reference to Question 9), he might use the same stem but include only one measure of scatter; or he might write a stem referring to (say) Standard Deviation, and offer options referring to what it does and does not measure.

Fourth, one might make use of what has been called the 'multiple-completion' type of question. (See, for instance, Macintosh and Morrison 1969.) Here is an example, based upon the substance of our Question 9 (p. 194).

Which of the following can be used to indicate the extent of a distribution's scatter?

I   *Standard Deviation.*
II   *Maximum Possible Mark.*
III   *Interquartile Range.*
IV   *Median.*

A   I *only.*
B   II *only.*
C   I *and* III *only.*
D   I, III, *and* IV *only.*

This format gets over the difficulties we have been discussing. The format of the second set of options (A, B, C, D) makes it clear that there may be more than one correct option in the first set (I, II, III, IV), and yet copes with the point that even when more than one of the first set are correct, yet there is only one 'correct answer'–namely 'C' in our example. It also simplifies the marking. It will nevertheless be apparent that it is unlikely that the second set (A, B, C, etc.) will cover all the possibilities. With four options in the first set, there are fifteen possibilities for the second set (sixteen if we include 'None of these'), and it would be quite impracticable to include them all. There is a danger, then, that by having to restrict the number of options in the second set the examiner may unwittingly allow the candidate (with the requisite acumen) to eliminate one or more of the options actually given. Even so, the 'multiple-completion' type would seem to have much to recommend it, especially when the other three suggestions fail to meet the examiner's requirements.

Finally, most of what has been said in this section would apply also to the practice of differential marking of options within a question. If the practice of having several correct (equally correct) responses is suspect, so also will be the more complex practice of having several options which are 'correct' to different degrees. Perhaps we should note also that in this section we have adduced only a small sample of the arguments applicable to the issue. The fact that there are many more, of a contradictory kind, but adds to our main points.

The wrong responses

Why there should be wrong responses at all is obvious: a question consisting of only a stem and the correct response would give itself away. But what form should the wrong responses take? Here again we must look first, not at content, but at function.

Whatever its particular content may be, the intention of a multiple-choice question is that the candidate who knows (or understands, etc.) what is required of him–that is, will *perform* as required–will select the correct option in response to the stem, and discard (or even ignore) the others. Negatively expressed, it is *not* the function of the wrong options to trick, or mislead, or catch out, or lay traps for the candidate who can do what is required of him by the examination's purpose. For this reason, despite the term's fairly common usage, we do not like the word 'distractors'.

It is not even an appropriate term for the function of wrong responses in respect of candidates who are *not* fully competent. Positively expressed, their function is to provide options which, *for such candidates*, are at least as *sensible* as the correct response. They are there, not to tempt these candidates away from what they would do correctly were they not so tempted, but merely to prevent them from receiving the correct response as a free gift, to preclude the possibility of their answering correctly in spite of their ignorance. If a candidate does not know, or understand something, or cannot do something, or is unable to apply something, plainly he cannot be 'tempted away' or 'distracted' from expressing or doing or applying it. The purpose of including wrong options is, in effect, to reveal those candidates who would not *give* the required response if the question were set in an open form.

It follows that while all the options should be 'plausible', yet the wrong options should be as plausible as the correct option only for candidates who are not thoroughly competent.

Such plausibility can be achieved in several ways. First, all the wrong options (and the right option too, of course) must make *sense*, not only in themselves but in relation to the cue given in the stem. For instance, if the stem indicates that the right response will refer to a *mark* of some sort, every one of the responses must refer to a mark. If the right response will obviously take the form of a plural noun, all the responses must be plural nouns. If not, the otherwise incompetent candidate, assuming that the examiner will not make grammatical mistakes, and that a correct response will not make nonsense, and the like, may be able to infer what the correct response must be.

Second, and related to the point just made, the set of options should be a *homogeneous* one, homogeneous, that is, except only in respect of the crucial feature which makes one of the options correct. In so far as the candidates are required to select *one* response, what the incompetent candidate is likely to do is to look for 'the odd one out'. And if the correct response is the 'odd one out' in respect of something other than the crucial feature, such a candidate may score a mark to which he is not entitled. Homogeneity of responses covers many possibilities. Some of the more common are now noted.

It often happens that wrong responses can be written in fewer words that can the correct response—because it may have to contain qualifications and the like. Examinees soon learn this, and when in doubt may choose whichever response is significantly longer than any of the others. Ideally, the set of responses would be homogeneous in respect of length, but this is rarely possible. The examiner should therefore strive to ensure that the correct response is not consistently the longest. (Deliberately to make one of the *wrong* responses the longest, in every question, would of course be quite reprehensible!) With these provisos, the best order of responses would seem to be one of increasing order of length—as in Question 6 (p. 190) and Question 7 (p. 192), where it so happens the correct response is *not* the longest.

In many subjects, especially the social sciences, only rarely can one say that something 'always' happens, or that something is 'never' the case, or that 'all' people do certain things, or that 'no one' has done something-or-other; and so the inclusion of terms like these in a response serves very well to indicate that it is probably false. If, then, it is necessary to use words like 'usually', or 'tends', or 'the majority' in the correct response, the same kind of words should be used in the wrong responses also.

Again, if the correct response is expressed in the technical vocabulary of the topic being examined, so also should the incorrect responses. In other words, the wrong responses should 'sound just as technical' as the right one. The alternative is, of course, not to use technical terms in *any* response.

A related point is that even if the correct response does not contain strictly technical terms, yet its *language* is likely to sound familiar – even to the candidate who is not very familiar with the *substance* of the topic. Accordingly, if the correct response cannot properly be written in an unusual style, the examiner should try to make the language of the wrong responses have the same familiar ring.

Finally, sometimes examiners have difficulty in devising wrong responses which are sufficiently plausible, or feel that by stating the correct response they are giving the answer away. In the former case they may write *several* correct responses, and as the last option write 'All of these'. In the other case they may write only wrong responses, and as the last option write 'None of these'. This particular breach of the homogeneity rule is to be avoided. If, in the first case, a candidate knows *two* of the responses to be correct, he can deduce that the required response is 'All of these' – without having to consider any other offered options. And if he knows enough about the topic to recognise that *one* of the options is *in*correct, he can thereby eliminate the 'All of these' option, and so cut down the number of options he has to consider. The basic objection to the 'None of these' form is somewhat different. If all the other options *are* incorrect, as we supposed, then even if the candidate does select the correct response (namely 'None of these'), all we have ascertained is that he has recognised that the other answers are wrong; which does not prove that he knows the correct consequence of the point contained in the stem. Since it is unlikely that the purpose of the examination is to ascertain only that candidates can recognise certain *wrong* answers as being wrong, such questions will lower the examination's validity.

Testing for understanding

In this section we shall try to show that, despite popular belief to the contrary, multiple-choice questions can test for understanding. Since understanding, as such, is not directly observable by the examiner, and since examinations can assess nothing but performance—no matter what form the examination may take, the fundamental question the examiner has to answer is what sort of *performance* can be accepted as *evidence* of understanding. To answer that question we must digress to consider the nature of understanding, for unless we have a rationale of understanding we have no criteria on which to base questions for testing it.

Elsewhere (Thyne 1966a) we have expressed the view that to understand something is to recognise it as a case of something which is already familiar. In other words, to understand something is to recognise what *kind* of thing (event, etc.) it is. For example, if one is to understand why doubling all the marks in a distribution doubles its scatter, one must recognise that this is but an instance of the general arithmetical fact that doubling any two numbers is at once to double the difference between them.

Now if one is to recognise some particular thing P as an instance of some other (necessarily more general) thing G, one must detect, in P, whatever feature, simple or complex, *makes P* an instance of G. For example, to answer the question, 'What number must be divided by $6\frac{1}{2}$ to give $4\frac{1}{3}$?', one must understand the question; and to understand it one must do more than notice the word 'divided'; one must attend to the more complex characteristic which makes it a 'multiplication' kind of thing.

Further, if one is to recognise P as an instance of G, one must be already familiar with G. One cannot *recognise* a certain physical problem as involving the Principle of Moments unless one is already familiar with that general principle.

To repeat: if one is to understand P, one must already know G, the more general thing of which P *is* an instance; and one must also detect, in P, the feature which identifies it *as* an instance of G. If these two conditions hold, understanding will occur. If either of these two conditions does not hold, understanding will not occur. A test of understanding must therefore be a test of whether these two conditions hold.

However, a candidate's recognising something as an instance of the more general thing is not directly observable by the examiner—a fact in accord with our previous comment that understanding as such is not susceptible of observation. A question aiming to test for understanding must therefore direct the candidate to undertake a task whose accomplishment *is* observable, and which *can be performed only if the candidate has understood.* More precisely, the performance he gives must provide evidence that he has recognised the identifying feature in the given instance. In other words, that performance must be such that only the identifying feature can give rise to it. In the terms we used before, the sort of performance necessary as evidence of understanding will be one which can be given as a response only to the cue consisting of the instance's identifying feature. If the candidate has not spotted the identifying feature he cannot take it as his cue, and so will not give the crucial response. And if he has detected the identifying feature, and takes it as his cue, he can give the crucial response. To that last statement there is nevertheless an important proviso.

Even if the candidate *has* recognised what kind of thing the instance is (by detecting the identifying feature), he cannot give the response required unless he has already *learned* to make that sort of response to this kind of thing. To revert to the problem about $6\frac{1}{2}$ and $4\frac{1}{3}$: a candidate who had indeed recognised it as a 'multiplication' kind of problem would still fail to give the correct answer if he had not learned to multiply numbers like $6\frac{1}{2}$ and $4\frac{1}{3}$. Had the question been somewhat different, 'If you were asked to find what number must be divided by $6\frac{1}{2}$ to give $4\frac{1}{3}$, what would you have to do?', and the candidate answered, 'I would have to multiply these two numbers!', that answer would provide reasonably good evidence of understanding. In contrast, if he gave a wrong answer to the question in its original form, it *could* be that he had failed to understand, but it *could* be only that he lacked the computational skill. In general, in so far as the question is intended to test understanding, and no more, the *response* selected by the examiner as crucial must be one within the learner's repertoire. But obviously an examiner would not set the question we have been discussing if the candidates had not already learned to multiply mixed numbers. The question could have used, not $6\frac{1}{2}$ and $4\frac{1}{3}$, but (say) 4 and 12.

A question intended to test understanding, then, must provide data susceptible of being recognised as a case of something more general, and it must direct the candidate to give a performance which can be given only in response to the feature, of the data, which identifies the data as being a case of the more general principle, or item of knowledge, or procedure, or law, or whatever it may be. In so far as the question is to be a test of understanding and not at the same time a test of some skill (mathematical, linguistic, and so forth), the performance required must nevertheless be one within the candidate's repertoire. Of course, there is no objection to a question's testing for understanding *and* for something else. If it does this, the candidate's giving the right response will be evidence of his understanding and of his skill; but if he fails to give the right response, there may be doubt about the locus of his failure.

With these points in mind we now consider multiple-choice questions for testing understanding. Questions 11 to 19 provide an extensive illustration.

Since a test of understanding necessitates the candidate's selecting the right option only in response to the identifying feature as cue, one has to ensure, in constructing questions like these, that he cannot give the right answer in response to a *wrong* cue. In illustration consider Question 11. The general principle here is that weight is proportional to scatter; and what the candidate has to note is which distribution has the greatest scatter. But if he thought that weight depended upon the marks' magnitudes, he would give the correct answer if the examiner had inadvertently made Distribution C have not only the greatest scatter but also the largest numerical marks. Similarly for Questions 12, 13 and 14. Likewise, since some candidates might suppose that Tom's best subject was the one in which he scored the highest numerical mark, namely D, the subject in which Tom had his highest *standing* should not be at the same time

Questions 11 to 19. To answer these questions refer to the data, below, from the four examination subjects, A, B, C, D.

	A	B	C	D
Maximum Possible Mark:	100	40	80	150
Upper Quartile:	70	32	71	130
Median:	61	20	53	116
Lower Quartile:	53	10	34	98
Tom's Mark:	62	38	40	87

11 If each candidate's four marks were added, which subject would have the greatest weight? (C)

12 And which subject would have the least weight? (A)

13 If, before the marks were added, they were all converted to percentage marks, which subject would then have the greatest weight? (B)

14 And which would then have the least weight? (A)

15 Which of these four examinations, taken by one and the same group of candidates, was the easiest for them? (D)

16 And which was the most difficult? (B)

17 From the information given, which distribution of marks appears to be the least symmetrical? (C)

18 In which subject did Tom give his best (norm-reference) performance? (B)

19 In which subject did Tom give his poorest (norm-reference) performance? (D)

the subject in which his numerical mark was the largest of the four marks he scored. See Questions 18 and 19.

These nine questions would seem to be of the appropriate form for testing understanding. In each question a principle or general item of knowledge has to be involved; and if he is to give the correct answer the candidate must notice (indeed *look for*-in these questions) the aspect of the data which is the characteristic of that general principle. We can be fairly certain that, if the candidate gives the right answer, he has understood the issue in question.

Two points are worth stressing. First, in none of these questions was the candidate told what the general principle was. If he had been, the test might more properly be called a test of 'application'—applying a *given* principle or rule to a given case. That kind of test may of course be perfectly legitimate–but the withholding of the general principle would seem to provide a more rigorous test of *understanding*. Second, none of these questions draws the candidate's attention to the crucial feature. For Question 11, for instance, the necessary data can be observed, namely the differences between the respective Upper and Lower Quartiles, but the candidate is not specifically directed to find these differences. He is not prevented from finding them, but neither is he prevented from noticing other, irrelevant, bits of information.

No question can of course guarantee that the correct answer is a proof of understanding; it is always possible, though in well-constructed questions highly improbable, that right answers can be obtained for the wrong reason. In particular, in multiple-choice questions (and some others) the completely ignorant candidate might select the correct option as a result of a lucky guess, a possibility applicable not only to questions for testing understanding. The problem of guessing is discussed in the next section.

The problem of guessing

A well-known objection to multiple-choice questions is that candidates may get the right answer by guessing. If they do, validity is lowered, because the marks will not be pure measures of what the examination was intended to assess; and the greater the incidence of guessing the lower validity will be.

Guessing is not peculiar, of course, to closed questions.

Intelligent but not very knowledgeable candidates can construct essay-type answers in such a way that the examiner is not sure whether they are cleverly hiding their ignorance. Even so, the problem of guessing in multiple-choice questions has to be dealt with.

At best, one would *prevent* candidates from guessing, perhaps by warning them that if they do not know the answer they should leave the question unanswered, and that marks will be deducted for wrong answers. However, this is essentially a problem of marking, and so is discussed in the next chapter. Another means of preventing guessing derives from the point that candidates will not resort to guessing if they are confident that they know the right answer. What prevents guessing here is, of course, not the candidate's actually knowing the right answer, but his belief that he does. Accordingly, the wrong options must be plausible for ignorant candidates, and so the examiner must know how to write plausible options. He must be *au fait*

with popular misconceptions, current prejudices, common fallacies, and the like.

This requirement is likely to be met by the examiner who is also the teacher, but can be met also by other examiners who have experience in examining the same topic by means of open questions and have learned from candidates' wrong answers.

It would be over-optimistic, however, to assume that guessing can be completely prevented. The most we can hope to do is minimise it. In particular, the chance of correctly guessing any question decreases as the number of its options increases. With only two options (one of them right) the chance is even. With three options it is 1 in 3, with four options 1 in 4, and so on. On the face of it, then, correct guessing can be minimised by our using a large number of options in each question, but the effectiveness of that procedure has severe limitations, because it depends upon all the wrong responses being plausible. (If, in a six-option question, three wrong options are not at all plausible, the chance of successful guessing rises to 1 in 3.) In some topics it may be possible to write a multiplicity of plausible wrong options, but in many topics it will not; and the examiner may find difficulty in writing more than two or three. We stress this point because it has become almost customary to regard four options as the minimum, whereas (as we have just illustrated) the plausibility of options may be as important as their number.

It might seem, therefore, that each question should contain as many wrong responses as can be made plausible. But this could result in different questions having different numbers of options —which would be very inconvenient for the treatment of results, particularly in determining the pass mark, discussed in the next chapter. We should recommend that the examiner should strive to construct four options for each question—three of them wrong but plausible.

Another way of minimising the effects of guessing is to have as many *questions* as is practicable. Were there only one four-option question, the chance of scoring full marks (1!) is 1 in 4. With two such questions the chance is 1 in 16; with three questions it is 1 in 64; and so on. With seven questions it is 1 in 16,384. The chance of scoring full marks decreases very markedly with an increase in the number of questions. And the greater the number of (plausible) *options*, the greater the decrease with the number of *questions*.

Since guessing is unlikely to be preventable, and at best merely minimised, one might be inclined to conclude that multiple-choice questions should not be used at all. It would nevertheless be shortsighted to reject multiple-choice questions solely on the ground that they allow of successful guessing. *Every* form of examination has weaknesses, but each has strengths not shared by some other forms, and one must balance this or this weakness against that or that strength in the light of one's purpose and the practical contingencies. In particular, multiple-choice questions, while they allow of guessing, can be constructed so that its effects are quite small, and (of greater importance, we think) have the great advantage of very wide sampling and very high marking-consistency and mark-relevance. These advantages are only too real when the number of candidates is large and essay-marking is likely to lose in consistency (and relevance) through the scripts having to be shared by several examiners—probably in haste.

However, our aim here is not to 'sell' multiple-choice questions to buyers who do not need them, but to stress the need to balance advantages and disadvantages, for as yet the perfect examination, sharing none of the current weaknesses and all the current strengths, is a dream.

Lay-out

We conclude this chapter with some practical points about the physical preparation of the question paper. Once stated, these may seem obvious, even trivial, but hours of careful composing of questions can be wasted by carelessness in the preparation of the paper itself.

First, it will almost always be necessary to provide each candidate not merely with the questions but also with a set of instructions as to how he is to proceed to answer them. The following points are particularly important.

a) Since multiple-choice question papers are much longer than essay question papers, and may run to several pages, stapled together, candidates should be asked to check that their question papers contain all the questions, numbered from (say) 1 to 70—in the correct order. (An office assistant may have omitted a sheet altogether, or stapled the sheets in a wrong order.)

b) The instruction sheet must also indicate the physical way in which the questions are to be answered. The candidates may have to draw a ring round the letter (A, B, C, etc.) of the correct response, and do so on the question paper itself—which then serves also as the answer paper. Or the letter may have to be underlined, or scored out, or have a 'tick' ('check') made beside it. This may not seem crucial, but if different candidates use different ways of answering, this can lead to mistakes in marking. Or the candidates may have to use a separate answer sheet, and they must be instructed how they are to complete it. (The use of separate answer sheets is discussed in the next chapter.)

c) Whichever method of answering is to be adopted (on the question paper itself or on a separate answer sheet), candidates must be told to write their names on the paper which is to be returned. All examiners who have used multiple-choice questions will confirm that this instruction is by no means superfluous. In aid of this requirement the answer sheet (which may be the question paper) should have a space clearly labelled for this purpose.

d)   If there is a separate answer sheet, with numbered spaces to correspond with the numbered questions, candidates should be asked to ensure that the number of the space they are completing corresponds with the number of the question they are answering.

e)   Since the examiners may wish to use the same questions on a later occasion (to measure student-progress, or to compare the performances of two groups), and so will want to have the question papers returned, candidates must be instructed to return them. Also if candidates are not to write anything on the question paper, they must be told.

f)   If marks are to be deducted for wrong answers (see 'Guessing-Correction', next chapter), this must be made clear before candidates begin to answer. Likewise if marks are *not* to be deducted. In the latter case, indeed, for a reason noted in the next chapter, they should be *advised* that since marks will not be deducted for wrong answers they should guess if they are not sure.

g)   The final instruction should indicate clearly what the candidates are to do when they finish – to leave the papers on their desks, or to hand them to an invigilator, or to put them in a certain tray, and so forth.

Second, since multiple-choice question papers contain a great many words, and a closely-packed mass of print can be confusing (even intimidating), the examiner should aim to present a paper with the most elegant format possible. In particular,

a)   The space between successive questions should be larger than any space within a question.

b)   The space between the stem and the options should be slightly larger than the space between any two options.

c)   The letters (A, B, C, etc.) of the options should form a vertical line, not only within each question but through all the questions.

d)   The letters of the options should be inset from the numbers of the questions (somewhat as in the Questions on p. 192).

e)   If certain data apply to a series of questions (as in our Questions 11 to 19, on p. 204), this should be indicated (as shown), though the separate questions must of course be numbered also.

f)   It is worth striving to ensure that all the questions to be answered by reference to certain data appear on the same page as the data themselves. Otherwise candidates have to keep turning back—to their own annoyance and that of nearby candidates also. When this is not possible it is desirable to provide a separate, if need be detachable, data-sheet—to which each question requiring it must make explicit reference ('From the data on Sheet III ...').

Third, should one question paper include questions of different types (eg. multiple-choice and True-False or Matching), the different types of question should be clearly separated.

These various points have been stated categorically—but solely for brevity's sake; they are intended only for guidance. Nor have we troubled to list obvious points—such as that the length of time allowed should be stated, the topic named, and the like. Further aspects of multiple-choice examinations are discussed in the chapter which follows.

15 Multiple-choice questions–marking and evaluating

The answer sheet

Candidates can be asked to indicate the selected response on the question paper itself–say by drawing a ring round the appropriate letter. This procedure eliminates the need to prepare a separate answer sheet, incidentally saves cost of paper, ensures that (if need be) every question paper is returned, and obviates the possibility of distraction by having to go from one paper to another.

A very practical advantage of multiple-choice questions, however, is speed of marking, and marking can be speeded up still further (an advantage when the number of candidates is large) if a separate answer sheet is used. A useful type consists of small 'boxes', one for each question, each of these boxes being divided into as many smaller boxes as there are options. The top line of a four-option answer sheet, of this kind, would begin like this:

```
  A B C D      A B C D      A B C D      A B C D
1 □□□□      2 □□□□      3 □□□□      4 □□□□
```

The advantage of this type of answer sheet is that it can be marked very rapidly by means of a stencil–which also makes marking more reliable. The stencil would be a facsimile of the answer sheet, though preferably on dark-coloured card, with a hole cut in each 'correct' square. Candidates would be instructed to shade, or put a heavy cross in the box corresponding with the response chosen. When the candidate's answer sheet is covered by the stencil, there will be white squares where the candidate is wrong.

Any answer sheet should, of course, have a space at the top for the candidate's name, section or class, date, and his score (and perhaps his scaled score also).

A further practical advantage of the separate answer sheets

(of any kind) is that they are easier to move about than are question papers each of many pages. And, since multiple-choice *question* papers tend to be long, single-page answer papers save storage.

Answer sheets need not be specially prepared for each and every examination. They can be printed or duplicated in large quantities, though the number of options should always be as great as one is likely to need in the foreseeable future.

There is a special difficulty, however, in using stencils: while one is marking it is not possible to see whether candidates have changed their minds. It is therefore desirable to scan each answer sheet after the stencil has been removed–to find out whether candidates have made little notes ('Not *A*, please, I meant *B*'), or, of course, have cheated.

A final point. Some education areas offer a computer service for marking objective examinations. If so, the form of answer sheet will be determined by the computer centre.

Marking

The simplest way to mark multiple-choice questions, and the way often recommended (see Ebel 1965), is to award 1 for a right answer, 0 for a wrong answer or no answer. On this system a candidate's mark is the number of questions he has answered correctly. (A possible exception is the application of a 'guessing correction', discussed later in this chapter.)

As Gronlund (1968b) comments, however, teachers often want to award more marks to some questions than to others–

because the former are regarded as more important, or more difficult, or require more time; but following Ebel (1965) he nevertheless recommends the simple 'o or 1' marking system, and suggests that if an area is to be more important it should be covered, not by awarding higher marks for the questions in it, but by having more such questions.

The issue is a mathematically complex one, but the following points are worth noting.

A good multiple-choice examination should contain a quite large number of questions, and it is on that assumption that most of the evidence is based. In particular, Ebel (1965) makes the point that differential weighting tends to have relatively small effects, and he quotes Wilks (1938) to the effect that weighting individual items is of little consequence in a long test of intercorrelated items; and Guilford et al. (1942), who found that it did not yield an appreciable gain in either validity or reliability; and Phillips (1943), that little is gained from weighted marking, and indeed is probably not worth the effort.

It is perhaps important to note that none of the above comments indicate that weighted marking has *no* effect; and herein may lie a danger we referred to in an earlier chapter. When, in comparing weighted with unweighted marking, the test is for validity, and that test refers to an external criterion, the difference in *correlation* may be slight, but as we noted before, even a small difference in correlation could account for a significant change of placing for a small number of candidates. And, when norm-reference is in order, a change of placing might mean Fail rather than Pass (or the converse). *If* a question deserves to have greater weight, then, strictly it ought to have it. And there is no evidence that weighted marking makes the examination *worse*–so long as the weighting is in accord with its purpose.

The crux of the matter, however, is whether any single question *does* deserve to have higher marks–say to be marked o and 2 (or o and 3 or 4 or 5). By its very nature a multiple-choice question deals with a very restricted piece of subject-matter, and not with what could reasonably be called an 'area'. What is much more likely to be 'more important', and to be justifiably so, is an area or sub-topic, not a single question. The suggestion

(Gronlund 1968a and Phillips 1943) that, instead of awarding higher marks for a question in a certain area we should set more *questions* in that area, would therefore seem an appropriate one. It has two advantages. First, the candidate's aggregate score will be the number of questions he has correctly answered–which can be useful. Second, as was shown in an earlier chapter, when we double the marks in a part of an examination (which is, in effect, what we do by marking on a 0 and 2 system instead of a 0 and 1 system), what we are doing is counting twice into the aggregate distribution the candidates' standings in the part so treated. But it would provide better sampling of the area in question to double the number of questions than to make the same question count twice.

To summarise the view we have been expressing: while the use of different marking systems (0 and 1, 0 and 2, etc.) is troublesome, yet there can be a case for weighting certain parts of the examination; but better sampling of 'important' areas is achieved, not by using higher marks for its questions, but by setting more questions in it–each question to be marked on a 0 and 1 basis.

Guessing-corrections–norm-reference

In a previous chapter guessing was discussed in connection with the setting of questions; now we raise it in connection with marking.

To avoid unnecessary quibbles we should state what discussions of this kind usually mean by 'guessing'. Sometimes referred to as 'blind guessing', it does not refer to candidates who are not absolutely certain of the right answer, or 'think' they know. Such candidates would usually be regarded as entitled to their marks. It refers to candidates who, in picking this response rather than that, might as well have tossed a coin. It is to eliminate the illegitimate advantage gained by such candidates that so-called 'guessing-corrections' are sometimes applied.

An important point is that if a guessing-correction is to be used, candidates must be advised that it will. If a candidate thought he would not be penalised for guessing, he would have grounds for complaint if he had not been told in advance.

There are two different forms of guessing-correction. We begin with the better known. In a four-option question the guesser has a 1 in 4 chance of being correct, and so the expectation would be that if he guessed several questions he would get one right for every three he answered wrongly. (The validity of that expectation is examined shortly.) The guessing-correction is based upon that expectation. For every three answers a candidate gets wrong, the mark of 1 is deducted from the number he got right, on the ground that he was not entitled to that 1 in the first place. For example, if Tom answered 64 questions correctly, 30 incorrectly, and left 6 unanswered, his corrected score would be 54.

In general, a candidate's 'corrected' mark, X, is given by

$$X = R - \frac{W}{n-1}$$

where R is the number of questions answered correctly, W the number answered wrongly, and n the number of options per question.

A basic fact about the application of this guessing-correction is worth stressing. If every candidate gives an answer, right or wrong, to every question, the application of the guessing-correction will lower the numerical marks of the candidates who gave some wrong answers, but the relative *positions* of the candidates will remain the same. Here is an example, in which there are 100 questions with four options in each.

	R	W	X
Alf:	100	0	100
Bill:	70	30	60
Charles:	61	39	48
Dick:	58	42	44
Ed:	43	57	24

It will be seen that the application of the guessing-correction, here, lowers the Mean and increases the scatter, but the inter-candidate differences remain in the same proportions.

In so far as we are concerned with norm-reference, then, the guessing-correction does not eliminate any sort of advantage *when there are no omissions.* The only advantage the guessing-correction can eliminate is the advantage gained by guessers over candidates who leave blanks.

The second form of guessing-correction has the same basic intention, but instead of deducting marks from the guessers, it adds marks to the omitters. For example, if a candidate left 24 four-option questions unanswered, the expectation would be that, if he *had* guessed them, he would have got 6 of them right. In general, the 'corrected' score, from this form of guessing-correction, is given by

$$X = R + \frac{O}{n}$$

where O is the number of answers the candidate omitted to give.

It will be apparent that this procedure too eliminates no sort of advantage if there are no omissions.

These two kinds of guessing-correction are, in a sense, equivalent. If there are some omissions, each form of correction may produce new relative standings, but these new standings will be the same no matter which form of correction is used. For example:

	R	W	O	Debited for *W*	Credited for O
Ian:	75	21	4	68	76
Joe:	72	0	28	72	79
Ken:	57	15	28	52	64

After either form of correction Ian and Joe change ranks, and the scatters change, but the two corrections produce sets of marks exhibiting the same relative standings.

These are the basic facts about guessing-corrections. Now we must consider two serious criticisms.

First, both forms of correction presuppose that all wrong answers were *guessed*. That this is so is more easily seen for the first form. If a candidate guesses 12 four-option questions, he will most probably get 9 wrong; but what this guessing-correction does is to assume that if a candidate gets 9 questions wrong he guessed them, which is quite another matter. He might not have guessed any.

Ebel (1965) agrees that this assumption (that all wrong answers were guessed) will usually be completely false, but suggests that this does not invalidate the guessing-correction which apparently rests on it. He argues that since the second form of correction does not involve the counting of wrong answers, yet produces the same standings as the first form (which in fact it does), the first form is acceptable. Now it is true that the actual *operation* of adding marks in respect of omissions does not itself refer to wrong answers; but the *justification* of that operation rests on the claim that it eliminates, nicely compensates for, the advantage gained by guessing. But exactly how *much* advantage can it be shown to eliminate?—the very advantage presupposed by the first form of correction, which is based on the counting of wrong answers! Our view, then, is that the identity of standings produced by the two forms, which Ebel accepts as evidence of the first form's innocence, is, on the contrary, evidence of the guilt of both.

It would seem, therefore, that *both* forms of correction presuppose that all wrong answers were guessed; and since that presupposition is difficult if not impossible to justify, one must surely have serious doubts about the legitimacy of using guessing-corrections at all.

The second criticism is that both forms of guessing-correction presuppose that all candidates who guess (strictly, who get wrong answers!) will get the *most probable* number of guesses right. For example, with 12 four-option questions guessed, the most probable score is 3. But, by the very 'laws of chance' on which the most probable score is 3, some candidates would score more, some less than 3. While 3 is the modal score, it is not the only one. Yet guessing-corrections presuppose that all candidates will be equally lucky–at the average, with the consequence that the correction (?) will overtax some candidates and let some away with tax evasion.

In view of these two criticisms we suggest that, so far as norm-reference is concerned, guessing-corrections should not be used at all. Candidates would be advised that their final marks will be simply the number of questions they answered correctly; and they should be encouraged to guess when uncertain, because guessing will not lose them any marks.

To that suggestion there could of course be objections. If it were objected that 'lucky' candidates will gain an advantage, this is true; but as we have just shown, guessing-corrections presuppose that all candidates are *equally* lucky, and so this is not a valid objection to our dispensing with them. Furthermore, the proposed invitation to guess makes guessing-corrections superfluous, because when there are no omissions the 'corrected' standings are the same as the initial standings.

The *invitation* to guess might raise stronger objections. But it is highly unlikely that any candidate judged fit to be taking this kind of examination would be foolish enough to guess blindly unless he was ignorant of the correct answer.

There nevertheless remains the indubitable fact that, whether we choose to use guessing-corrections or to dispense with them, some candidates will be luckier than others in their guessing. We have just argued that guessing-corrections do not meet that possibility, and so we suggest that the problem of guessing must be dealt with, not at the marking stage, but in the setting of questions–by means of procedures described in the previous chapter.

Guessing-corrections–criterion-reference

The problem here is that a candidate may obtain a mark as high as the standard, not solely by his giving the performances comprising the criterion, but with the aid of answers he has guessed. The substance of the foregoing section is therefore largely irrelevant here, because it was concerned with candidates' obtaining a spurious advantage over other candidates, whereas now the relevant comparison is with a predetermined numerical mark–the measure of the criterion.

For convenience we shall refer to the mark a candidate actually obtains (perhaps with the aid of lucky guesses) as his 'actual' mark, and to the measure of what he really knew as his 'true' mark. Thus, if a candidate 'really knew' only 32 answers, but successfully guessed an additional 8, his actual mark would be 40 but his true mark would 32. If the standard were, say, 36, the difference would be crucial. The problem is, of course, that all the examiner can know for certain is the candidate's *actual* mark.

Irrespective of the standard's particular value, however, we can be certain that any candidate whose actual mark is less than the standard has truly failed to reach it–because his actual mark cannot be *less* than his true mark; and so the problem is restricted to actual marks which do reach the standard. What is the chance of a candidate's reaching the standard when his true mark is below it?

That chance depends upon the proximity of the standard to the maximum possible mark: for a candidate who cannot answer all the questions the standard requires, the chance of his reaching a predetermined standard with the aid of guessing will decrease with the number of questions left for guessing. For instance, in an examination with a standard of 40, a candidate knows 32 answers. With 100 questions in all, he would therefore have 68 questions available for correctly guessing the requisite 8. In contrast, were there only 60 questions, he would have to guess 8 questions correctly out of only 28. A somewhat different case: again the candidate knows 32 of the total 60. Were 40 the standard, he would have to guess (correctly) 8 from the remaining 28; but if the standard were 50, then from the remaining 28 he would have to guess correctly as many as 18. To repeat the main point: the closer the standard and the maximum possible mark, the lower the chance of a candidate's reaching the standard with the aid of guesses.

The effects of successful guessing, for criterion-reference, will therefore be minimal when the standard *is* the maximum possible mark. At first sight the implied recommendation may seem unreasonable. It is probably unusual—but at present so is

criterion-reference. And if an examination is planned with a view to criterion-reference, what is the point of incorporating in it performances the examination's consequences do not require?

What we have been arguing, however, is only that when the maximum possible mark is the standard the effects of successful guessing are at a *minimum, not* that there are no effects at all. It is quite conceivable that a candidate who answered correctly every one of the four-option questions did indeed guess some of them. It is highly unlikely, however, that he guessed many. If he knew all but three, the chance of his guessing these three correctly is 1 in 64; if all but four, 1 in 256; if all but five, 1 in 1024. These 'chances' may be regarded as representing 'levels of confidence' on the part of the examiner. If the chance of 1 in 1024 were regarded as sufficiently remote, as it might well be, but the chance of 1 in 256 were not, we should be accepting, and could base our judgment on, the former level of confidence. This would mean that, for instance, we should have to consider that a candidate who got all of the 100 four-option questions right *might* have known only 96, but that we should reject the suggestion that he knew only 95 or less.

This example illustrates a further point, namely that the seriousness of successful guessing here depends upon the number of questions. In that example we should confidently assume (at the 1 in 1024 confidence level) that a candidate's true percentage mark was at least 95 per cent. But if there were only 20 questions, we should be confident only that he knew at least 75 per cent of the answers.

We have supposed, so far, that the standard is the maximum possible mark, because (as we argued earlier) there is good reason for it. But there could be occasions when candidates need not have mastered *all* the performances required. This would presuppose, however, that the 'consequences' (pp. 106ff.) were such that it would be in order for a candidate to do this and this and this *or* do that and that and that. Nevertheless, even on such occasions it does not follow that the candidate is to be free to reach the standard (say of 50) by answering correctly *any* 50 of

FOR THIS POST, MISS JONES, YOU MUST BE EFFICIENT OR ORNAMENTAL, BUT, NOT HALF OF EACH.

the 100 questions. It is likely that in some examinations candidates would be obliged to demonstrate complete competence in this *area, or* in that *area,* and the like. If so (and in our example), the candidate would not pass by scoring 30 in one area and 20 in the other; he would have to score 50 in *either.* But to speak of this kind of case as having a pass mark of 50 per cent would be quite misleading, because such an examination really consists of two alternative papers, each of which sets the maximum possible mark as standard.

On the other hand, if the examiner had declared any of the 100 questions to be equivalent to any other question, and the 'consequences' allowed of such a declaration, the standard would not be the maximum possible mark, and the treatment would have to be different. We now suggest that in this kind of case it will be appropriate to apply a 'guessing-correction'—but not to the candidates' raw marks. As is now argued, it would seem to be more appropriate to apply the guessing-correction to the standard itself.

For example, in a paper with 60 four-option questions and a true standard of 40, a candidate's *true* (unaided by guessing) mark must reach 40. But if he knew exactly 40, and guessed the remaining 20, his most probable actual mark would be 45. If, then, candidates had been advised to guess when uncertain, there would be a case for making the standard 45. Any candidate with a true mark less than 40 (and who *should* fail) would have, as his most probable actual mark, a mark less than 45—and *would* fail. Any candidate with a true mark between 40 and 45 would have, as his most probable actual mark, a mark above 45—and would pass, as he should. In general, this procedure entails raising the true standard by one nth of the difference between the true standard and the maximum possible mark, n being the number of options per question.

This kind of guessing-correction is much simpler to operate than are the two kinds already described, because only one calculation is required—namely raising the standard; the candidates' marks are not changed at all. Further, it is not open to the criticism that it assumes that all wrong answers were guessed—for it does not; though it does assume, reasonably, that some *right* answers were. But it does presuppose that all guessers will receive their *most probable* mark for guessing–a presupposition we have already deplored. Again, a difficulty arises in connection with cases of omission, a crucial case being the candidate who (in our example) knows 40 and leaves the remaining 20 unanswered, for with this correction he would fail.

The last of these points can be dealt with by instructing candidates to guess when they do not know the answer. This may seem odd for criterion-reference, but some candidates will guess anyway, and the instruction is perfectly in order when this kind of guessing-correction is to be applied.

The problem of 'differential luck' can be tackled by trying to devise the examination in such a way that the standard is as near as possible to the maximum possible mark; that is, to cut down the candidate's freedom to choose between alternatives. Since the standard will be determined by the criterion, and the criterion itself is determined by the examination's 'consequences', one cannot raise the standard from (say) 50 to 75 per cent in an arbitrary way merely to cope with this particular problem. Guessing is most likely to occur, however, when the questions are difficult; and the examiner might well question the sense of setting questions which, in the main, will almost certainly produce guessing. As Gronlund (1968b) comments, widespread guessing is unlikely to happen in a sound test of achievement on a course. If one suspects widespread guessing, then, one might have to reconsider the relevance of the criterion to the candidate-group.

Some readers may have decided that we have spent an unduly high proportion of the book in dealing with the problem of guessing. Its coverage is nevertheless deliberate. For one thing, relatively little seems to have been written elsewhere about the problem of guessing in connection with criterion-reference. Second, many prospective examiners, on first meeting with multiple-choice questions, tend to be very much impressed by the possibility that a candidate may get 'a very good score just by guessing'. Since we believe that multiple-choice questions can be extremely useful, we believe also that the question of guessing must be closely scrutinised. It may be true that examiners are not as excited about guessing as they used to be; but as we have tried to show, this is not necessarily to be welcomed. To assume, for instance, that we can dismiss the problem by resorting to guessing-corrections, would be quite wrong.

Item analysis[30]

So far, our discussions of evaluation have been concerned with the marks candidates obtained for answering the questions; but it is relevant also to evaluate the questions the candidates had to answer. When these questions are of the multiple-choice or true-false type (when they are frequently known as 'items'), this latter kind of evaluation is customarily known as 'item analysis'.

Broadly, item analysis involves finding out what percentage of candidates got each question right; that is, discovering the relative difficulty of each question (see again pp. 56ff.). Thus, if as many as 83 per cent of the candidates were right in Question 1, but only 32 per cent of them were right in Question 2, Question 1 was patently much easier for this group of candidates.

This kind of information has several uses. If the examination's results are to be discussed with the examinees, the time will be most profitably spent in discussing the questions found to be most difficult. Also, if the examination were based on a course of instruction, information about the difficulty of the items could be used for the improvement of the course: topics found to be very difficult could be given greater emphasis or different treatment. Further, the information could be used for the improvement of the examination. If the results are to be subject to norm-reference, questions which everyone gets right, or which everyone gets wrong, are fulfilling no function, and so may be eliminated or altered.

Usually, however, item analysis will provide information of a more refined kind. It will reveal the percentage of candidates choosing each of the *options* within each question. (The percentage choosing the correct option is, of course, the measure of difficulty we have just been discussing.) For a particular question it might be found that A was chosen by 33 per cent of candidates, B by 65 per cent, C by 2 per cent, and D not at all. Were B the correct response, the analysis would show that about two thirds of the candidates knew what they should have known. But it would show also that as many as one third chose the *same* wrong response–which is significant. It could of course mean no more than that Responses C and D lacked plausibility; but even so, it suggests that a fair proportion of candidates were not merely ignorant but were misinformed. Such a result would seem to indicate two procedures. Since as many as a third of the candidates chose the same wrong option, the examiner should ensure that it was indeed wrong! If it was, however, he would probably have to put more emphasis on its subject-matter in the next course. Note also that if no candidate chooses a certain option, one's assumptions about the chances of guessing correctly are likely to be mistaken.

There is a further refinement, concerned with 'discrimination'. It would surely seem odd if (of 60 candidates) a certain question were answered correctly more often by the *bottom* fifteen candidates than by the *top* fifteen–top and bottom, that is, in the examination as a whole. In other words, it would seem very odd if there were a question answered better by the 'poor' candidates than by the 'good' ones. Admittedly, there is not *necessarily* anything fundamentally wrong with such a question: if the examination's purpose requires it, it must be included. But such a question would nevertheless give the examiner cause for thought, for while we should not expect every examination to be testing some single 'ability' (when such a question *would* be out of place), yet it is unusual, and the examiner might well have made a mistake in writing it–even to the extent of omitting the word 'not'. Similarly, if it were found, of the bottom fifteen candidates, that ten got a certain question right, and that the same number of the top fifteen candidates got it right, that question would not be 'discriminating' among the (generally) best and worst candidates. It is therefore desirable to *test* the discriminating power of each question.

To test for discrimination it is not necessary (and not even desirable) to consider every candidate's result. Ideally, one would make comparisons between the candidates comprising the top 27 per cent in the examination and the candidates comprising the bottom 27 per cent. For most examinations, however, it will be adequate, and simpler, to select the top and bottom quarters or the top and bottom thirds. Two samples of this sort are *necessary* for a test of discrimination, but while not necessary for testing the other two issues we have referred to, they will be *sufficient* for them. Obviously it is quicker to base one's calculations upon two quarters, or two thirds, of the candidate-group than upon all of it.

We shall not spell out in detail the practical details of item analysis—such as the form in which one would tabulate the results. Each examiner will use the system he finds most appropriate, but we shall outline the basic steps. To shorten the exposition we shall assume that there are, in all, 60 candidates, and that it is the top and bottom quarters which are to be used.

General

1 Pick out the top 15 and the bottom 15 candidates' scripts.
2 Note how many of the top 15 choose each option in each question.
3 Note how many of the bottom 15 choose each option in each question.

To assess each question's difficulty

4 Within each question, and for all 30 candidates, note the number of candidates choosing the *correct* option. (This information is already provided by Steps 2 and 3. All that is to be done in the present step is to add the appropriate numbers for the two samples of candidates.) The sum for each question indicates the question's degree of difficulty.

For diagnostic or remedial purposes

5 Note, within each question, the number of candidates (across both samples) choosing each wrong option. One might find that, for instance, more candidates chose wrong option A than chose correct option B, or that one of the wrong options was not chosen by anyone, and so forth.

To test a question's discriminative power

6   Compare the number in the top sample who answered the question correctly with the number in the bottom sample who answered it correctly. (The numbers to be compared in this way are already provided by Steps 2 and 3.)

True-false questions

In this chapter we consider three other forms of closed question—
True-False, Matching and Rearrangement.

A true-false question consists of a statement which the
candidate has to judge as true or false—usually by his circling the
letter T or the letter F printed alongside the question. For example,

*In scaling marks it is legitimate to alter their standings
but not their numerical values.*   T Ⓕ

*The greater a distribution's scatter, in relation to other
distributions' scatters, the greater its weight.*   Ⓣ F

*A correlation of — 1·0 between two distributions indicates
that between these distributions there is no sort of correspondence
at all.*   T Ⓕ

Questions of this type have some obvious advantages. They
are very easy to mark, and the marking can be very consistent.
Compared with multiple-choice questions, there can be a great
many of them, and so they can provide even better sampling of
the topic. They can be easier to write, because (again in comparison with multiple-choice questions) the examiner does not
have to invent plausible options. And for virtually all topics they
can be relevant, because every topic demands knowledge of
whether something is or is not so.

But they have obvious disadvantages too. A great many
statements are unequivocally true (or unequivocally false) only
in certain contexts or on certain assumptions; whereas in a true-
false paper each statement stands in isolation. This may lead to a
further disadvantage: in order to find statements which are
unequivocally true (or false), the examiner may be reduced to
testing what is relatively trivial—if not downright irrelevant. A
further common objection to true-false questions is that they are
testing no more than verbal memory—of 'quotes' from a text-

book, for instance. And may it not be educationally undesirable to present students with assertions which are untrue? Also, as will be apparent from our previous discussions of guessing, the chance of a candidate's guessing a true-false question correctly is much higher (evens) than the chance for a four-option multiple-choice question (3 to 1 against). These points must be dealt with.

First of all, it would be most unwise of the examiner to use statements lifted from a textbook, not merely because of the danger of testing no more than verbal memory, but because textbook statements are usually made in a context—of a paragraph, or a page, or even a chapter. Authors who have gone out of their way to make statements which are self-contained truths (or falsehoods) are somewhat rare. The problem of 'quotes', therefore, is largely the problem of context or underlying assumption.

To that problem there are some obvious solutions. For example, while there may be doubt about the truth of a statement some authority has made, there may be no debate as to whether he made it. One might therefore quote the *source* of the statement: 'According to Freud's theory of . . .', 'In B. F. Skinner's sense of *reinforcement* . . .'. Also, there are occasions when the context or underlying assumption can be included in the statement without its becoming unduly lengthy. For instance, 'Assuming that the current income tax laws remain operative . . .'. One can of course be over-censorious here. The statements offered in a true-false paper, while they *can* be extracted and analysed one at a time, are *not* presented in isolation; they appear in the context of the topic being examined, and in that context it would be unrealistic to argue that in some other context the statements could mean something else. Nor is this problem peculiar to true-false questions. It arises in open questions too—though there it has a different locus: it is the *examiner*, reading the candidate's essay-type answer, who may be in doubt about the context in which the *candidate* wishes his statements to be interpreted. Even so, the problem is a real one, and the best solution would seem to lie in the examiner's being very conscious of it and in his submitting his questions to other experts. If a *panel* of examiners are satisfied that there is no genuine cause for complaint, on this account, the paper will be as fair as any paper can be.

As for the possibility of one's misinforming students by presenting them with false statements, surely one would not use this kind of question at all unless the candidates were mature enough to realise that some of the statements *are* false?

Of all the criticisms made of true-false questions, those citing the probability of success by means of guessing are probably the most common and, in the eyes of the critics, the most serious. To pinpoint the difficulty let us assume that the paper has 100 questions, and that every one of the large number of candidates guesses every question. This is a highly improbable event, but to tackle the criticism it is reasonable to consider the worst possible case. Then the average score would be 50; about half the candidates would be expected to score 50 or more. Also, about a sixth of them would score 55 or more; and fully 2 per cent of them would score 60 or more–and all of this when no candidate knew anything at all about the topic.[31]

With these facts in mind, then, the examiner could set the pass mark to be in accord with his 'confidence level'. It would obviously be inappropriate, for instance, to set the pass mark at 50 per cent–because that is the most probable score for a candidate who guessed every question. If the confidence level were 5 in 1000, the pass mark would have to be 63; if it were 1 in 1000 the pass mark would have to be 65.

There is, however, an entirely different way of dealing with the problem. It also involves 'confidence', but now it is the *candidate's* confidence which is at stake. 'Stake' is a pertinent term, because in effect the candidate is obliged to 'bet' on how confident he is about his answer. In this system the candidate can answer in five different ways. The wording of the five options is not crucial, but in effect this is what the options amount to.

Optional Responses to the Statement	Mark Awarded		
	If Right	If Wrong	If Omitted
I am sure it is true.	2	−2	
I think it may be true.	1	−1	
I don't know.			$\frac{1}{2}$
I think it may be false.	1	−1	
I am sure it is false.	2	−2	

The technicalities involved in determing just what the different marks should be will not be discussed here. (The reader wishing more details is referred to Ebel 1965.) A few points nevertheless deserve mention. The candidate who is right, and is fully confident about his answer, gets 2; whereas the candidate who is not very sure gets only 1. On the other hand, the candidate who is very sure, but wrong, gets − 2 − and so loses more than the candidate who, while wrong, was less sure of himself. The candidate who says, 'I don't know', and in effect is 'omitting' the question, gets $\frac{1}{2}$ − because this is the score he could expect, on average, for blind guessing, and so he is not penalised for refraining from guessing. This system, known as 'confidence weighting' would seem to have much to recommend it − not only on statistical grounds, or on the ground that it improves the examination's reliability, but also on what might be called commonsense educational grounds. It seems reasonable that the candidate who is sure of his knowledge should score more than the candidate who is doubtful − and that the candidate who is sure of himself, but wrong, should score less than the candidate who, though wrong, is unwilling to commit himself very strongly. Systems of marking, different from the system just quoted, are of course possible; but while the above system might be justified on commonsense grounds, common sense alone does not provide an adequate basis for a different system; and the prospective examiner would be well advised to study 'the odds' very carefully before using marks different from those we have quoted.

Some final comments on setting true-false questions. Ensure that the statement is not so complex that part of it could be true and another part false; such statements are often ambiguous. As far as possible, avoid negatives; and in particular avoid turning a true statement into a false statement by inserting the word 'not', for that kind of negative statement is likely to be confusing. Try not to use statements with 'never', 'always', 'impossible', and the like, because such statements are more often false than true. Avoid a regular pattern of answers − such as True and False alternating: it is preferable to toss a coin, Heads meaning insert a true statement, Tails a false one. Ensure that a team of experts would agree with the falsity of your false statements, with the truth of your true ones. If the substance of a statement is taken from a text or published notes, do not use exactly the same words.

Questions of the 'matching' type

This type of question consists of two sets of items, items in the one set having to be matched with items in the other. Here is a very simple example.

Set A		Set B					
A	M	Correlation Coefficient.	A	B	C	Ⓓ	E
B	Q_3	An obtained mark.	A	B	C	D	Ⓔ
C	σ	Upper Quartile.	A	Ⓑ	C	D	E
D	r	Standard Deviation.	A	B	Ⓒ	D	E
E	X						

As in all questions of this type the candidate has to indicate what goes with what–in the present example symbols with terms. Various formats are possible, and the style of the above example is but one of many. Thus if, as in our example, the items in Set A are very short, the candidate could be asked to *write* the item in the space provided opposite the B-item. But not every question of this kind will have such short items, and the system illustrated allows of marking by stencil or machine.

Matching-type questions can of course cover *any* area in which the student is expected to know 'what goes with what'– not only symbols with terms, or authors with books, or events and their dates, but also more complex issues of processes with products, assumptions with deductions, skills and jobs, tools and tasks, and so forth.

Several technical points are nevertheless worth noting, for our example, while illustrating what a matching question is, is in some respects over-simple.

First, if (as in our example) each A-item is to be used only once, there will have to be more items in one set than in the other, for otherwise a candidate who knows all but one gets that one as a free gift. Theoretically it makes little difference which set is the longer, but if Set B had more items than Set A, and Set B's items are to have the answers appended, the candidate could be disconcerted to find he had left some answer-spaces empty. For practical purposes it is obviously better to have every answer-space completed–and have some of the A-items unused.

But second, there is a strong case for *not* having each A-item usable only once. As may have been apparent, the matching-type question is but a variant of the multiple-choice question. Our example is, in effect, four multiple-choice questions in one. The material *could* have been separated out into four multiple-choice questions, each with five options, but the same five options would have appeared in each of the four questions; and so the matching form saves unnecessary repetition. However, the main point is that, if each A-item is used only once, a candidate who knows *some* of the matches has a higher chance of guessing the others correctly. Were this procedure adopted, then of course candidates would have to be advised accordingly.

It will be obvious that not every area of knowledge will be amenable to the multiple-usage of A-items. When this is so it may be just as appropriate to use a series of multiple-choice, or of short-answer open questions.

When the subject-matter does allow of matching-type questions one further point is worth stressing: each question should deal with a quite restricted aspect of it, for two reasons. For one thing, the candidate is likely to become confused if he is asked to match, within one question, items of very diverse sorts–towns and populations, countries and products, geographical areas and weather conditions, and the like. For another, a mixed bag of this kind is unlikely to meet the requirements of plausibility, because some A-items will obviously have nothing to do with some B-items.

Finally, the simplest form of marking is to award 1 for each B-item correctly matched. The maximum possible mark for a question, then, will be the number of B-items there are–probably not less than 5 and not more than 10.

Rearrangement questions

In many subjects the student is required to know the correct, or best, or customary *order* of things–historical events, fault-tracing techniques, procedural points in debates or board meetings, stages of child development, and so forth. In general, he is required to know 'what comes after what'.

It may be, of course, that he is required not only to know the order in which the things occurred (or are to occur, etc.) but also to recall what these things are. If so, an 'open' form of question may be appropriate. ('Give an account of the steps you would take. . . .') But when, as is often so, he is required to order *given* items, the 'rearrangement' form of question may be the most suitable.

In this kind of question the candidate is presented with a list of items which are *not* in the required order, and has to indicate what the required order is. He might be asked to *re-write* the items in a column, beginning with the item to occur first, but the labour of writing out what is already printed on the question paper is unnecessary. The simplest procedure is for the candidate to write, in a space provided beside each item on the question paper, the figure representing what he believes to be its correct position–1 for first, 2 for second, and so on. Here is an example:

	Marking the candidate's answers.
	Setting the questions.
	Weighting the questions in accord with their agreed importance.
	Listing a representative sample of the performances the examination's purpose requires.
	Drawing up a detailed marking scheme.
	Combining the marks in the various questions.

(Read downwards, the correct order is 4 2 5 1 3 6, though of course the candidate would begin, presumably, by writing 1, then 2, etc.)

As for the marking of questions of this kind, we do not recommend that the examiner should memorise the correct order and check candidates' orders against it, because that procedure is too liable to error. Probably the most reliable method of checking is to cut out, in a spare question paper, the spaces where candidates are to enter their answers; to write, alongside the slots, what the correct answers are; and then to check each single answer by fitting this prepared stencil over each candidate's paper.

This still leaves open the question of the mark to be awarded. Obviously, no candidate who makes errors can make less than two—because if one item is misplaced another must be misplaced also. But is a candidate who transposes only two items to be given more marks than a candidate who misplaces more than two? Or might the switching of the first and last items be more serious than the switching of three in the middle?

As we saw in a previous chapter, there *is* a way of ascertaining how close one order is to a required order—namely by calculating a correlation coefficient. In the present case, however, such a procedure would be absurd. For one thing, the examiner would have to calculate a coefficient for every candidate's every wrong answer—which could involve him in hundreds of calculations. For another, as we hinted a moment ago in connection with the number of misplacements, it may be that the seriousness of a wrong order does not necessarily run parallel to the sort of correspondence a correlation coefficient measures.

We suggest that each question of this kind should be marked simply as 1 or 0. A correctly answered question gets 1; any other gets 0, no matter how many misplacements there are. An obvious advantage of this way of marking is that as soon as the examiner finds *one* discrepancy in a candidate's answer, he awards that question the mark of 0.

At first sight this simple marking scheme might seem to be unduly simple. In particular, is the mark of 1 large enough for complex questions of this kind? Well, first of all one has to recall that a mark's value, whether by norm-reference or criterion-reference, is relative; and that 1 is not 'small' if all the other questions of this kind are marked in the same way. Second, our main point was, not that the two possible marks must be 0 and 1, but rather that there should be only two different marks. One of these might as well be 0, but the other could be 2, or 3, or $\frac{1}{2}$.

Accordingly, if it were agreed that questions of the matching type should have greater weight than questions of other kinds, the marks for matching questions could be 0 and 2, or 0 and 3, etc. As we commented earlier, however, in a similar connection, it is usually better to increase 'importance' in these circumstances, by increasing the number of *questions*. This is easily arranged for matching questions, because not all the items of an ordered series need be included in one single question; they can be spread over several 'smaller' questions. Indeed, one question may overlap with another.

In the last three chapters we have discussed some possible types of 'closed' question. Plainly, not every type is suitable for every kind of subject-matter. Indeed, some performances may not be properly tested by closed questions at all. We have spent some time considering them, however, because many questions customarily set in an 'open' form could just as easily be set in a 'closed' form, with the advantages of greater consistency of marking, greater relevance of marking, and often better sampling. Also, when closed questions are used, the marking-scheme is simply devised, and the results tend to have a better spread, and to be more amenable to item analysis—and more quickly marked.

Length of answer

An obvious characteristic of open questions is the variety of answer-length they allow. An answer may be a short essay, a few paragraphs, one paragraph, a sentence, a phrase, a single word. Probably for this reason answer-length is often made the basis of the classification of open questions: essay questions, sentence-answer questions, and so on.

Emphasis on answer-length can nevertheless lower the examination's validity. All questions must be directives to the performances required by the examination's purpose. Some of these, such as arguing a case for something, will be relatively long and need a relatively large number of words; other performances, such as defining a technical term, will be relatively short and need relatively few words. But, as these examples illustrate, the length of an answer will be determined by what the *performance* needs, and not by anything else. It would be improper to decide, on any other ground, 'I'll set essay questions this time!', or to use sentence-answer questions on the sole ground that their marking is more consistent. Such decisions could lead to the examiner's asking for performances to fit the predetermined answer-length, whereas if the condition of Question-Relevance is to be fulfilled, it must be answer-length which has to fit the required performance.

Even when the dependence is the right way round, however, it does not follow that the required performance will *prescribe* (determine in detail) what the length of answer has to be. Such a prescription will be in order only when answer-length is itself part and parcel of the performance the purpose requires. If candidates are directed to write out a talk to be given in thirty minutes (a performance, we may assume, relevant to the examination's purpose), that directive does put limits on the number of words to be used. If candidates are asked to summarise the findings

of a certain research, the term 'summarise' does indicate, if only rather roughly, that the answer is not to run for a dozen pages. (And, of course, the time allowed will also give some indications.)

In all other cases, likely to be in the majority, where answer-length is not an integral part of the required performance, the mark awarded must not depend upon answer-length *per se*. If some required performance is expressible in a paragraph, a candidate who writes three pages will not have marks deducted (if he had any!) solely on the ground that he used too many words—unless the question is, for instance, a test of conciseness of writing, that being part of the required performance. If, within his three pages, he has given the performance required, he will get the mark for it. If, in addition, he has included some irrelevant remarks, then in accord with the condition of Mark-Relevance (p. 12) these superfluous performances must be ignored. And if, despite his writing at great length, he has not given the required performance at all, he will gain no marks—but simply because the required performance was not given, and not as a punishment for writing rubbish.

Likewise, if a candidate contrives to express the required performance in fewer words than were expected, he will not get fewer marks on that account. Nor will the examiner's delightful surprise warrant a bonus—unless conciseness is part and parcel of the required performance.

These considerations indicate that, if the question is clearly directive to the *performance* required, any additional instruction about length of answer is unnecessary–and perhaps worse. It would be absurd (except for single-word answers) to stipulate the exact number of words to be used, because the candidate would be distracted from his main business by having to keep a running count. Also, 'in about 100 words' not only has that same disadvantage but also may cause the candidate to wonder how generous the word 'about' is meant to be. Phrases like 'in a paragraph', or 'in a few words' are perhaps preferable, but even those may well be interpreted by some candidates in highly idiosyncratic ways. Even so, the marking must conform to the

condition of Mark-Relevance, for which idiosyncracy is not necessarily criminal.

Since no one can be aware of all possible questions, it would be presumptuous to assert that open questions will *never* need to include a specific directive about length of answer. The foregoing points nevertheless suggest strongly that this is so. Indeed, we dare to suggest that injunctions about length of answer are most likely to be given when the question (that is, the examiner) does not provide a very clear directive about *how* the candidates are to *perform*. But to prescribe a length is not much use if the candidates are not clear about what they are supposed to do in it.

To summarise: the primary function of a question is to indicate, not what length the answer should be, but what the candidate has to do. If that primary function is well served by the statement of the question, the other function is of very little importance, perhaps none at all.

Directiveness

A 'weak' or 'poor' question is essentially one which fails to direct the candidate to give a performance required by the examination's purpose. Failure in this respect has two aspects. The performance to which the question directs the candidate may not be a performance the examination's purpose requires. However, we have already discussed this point, in previous chapters, at some length, and so we need not pursue it further. The other aspect is this: the performance the question is *intended* to ask for may be perfectly relevant, but the question may not make clear what that performance is. In other words, the question's 'directiveness' is inadequate. We have already referred to a 'non-directive' stem; open questions too are prone to the same basic fault.

Within the 'directiveness' issue also there are two basic difficulties–which we look at in turn.

Consider the question 'Give an account of the scaling of marks.' A possible weakness here is the question's failure to specify what performances will be necessary. Is the candidate merely to say what scaling *is*? The word 'account' suggests that that would not be enough. Is he to describe how scaling is *done*? If so, is he to give a general description, or will he gain more marks by providing a worked example? And should he describe *several* methods of scaling, commenting on the characteristics of each? Is he to explain *why* marks are scaled? And why scaling is *appropriate*? Is he to point out what may happen if marks are *not* scaled? Should he deal with possible, even naïve, *objections* to scaling? If he is expected to do all, or some, of these things, surely the question should *direct* him accordingly, not leave him wondering what the examiner wants? Those least likely to be concerned will be the candidates who know very little: they have no problem; they just write what little they know. In general, a question may lack directiveness in being too general, in failing to be specific about what the candidate has to do.

It could of course be objected that by giving the candidate specific directives we are giving too much away. If we ask him *why* marks are scaled we are reminding him that this is an issue worthy of comment; whereas (it might be objected) he should think of this for himself. Objections of this kind may be perfectly valid—but only if it is part of the required performance to recall *what* the crucial issues are. In our illustration, for instance, the objection might be valid if the candidates were prospective teachers of examining-technique (!), and the aim were to find out what they would include in their course. But if so, would it not be more appropriate to ask a different, yet specific, question directing them to list the issues the course would cover? In contrast, if the examinees were prospective examiners, would it not be more relevant to find out whether they could deal with *given* problems which they would eventually be faced with anyway while on the job? Very similar questions are pertinent to most other topics. We suggest that what the setter of questions has to justify is, not the giving (or giving away) of directives to specific performances, but rather their omission. In other words, unless the examination's purpose forbids it, be quite specific about what the candidates are to do.

A second cause of inadequate directiveness is ambiguity. A question may be, arguably, a directive to a required performance, but because of its form it may direct some candidates to an irrelevant performance. For instance, to many candidates the word 'compare' means only that *differences* are to be discussed; whereas for the examiner it means more. If so, would it not be clearer to ask for a description of the ways in which the (to be compared) things are alike and the ways in which they differ? Again, does a question asking for an 'explanation' of something presuppose that the thing is to be *described* too? If so, the question should say so. If not, the candidate who does give a description is wasting time he might have spent more profitably.

A related difficulty arises when the examiner uses unusual words—familiar enough to him but having no clearcut meaning for the candidates. In general, unless part of the required task is the interpretation of words in the question, the language of the question should be as simple as possible.

In discussing points like these Gronlund (1968a) suggests that the examiner should write out a model answer to each of his questions, and also recommends that the question should be submitted to colleagues. We should go farther, suggesting that both question and model answer should be read by a colleague–who should be invited to be downright awkward about both–offering answers which, though not the answer the examiner intended, would nevertheless qualify as legitimate answers to the question. Most teachers should be able to find a colleague who would not refuse such an invitation! If one does not submit oneself to this ordeal at the hands of a colleague (with whom one could change roles), one is likely to be submitted to it at the hands of candidates. And they may well have a case.

Setting open questions to test understanding

In an earlier chapter (p. 201) we outlined some basic principles of understanding and suggested how they might be applied to testing for understanding by means of multiple-choice questions. The same principles apply to open questions, though the actual applications will be somewhat different.

Because multiple-choice questions are difficult to construct, especially if they are to test understanding, the examiner may decide to use open questions which ask candidates to provide an *explanation*. ('Explain why . . .') The presupposition here, in so far as understanding is to be tested, is that a correct explanation is evidence that the candidate has understood. But this is not necessarily so. It is possible for candidates to have learned explanations by heart without their understanding either the thing to be explained or the explanation itself. Here is a simple example.

The question, which adequately describes the apparatus illustrated, asks the candidate to explain why the given arrangement of rod, fulcrum, and weights will balance. If he replies, 'It

will balance because it obeys the principle of moments', he is right; but it does not follow that he has understood. He might merely have learned the fact that levers balance when they obey the principle of moments – and have little or no idea of what the principle of moments is. (We could have asked him *whether* it will balance–but that is, in effect, a multiple-choice question with only two options. And if we ask him to explain his answer, all we can be sure of is that if his answer is wrong ('It will not balance') he has *not* understood. If it is right, we are back to our original question.)

A more appropriate form of question would ask the candidates to give the explanation *in terms of the given instance.* In particular, they would have to include in their answers the specific fact that $5 \text{ gm} \times 6 = 2 \text{ gm} \times 15$.

We need not discuss the precise form the answer to that question must take; the example was intended only to illustrate the principle that, to provide evidence of understanding, the candidate must recognise *in the instance* the feature which identifies it *as* an instance of the relevant general principle, or procedure, or item of knowledge. Obliging the candidate to answer in terms of the given instance is a way of ascertaining whether that requirement has been met.

Another example: if a question which presents two distributions of marks asks why Distribution A will have greater weight than Distribution B, a candidate may answer, 'Because A has the greater scatter', yet have no idea what either 'weight' or 'scatter' means. The statement constituting his answer might be no more than an isolated and virtually meaningless fact picked up in a moment of insomnia during a lecture. Here also it would be necessary for the candidates to demonstrate how they knew that this particular Distribution A had greater scatter than that particular Distribution B. (For example: 'Since the interquartile range of A is 13, and the interquartile range of B is only 7, and weight is directly proportional to scatter, A will have the greater weight.')

This latter example illustrates a further point, namely that there may be occasions when the 'general' item of knowledge *also* must be cited in the explanation.

The mere repetition of a previously learned explanation may nevertheless be appropriate in many cases. As we keep emphasising, it all depends upon one's purpose. Whether such cases constitute understanding is debatable, but they might be more aptly called cases in which the candidate 'has to know the explanation of . . .'. Questions with that purpose would perhaps be exemplified by 'Give an account of the causes of the American War of Independence', or 'Explain why it is a distribution's scatter, and not the magnitude of its marks, which determines its weight'. In cases like these it might be unreasonable to expect candidates to understand from scratch, as it were; one is more likely (for most purposes) to be content with a knowledge of explanations already current.

The questions with which we began this section called for fairly short answers; the answers for the last two questions would presumably be rather longer; but the same basic principles will apply no matter what length the answer is. Since an examination can assess performance, and nothing other than performance, the examiner who sets a question intended to test for understanding must make clear to himself, at the outset, precisely what performances the candidates must 'give in evidence'. If he does not do this, he has no criteria to refer to in framing questions which will be adequately directive *to* the requisite performances. Nor, of course, will there be any guarantee of mark-relevance when he is assessing the performances the candidates have actually given.

'Processes' and 'performances'

In the previous section, and in a section of a previous chapter, we spent some time considering Understanding and what sorts of performance might be accepted as evidence of it. But Understanding is only one of many 'mental processes' examiners often wish to assess. There is Comprehending, Analysing, Synthesising,

Organising, Recalling, Recognising, Applying, and doubtless many more. But if we follow the same line as we took for assessing Understanding, the fundamental principle will be the same: the examiner must specify, at the outset, the *performances* to be accepted as evidence of Comprehending, or of Analysing, or whatever 'process' he wishes to assess, because examinations can measure only performance, not mental process.

The examiner who follows this line may nevertheless find himself in difficulty in that he may sometimes have doubts about whether a performance he initially intended to be evidence of (say) Understanding may be evidence of something different—say Analysing, or even Recall. But does it really matter? We venture to suggest that it does not. In the foregoing discussion of Understanding we assumed something called 'understanding', and then considered performances which might be accepted as 'evidence' of it—largely because this is the way many examiners envisage the issue. And we would not have taken so much time to discuss it in this way unless this way were of some value. As we have just mentioned, however, there can be doubts about just what process a particular performance is evidence *of*, and so there may never be certainty that we have been assessing the process we thought we were assessing. What we are now suggesting is that this problem need never arise, because it is the outcome of a way of thinking which, though very common, is by no means obligatory. There is another way of thinking. We shall not elaborate it here, nor try to be very persuasive about it, because to justify it would take a much longer time than would be appropriate in this account. One example will have to suffice.

Consider again the example (illustrated on p. 244) of the rod, fulcrum and weights. No matter what his views about 'understanding' might be, an examiner would not set such a question unless what the candidate had to do exemplified a sort of *performance* which was, so to speak, worth while in its own right. (And, of course, in accord with the examination's purpose.) By 'sort of performance' we mean, not an 'understanding' sort of performance, but a sort exemplifiable by reference to a variety of instances of *rods, fulcrums* and *weights*—different weights, different lengths of rods, different positions of the fulcrum. If we chose to speak of 'understanding', it would probably be correct to say that such cases demanded understanding, or even provided evidence of it. But surely the examiner who sets such problems does so, not for the primary and specific purpose of finding out whether the candidate has been 'doing some understanding', but to find out whether he can deal satisfactorily with arrangements of rods, weights and fulcrums? Surely the 'evidence' the examiner wants is, not evidence of a psychological process of understanding, but evidence that the candidate can deal with (perform!) certain sorts of tasks, tasks conveniently classifiable under the head, Principle of Moments.

On this view, the examiner would not begin by devising some tasks for testing Understanding, some tasks for testing Application, some tasks for testing Organisation, and so forth. On the contrary, he would begin by listing tasks the candidates should be able to perform. Doubtless some of these tasks might be *said* to require Recall, others to necessitate Analysis, and the like; but interesting as it might be to say such things, there is really no obligation to say them. Nor would there be any cause to wonder whether one was testing the right 'process'–because the testing of mental processes would no longer be a pertinent aim. All that would matter would be whether the *sorts of performance* asked for were in accord with the ulterior purpose of the examination.

As we said, however, many examiners do think in terms of these processes; and, when they do, a consideration of the possibilities of testing for Understanding, Application, Organisation, Synthesis, and so forth, may be of value in drawing their attention to sorts of *performance* they might otherwise have omitted to ask for.

In concluding this chapter we should repeat once more the fundamental principle that the setting of questions must be based upon the 'list' of performances the examination's purpose requires, and that the questions should be directives to a representative sample from that list. That demand overruns any system of classification (such as Understanding, Recall, and so on), and any distinctions in terms of length of answer.

The marking scheme

If the validity of an examination's results is not to be lowered by
the method of marking the candidates' answers, it must conform
to the conditions of Mark-Relevance (p. 12) and Marking-
Consistency (p. 8), no matter what particular method of
marking may be adopted. At the outset, therefore, the examiner
must specify, by reference to his purpose, what performances are
to be marked and what marks are to be awarded to them. And if
that demand is to be translated into effective action, it must give
rise to a set of rules – a marking scheme. The necessity of such a
marking scheme is obvious when the scripts are shared among
several examiners; but unless there are only a very few candidates
a sole examiner will need a marking scheme too, because otherwise he might forget, from one hour (or day) to the next, just
what he previously awarded marks for, and how many marks he
awarded.

Although that demand applies to examinations generally,
the marking scheme for any particular examination will be highly
specific to it, and will be based upon the performances set out in
the 'list' (pp. 13ff.) from which the questions were drawn. For
instance, it would be inadequate to decide to 'award the mark
of 1 for each significant point'; he would have to make clear what
the significant points are.

The more precisely the relevant performances are described
in the marking scheme, the more relevant and consistent the
marking is likely to be; but the degree of precision possible will
depend upon the nature of the performances the questions have
required.

For example, in some examinations it will be possible for
the examiner to spell out in detail what the relevant performances
are – down to the very words, figures or symbols to be used. In

such cases even the slightest deviation from the performance detailed in the marking scheme could be irrelevant and awarded no marks. This kind of marking scheme might well apply when the answers were place-names, the names of people, dates, materials.

In many other examinations, however, what matters are not the particular words or even the particular calculations the candidate has used, but what these *mean*. In some questions, for instance, where the term 'scatter' or 'spread' or 'dispersion' was expected as answer, it might be relevant to accept the longer phrase, 'the extent to which the marks are clustered around the Mean'. Again, if a question asks candidates to provide an example of some principle, some candidates may give examples the examiner himself had not thought of. A marking scheme must allow for such contingencies; but while it cannot spell out the details of specific examples, it would nevertheless have to make clear (except in the simplest of instances) the criteria a given example must meet. (In effect, anticipating the question, 'When is an example not really an example?') One more example: if the candidates are writing in Spanish, quoting a gentleman's reference to 'my wife', would one accept 'mi esposa', or 'la señora', but perhaps reject 'mi mujer'? Although one is marking for what the words mean, one might nevertheless have to specify the latitude of the meaning itself. Even in relatively brief instances like these, it will be apparent, there is room for difference of opinion among examiners unless the marking scheme provides the necessary rules; and as the latter examples illustrate, the devising of a marking scheme may itself be extremely difficult.

The difficulty will almost certainly increase with the extent to which the candidate is 'free' to express himself–as he would be if what is to be assessed is 'creative expression', or 'originality', or something of that kind. If such performances are presupposed by the examination's purpose, it would be a breach of the condition of Question-Relevance if the questions did not ask for them. But how are such performances to be assessed? When is an answer truly 'creative'? And is 'originality' all that is to matter?

Obviously, in this kind of case, model answers written by

the examiner will be inappropriate. But if the marking is to be relevant and consistent, here also he must set out criteria by which all candidates' answers are to be judged. Admittedly, this may be very difficult, but if the examiner does not *have* criteria by which to assess originality, creativity, organisation, expressiveness, and so forth, how can he claim any validity for his marks? And one would seem to have cause to be suspicious of an examiner who assures us that he does have criteria, but cannot say, even to someone expert in the topic, what the criteria are.

In this sort of discussion one sometimes hears reference to 'imponderables', and assertions that in such cases the rules of examining, which may be good enough for mundane issues, cannot possibly apply. We can but reply that if something is believed to be 'imponderable', then one should have the courage of one's beliefs and stop trying to weigh it. It may be that some, perhaps many, human activities are not susceptible of measurement; and if the critic is saying that such activities should not be subjected to assessment, his logic is faultless. But if he is saying (or, as indicated by his actual practice, *in effect* is saying) that *he* can assess them by some occult means known only to himself and incommunicable to anyone else, one has every right to ask him to subject his marking to a consistency and relevance test at the hands of other examiners.

It is a different matter, however, to suggest that some sorts of performance may not lend themselves to such *fine* assessments as others. A spelling test, consisting of a hundred words, and taken by a large number of candidates, might well produce a hundred different marks. But many examiners would be doing very well if they could consistently allocate English essays to as few as ten different categories, or even to as few as five; and results do not necessarily become useless or completely invalid merely because they are not as precise as some others.

Even if a fairly low degree of precision is allowable, the examiner must nevertheless have criteria of judgment. The difference will be, not that he abandons criteria in these cases, but simply that the sorts of performance he has asked for do not allow him to set up criteria of a high degree of refinement.

In the following section we shall look at three different 'methods' of marking, but these should be considered in the light of the points made in this present section, because the examiner is not really free to choose the method he personally takes a fancy to. These three methods correspond with degrees of precision achievable in the marking scheme. If the marking scheme is one in which the required performances are spelt out in detail, the marking will be most valid if he adopts a 'unit-counting' method. At the other extreme, he would be advised to use a 'grading' method.

Marking by unit-counting

This method consists in the examiner's counting the number of relevant, required performances each candidate has given. If the candidate correctly spells twelve of twenty dictated words, his mark is 12. If he correctly answers sixty-five short-answer questions, his mark is 65.

This kind of method is known by several names – 'enumeration', 'count scoring', 'point scoring'; but we have suggested the term 'unit-counting' in order to make explicit what the method entails. The main point is that counting the number of performances in this way presupposes the *equivalence* of all these performances; and, more precisely, that each of them is to be treated as a *unit*. Strictly, then, a 'declaration of equivalence' (p. 154) must already have been made, in accord with the purpose of the examination.

This does not mean that no performance must ever be awarded a mark greater than 1. But it does mean that if the mark of (say) 3 is awarded to a (*sic*) performance, there must have been agreement that it is equivalent to any three unit-performances. And the surest basis for such an agreement would be the demonstration that it *consisted* of three performances each of which was agreed to be a unit. It might be, for instance, that it required three distinguishable pieces of information. But it would be out of order to award 3 in such a case if these particular pieces of information were asked for in other questions, because then the same unit-performance would be marked twice (or more). (This is the sort of issue we referred to earlier when we said that the declaration of equivalences was not entirely free.)

It will be apparent that this method of marking is not only possible but obligatory when the 'list' of performances (required by the examination's purpose) contains specific performances, each precisely described or stated, because to fail to take each and every one of these into account (or into *the* count) would be to fail to observe the condition of Mark-Relevance.

Many performances, however, cannot be (or usually are not) described precisely enough to allow of unit-counting. In these cases some other method must be used.

Before we look at other methods, however, we suggest that even in subjects commonly believed to be unsusceptible of a Unit-Counting method of marking, that method may be applicable. In some aspects of English, for instance, candidates are given considerable scope to express things in their own ways—which precludes reference to a list of highly specific performances. Candidates might have been asked to contrast the styles of two authors, as exemplified by two given excerpts from their works. Here, surely, there would be no 'set answers'. But a candidate's answer could not be assessed at all, by *any* method, unless the examiner had in mind, and referred to, certain *criteria* of style. And if he made these criteria explicit, he could count the number of *criteria* the candidate's answer met.

We quoted the instance just given because the Unit-Counting method of marking is likely to be the most *consistent* method, and in so far as the criteria have been properly constituted, also the most *relevant*. It also allows of greater *precision* than the methods described in a moment. It is also the most likely to prevent a candidate's obtaining a (spuriously) high mark by his multiplying illustrations of a very few criteria, instead of his giving an adequate coverage of the topic in question. Of course, as we said, *any* method of marking requires reference to some criteria; but if the examiner sets out his criteria in advance, and sets out as many as are relevant, he will almost certainly produce better *sampling*, and so in a somewhat indirect way go further to satisfy the condition of *Question*-Relevance.

Marking by grading

The essence of the Grading method of marking is what is sometimes called 'impression marking'. Instead of analysing the candidate's answer and counting up the unit-performances, the examiner tries to gain an impression of the answer as a whole. The assessments of paintings, poems, and handwriting, would probably be cases in point. So also might be the assessment of style, originality, organisation, humour, lay-out. Having studied the candidate's answer in this 'impressionistic' way, the examiner would then allocate it to a 'grade', A or B or C or D, or something of the kind. Note that we referred to grades in an earlier chapter; but there we were speaking of ways of *reporting* marks, not of methods of awarding them. Unlike a *report* in terms of grades, which could be derived from a distribution of very precise numerical marks, the Grading method of *marking* does not involve fine numerical marks at all. The examiner studies the answer and then awards it B–or some other grade.

Now although the above description of the Grading method of marking would seem to be the normal one, it is very doubtful if in fact the matter is so simple. Certainly the examiner may try to obtain an overall impression of the candidate's performance, but he is bound to be influenced by this and that detail. Sometimes these details may be quite irrelevant–such as an essay's being beautifully typed. But even when the details are relevant, one or two of them may have undue influence, so that what purports to be an 'overall' assessment is badly biased.

One way out of this difficulty is, of course, to pay attention to *all* relevant details, one by one–which takes us back to the Unit-Counting method.

It is nevertheless valid, we believe, to point out that a 'whole' will have characteristics not to be found in its constituent parts. A poem has characteristics not discoverable by one's examining each line in isolation from the others. An essay changes if we re-arrange its sentences or paragraphs. Even a simple joke loses its appeal if the teller provides the punch-line at the beginning. But if 'structural characteristics' of this kind are to contribute to the assessment, the examiner must have specified what they are, preferably by specifying the criteria by which they are to be judged. In this case, the 'list' would be a list of criteria–and so the same basic principles would apply: the candidates' performances would be compared with the items of the 'list', no matter what the nature of the items might be.

In many examinations, however, even criteria-counting will be inappropriate, if not impossible, and the standard of judgment will have to take a different form. The following procedure is well known and has often been recommended.

The examiner decides (or has decided for him by current regulations) the number of grades to be used. For the sake of illustration suppose there are five–called A, B, C, D and E. He then reads the scripts in an 'overall' way (or if there are a great many, reads a reasonably large sample of them–say thirty or more) but only in order to get an impression of the general run of the group's performances. He then selects the best of the scripts he has read, and calls it 'A'; and the poorest, calling it 'E'. The next step is to find a script which seems to him to lie about halfway between the two scripts already selected, and to call it 'C'. Finally, he selects a script whose quality is about halfway between the 'A' and 'C' scripts, calling it 'B'; and a script about halfway between the 'C' and 'E' scripts, calling it 'D'. These five scripts then serve as the criteria for judging the rest. With the five selected scripts before him, the examiner reads each of the remaining scripts, and decides which of the five it most resembles, allocating to it the appropriate grade. Note that the five initially selected scripts remain available, for reference, throughout the marking.

The marker who takes his job seriously will almost certainly find this task difficult. In particular, he may have considerable difficulty in finding a script which, in his confident opinion, lies halfway between the best and the worst; and scripts halfway between A and C and between C and E. And yet, all he is being asked to do is differentiate five qualities of script—with about the same difference between successive pairs. If he cannot do this, what sort of confidence can we have in the marker who, having scanned a script in the 'impressionistic' way, awards it 21, awards the next script 17, the next 23, the next 10, and so on? Numerical marks like these presuppose the possibility (indeed actuality) of very much finer differentiation. Our own opinion is that an examiner who can allocate a large number of scripts, by impression marking, to five grades, and produce the same marks on re-marking, is to be complimented.

If the five 'criterion scripts' have been carefully chosen, it is likely that the examiner will find that on completing the marking he has a relatively small number of 'A' scripts and of 'E' scripts, a relatively large number of 'Cs', and intermediate number of 'Bs' and 'Ds'. This shape of distribution will suit many purposes, but of course it would be improper of him to keep an eye on the numbers and contrive to produce this conveniently symmetrical shape.

As we have said, the nature of the performances to be assessed may make this method of marking almost obligatory; but it is well known to be prone to inconsistency, and so if it has to be used, it is highly desirable that all the scripts should be read by at least two examiners. At the least, a *sample* of scripts should be 'cross-marked'.

Higher consistency is likely also if, when several issues are to be discussed, the scripts are assessed in respect of each issue in turn. For instance, one might grade each script for content, for organisation, for evidence of background reading, and the like. Or, if more than one examiner is available, one examiner can deal with one issue, another examiner with another issue, and so forth. This kind of procedure lowers the probability of the examiner's being unduly influenced by the candidate's expertise (or ignorance) in one area.

A similar procedure is sometimes recommended if there are several open questions in the one paper. Consistency of marking is likely to be greater if the examiner marks Question 1 for every candidate, then Question 2 for every candidate, and so on. Or, if the marking can be shared, Examiner A would mark Question 1, Examiner B would mark Question 2. . . .

The procedures suggested in the two foregoing paragraphs nevertheless raise difficulties of combination. If Tom gets A for content, C for organisation, and D for some other issue, how is one to arrive at his mark for the question as a whole? Similarly for combining grades in different questions. There are two possibilities. First, it is worth considering whether combination is necessary at all. As we argued in an earlier chapter (p. 147), combination is necessary only when compensation is required; and if serious examination of one's purpose indicates that there is no case for compensation, then there is no case for combination; and it may well be that the most appropriate kind of information is obtainable without it. The second possibility is to allocate numbers to the grades, as follows.

If there are five grades, and these have been 'equally spaced' as suggested on p. 254, the grades A, B, C, D and E can be given the numbers 5, 4, 3, 2, 1. Any other series of numbers forming an arithmetic series (such as 14, 11, 8, 5, 2) would do just as well— but why use large numbers when small numbers will serve? In themselves, these numbers have no more significance than the initial grade-letters; but they do provide a basis for 'fairness' when grades are combined. For instance, is A+C+D equal to, or better than, or worse than A+B+E? Without reference to numbers, how can one know? Indeed, numbers are the *only* things susceptible of addition, and so if combination is required, numbers must be used.

The same system is applicable when the marking is, or approximates to, criterion-reference. For example, in the six questions in a paper a candidate is awarded Clear Pass, Fail, Just Pass, Just Pass, Pass, Clear Pass. The five 'categories' illustrated can be allocated numbers, and the five 'marks' added. (There may of course be a regulation to the effect that if a candidate fails in one question he fails altogether.) But we do stress that such numbers, by themselves, are of no value whatsoever, and that the names given in the first place (such as 'Clear Pass') are the significant indicators of merit. The allocation of numbers is for the sole purpose of achieving consistency in combination.

In concluding this section we should perhaps include the obvious point that, whenever possible, candidate's answers should be marked without the examiner's knowing who the candidates are. The most scrupulous honesty is not always proof against the power of the 'halo effect', or whatever may be the halo's inverse.*

Marking by ranking

Here again we should note the difference between issuing a *report* in terms of ranks (when numerical marks may already have been awarded), and ranking as a method of *marking*, when numerical marks of the usual kind are not awarded at all.

This method also is based upon 'impression marking'; but instead of the examiner's allocating the scripts to (say) five categories, he arranges the scripts in order of merit—as judged impressionistically. It will be apparent that if it is difficult to assign five grades it will be even more difficult to assign as many ranks as there are candidates; and that this method has the same sorts of disadvantages as the Grading method.

---

* In assessing someone in respect of one characteristic it is only too easy to be influenced by one's familiarity with other characteristics he has previously displayed.

Its value lies in its being applied to small numbers of candidates. For one thing, if the numbers are small, one can examine each script in greater detail, and make finer comparisons. For another thing, if there were only about half a dozen candidates it would be inappropriate to assign them to equally spaced grades – for the simple reason that the differences would almost certainly not be equally spaced.

In addition to the disadvantages this method shares with the Grading method, it has the disadvantage of not being susceptible of subsequent norm-reference – in so far as the method is used only when the number of candidates is small. Pass and Fail decisions will have to be based upon criterion-reference. Nor would it be appropriate to add ranks (by allocating numbers in the way just recommended for Grades), because there is no guarantee that equal rank-distances correspond with equal performance-differences. (This difficulty was avoided in the Grading method by the examiner's choosing, as criterion-scripts, performances he judged to *be* equally spaced.)

Except when the number of candidates is very small, then, and when a Unit-Counting method is precluded, the Ranking method would seem to have little to recommend it. The general conclusion would seem to be that whenever possible a Unit-Counting method should be employed – even if what one is counting are criteria fulfilled. But if that is not possible, a Grading method is to be preferred to a Ranking method – though in every case the marker must determine his 'criterion-scripts' in the first place by reference to the sorts of performance his purpose requires, and must continue such reference when 'matching' the remaining scripts with them.

Question analysis

Although the *term* 'item analysis' customarily refers only to objective questions (commonly called 'items'), there is no good reason why the sort of *procedure* denoted should not be applied to open questions too. However, such a procedure does not appear to have reached the degree of formalisation attained by item analysis. We may nevertheless make a few comments.

For short-answer questions (single words, phrases, sentences expressing a single fact or idea), the analytic procedures can be very similar to those we have already described (pp. 225ff.). If each question is awarded 1 (correct) or 0 (incorrect or omitted), we can calculate the number of candidates answering each question correctly, and so obtain a measure of difficulty in exactly the same way as for multiple-choice or true-false questions. Also, we can make a test of discriminative power for each question.

For longer answers, such as essay-type, these operations are scarcely feasible—and probably not very useful anyway. But the examiner can note, during marking (so long as he is not distracted from his main task), those questions in which correct or sensible or informed answers were relatively rare.

And, irrespective of answer-length, the examiner can make notes of wrong answers the candidates gave. (We strongly suggest that he does make notes. Funny wrong answers have a tendency to take priority, in one's memory, over mundane wrong answers which may nevertheless be more common and demand more attention.) This procedure is analogous to, though less precise than, the part of item analysis involving wrong options.

Of course, many examiners do all these things. What we are now suggesting is that they should be done deliberately, and systematically, and not just turn up casually during marking. If examinations are to be improved, and if their results are to be used for the improvement of courses, assessment of the candidates is not enough; the examination too must be made the object of evaluation.

Appendix I
Some elementary statistical formulae

The standard deviation

The Standard Deviation is a measure of scatter; that is, of the extent to which the marks are spread out around the Mean. If the marks are closely clustered around the Mean, the Standard Deviation will be relatively small in value; if the marks are well spread out, going far below and far above the Mean, the Standard Deviation will be relatively large. It is customarily symbolised by the small Greek letter 'sigma', σ, or by its initial letters, SD.

Unlike the Range and Interquartile Range, the SD takes every mark into account. It is more useful, in some respects, than other measures of scatter, largely because it is incorporated in the formulae for other measures—such as the formula for the product-moment correlation coefficient, and the formula for the normal distribution curve.

The Standard Deviation is given by the formula

$$\sigma = \sqrt{\frac{\sum x^2}{N}}$$

The symbol x represents any mark's 'deviation' from the Mean; that is, the difference between a mark and the Mean. If the Mean were 47, the mark of 52 would have a deviation of $+5$, the mark of 39 a deviation of -8. The mark of 47 would have a deviation of 0.

The symbol $\sum$, which is the Greek capital letter 'sigma', is a summation sign, indicating that the items following the sign are to be added together. Thus $\sum x^2$ means that all the deviations are to be squared, and these squares totalled.

N is the number of marks—or candidates.

In order to find the SD of a distribution of marks, therefore, one has to

a) Calculate the Mean.
b) Calculate each mark's deviation from the Mean by subtracting the Mean from the mark.

c) Square each of these deviations.
d) Add all the squared deviations.
e) Divide that sum by N.
f) Find the square root of that quotient.

Most elementary textbooks on statistics describe convenient methods of effecting these calculations.

One aspect of the nature of the SD is worth noting: the SD is given in the same unit-system as the marks themselves. Were the measures in inches, the Mean and all deviations from it would also be in inches. The squared deviations, that is x^2 terms, would be in inches-squared. Division by N, a pure number, produces inches-squared, but extraction of the square root brings the final measure back to inches. The reason for mentioning this point will be apparent when we look at Normal Distribution and z-scores.

Standard scores (or z-scores)

The text has described how a mark's standing can be assessed by comparing the mark with the Median and Quartiles; and it was suggested that its standing might also be indicated by quoting the mark's percentile position. The Standard Deviation provides another form of indication, namely in terms of 'standard scores', sometimes known as 'z-scores'.

As we noted above, the SD is given in the same units as the marks themselves. Suppose, then, that the Mean of a distribution of lengths were 47 inches, and that the SD were 5 inches. Then the mark of 52 inches, which is 5 inches above the Mean, would be at a distance of 1 SD above the Mean. The mark of 57 would be 2 SDs above the Mean. The mark of 32 would be 3 SDs below the Mean. Instead of reporting that these marks were 52, 57 and 32—which would give no indication of their standings, because no account is taken of either Mean or Scatter—we could say that these marks were +1 SD, +2 SD and −3 SD. In fact, the term 'SD' is dropped, and these particular scores would be referred to as 'standard scores' of +1, +2, and −3 respectively.

Thus, a standard (or z) score of +1·5 would indicate that the candidate's mark was one and a half standard deviations above the Mean. A standard (or z) score of −2 would indicate that the mark was two standard deviations below the Mean.

Note that z-scores in different examinations are, like percentile positions, directly comparable, because the different Means and different SDs have been taken into account.

A particular use of z-scores is described in the next section.

Normal distribution

As was noted in the text, a distribution may be symmetrical, or skewed. One particular form of symmetrical distribution is the 'normal distribution'. The marks pile up at and around the centre, and thin out towards the ends. Not all symmetrical distributions with these characteristics, however, are normal distributions. The normal distribution is the 'distribution of chance', the 'Gaussian' distribution, and has a defining formula–including the SD as a parameter. Many examinations nevertheless produce distributions approximating to normal distribution–if the number of candidates is fairly large, say 100 or more, and the questions have been set in order to produce it. In such cases certain characteristics of normal distribution can be exploited.

A normal distribution curve looks somewhat as follows:

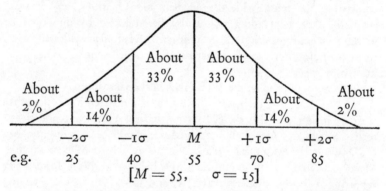

As with other curves, the area under the curve represents the total number of candidates. With normal distribution, the Mean value is also the Median value, irrespective of the particular numerical value they may have. But further, no matter what particular value the SD may have, the proportions of candidates above (or below) given z-scores are the same–for any normal distribution curve. These proportions can be expressed very precisely, but for our purpose here the following approximations (which are easy to remember) will suffice.

Between the Mean and 1 SD above the Mean–about one third of candidates.

Between 1 SD above the Mean and the top end–about one sixth of candidates.

Between 2 SD above the Mean and the top end–about 2 per cent of candidates.

If, for example, the Mean were 55 and the SD were 15, half the candidates would score 55 or more; about one third would have scores between 55 and 69; about one sixth would have scores of 70 or more; and only about 2 per cent would have scores of 85 or more. Similarly, only about 2 per cent would score less than 25.

Proportions above (or below) any particular z-score can be found by consulting tables or graphs (e.g. in Vernon 1940).

It will be apparent that, when the distribution is approximately normal, quotation of a candidate's z-score will indicate very clearly how good the score is–that is, how it stands in relation to the other scores.

The rank-order correlation coefficient

This coefficient of correlation, based upon candidates' ranks in two distributions, is given by the formula

$$1 - \frac{6\sum d^2}{N(N^2-1)}$$

In this formula, d is the difference between a candidate's two ranks (one in each of the two distributions).

Clearly, if each candidate has the same rank in the one distribution as he has in the other, all the d's will be zero, the fractional part of the formula will be zero, and the coefficient will be 1.

It is not immediately obvious that, when the rank orders are reversed, the coefficient will be −1. If, however, the reader cares to work out a simple case, say with $N = 8$, in which the candidates' pairs of ranks will be (1, 8), (2, 7), (3, 6), (4, 5), (5, 4), (6, 3), (7, 2) and (8, 1), it will be seen that the fractional part of the formula becomes 2, giving a coefficient of 1−2, namely −1.

The product-moment correlation coefficient

This coefficient is based, not upon ranks, but upon z-scores, and *could* be given by the formula

$$r = \frac{\sum z_1 z_2}{N}$$

in which z_1 is a candidate's standard score in Distribution 1, z_2 his standard score in Distribution 2. This version of the formula makes it explicit that it is upon z-scores that the formula is based, but if one were to base one's actual calculations upon it, one might do more work than is necessary, for it is not necessary to calculate each candidate's z-scores. More frequently the formula is written

$$r = \frac{\sum x_1 x_2}{N \sigma_1 \sigma_2}$$

where x_1 and x_2 are a candidate's deviations in the two distributions, and σ_1 and σ_2 are the SDs of the two distributions. The two formulae are nevertheless algebraically identical, because a candidate's z-score is his deviation divided by the SD. (Indeed, z-scores are customarily defined in this way, but the way in which we introduced z-scores in this Appendix appeared to make more clear what a z-score actually is.)

It is easy to see, from this second formula, that r will be $+1$ when there is perfect positive correlation, and -1 when there is perfect negative correlation. If every candidate's x_1 has the same value as his x_2, then although the *Means* of the two distributions may be different, yet the *scatters* will be the same; that is $\sigma_1 = \sigma_2$. The denominator of the fraction then becomes $N\sigma^2$. And the numerator becomes $\sum x^2$. The formula then reads

$$r = \frac{\sum x^2}{N \sigma^2}$$

But $\dfrac{\sum x^2}{N}$ is σ^2, and so $r = +1 \cdot 0$

Somewhat similarly, if there is perfect negative correlation, each x_1 will equal each x_2, and so the formula will become

$$r = \frac{-\sum x^2}{N \sigma^2} = -1 \cdot 0$$

Appendix II
Notes

1   This view of validity is in accord with the views expressed in the APA Bulletin on *Standards for Educational and Psychological Tests and Manuals* (1966), and also with those of Ebel (1965), Gronlund (1965), Wiseman (1961), and others. It is wider than the 'traditional' definition, namely that an examination is valid in so far as it measures what it purports to measure. When, however, an examination is envisaged (as in this account) as a means of measuring *performance*, it can be seen that the two views are by no means contradictory.

At this stage we have not distinguished various 'kinds' of validity, but Content Validity and Criterion-related Validity will be referred to later (p. 30).

2   'In the wide sense' because the measurement of human performance does not necessarily presuppose measurable equality of units, but may take the form only of counting items which have been *defined* to be *equivalent*–meaning that they are interchangeable.

For example, if it were agreed that the magnitude of a family consisted of the number of children (suitably defined) which it contained, a family of 6 children would be larger than a family of 4 children, and to the same extent as a family of 10 children exceeded a family of 8. Here, the units are children, and in measuring the family's magnitude by counting the number of its children it is irrelevant to ask whether these *units* are equal one to another, because within a unit no such counting is possible. (Unless, of course, we subdivide a unit into smaller units–which takes us back to the same problem again.) To underline the point: 'magnitude' refers to the class containing the units, and not at all to the units themselves, and so it is improper to ask about equality of units.

The vexed question of equality of units in examinations becomes irrelevant, then, if we regard measurement simply as the counting of defined performances. The magnitude of a candidate's 'answer', then, becomes the number of unit-performances it contains.

For the present, one other comment will suffice. Here and there in the text we have illustrated aspects of measurement by reference to units of height–to which it may be relevant to speak of 'equality', but we think that the pertinence of the illustrations is not affected by that possibility.

3   Even if (see Note 2) we are only 'counting'.

4   For example, in counting family-size: counting a pair of twins as 1, and later as 2.

5   This 'list' does not constitute an additional condition of validity, for it is presupposed by the condition we are discussing.

6   We take the name 'Relevance' from Ebel (1965). He uses the unqualified term 'relevance' to refer to what the candidate is required to *do*–which is the sense of our term 'Question-Relevance'; but since he is speaking of *tests*, in which the relevance of the marking is built into the framing of the questions, the term 'Mark-Relevance' is not required–as it is for *examinations*.

7   See, for instance, English and English (1958), who note that representativeness of sampling must refer to the *extent* to which a sample depicts what is true of the population from which it is drawn.

8   What is required here is, in effect, a test of 'content-validity', and it seems to be generally agreed that quantitative evidence of content-validity is rarely if ever obtainable. The best one could do would be to check the correlations between and among *various samples* drawn from the list, but for examinations (at least) such a procedure is impracticable. The nature of content-validity is briefly described in Chapter Three, but for a comprehensively critical account see Lennon (1956), or Gronlund (1968a) in which Lennon's article is reprinted.

9   Although he does not use the term in quite the same way, and does not say explicitly that Balance is a *condition* of validity, the similarity of usage would seem to justify our adopting his term rather than inventing a new one.

10   It is of course true that an examiner might not stick to these rules, but the point is that maximum validity is ensured not by the *making* of the rules but by their observance; that is, the rules are *conditions* of validity. Similarly for other rules.

11   Correspondence between odd-numbered and even-numbered items is but one possibility. The 'any half' possibility is covered by the Kuder-Richardson type of test.

12   Accounts of criterion-related validity tend to suggest that the criterion is something with which the results in question should have

a high *correlation*. In many cases this will be so, but while correlation provides the (so far) only accepted quantitative judgment of criterion-related validity, it would nevertheless seem illogical to exclude other possible criteria (such as precision) from the 'criterion' class. Indeed, there would seem to be no good reason why precision itself should not be measurable. See also pp. 54ff.

13   In defining the Median as the middle mark we follow Vernon (1940), but it is often defined as the mark below which 50 per cent of the marks fall. The two definitions have the same *general* meaning, but the latter raises practical difficulties when the marks are whole numbers. If the middle mark were one of *several* equal marks (as in Table IV), there might not *be* 50 per cent of the marks below it (or above it). The latter definition gets over that point by treating a mark as an interval, and assuming that the marks are distributed at random within it. On this view the Median could have a fractional value, such as 67·8. But if the marks are in fact whole numbers, all the marks of 67 are indistinguishable one from another, and it would be impossible to say which of them were below 67·8 and which were above it. For examinations it would seem to be preferable to regard the Median as the *middle* mark (or the mark of the middle candidate–which comes to the same thing), even if it has the same value as some other marks, for then it is possible to say which marks are above and which marks are below it.

14   The question of definition here is similar to that of the Median. See Note 13.

15   In terms of 'counting of items' (see Note 1) the argument would be, briefly, as follows. Even if, within Examination A, what constitute equivalent performances have been specified, and likewise for Examination B, it may not have been agreed that a unit-performance in Examination A is to count as equivalent to a unit-performance in Examination B. Indeed, if the two examinations are concerned with very different kinds of performance (as in English and Chemistry), it might be virtually impossible to find any reasonable basis on which agreement could be reached.

16   It would be, in effect, a form of 'scaling'. See Chapter Seven.

17   Here again we follow the style of Vernon's definition. See Note 13.

18   That is, approximating to normal distribution.

19   Except in the (at present) unlikely event that we had based the examination upon a 'Guttman scale' (Guttman 1944).

20   When a, b, and c refer respectively to the two components and the composite, the value of the composite standard deviation is given by the formula

$$\sigma_c = \sqrt{\sigma_a{}^2 + \sigma_b{}^2 + 2r_{ab}\sigma_a\sigma_b}$$

21   If $SD_a = p \cdot SD_b$, it can be shown that

$$r_{ac} = \frac{p + r_{ab}}{+\sqrt{p^2 + 2pr_{ab} + 1}} \qquad r_{bc} = \frac{pr_{ab} + 1}{+\sqrt{p^2 + 2pr_{ab} + 1}}$$

which equal $+1 \cdot 0$ when $r_{ab} = +1 \cdot 0$, irrespective of the value of p.

22   By means of the formulae given in Note 21 it can be shown that, when p is greater than 1, the first derivative of $r_{ac} - r_{bc}$, with respect to p, is positive for all values of r_{ab} except $\pm 1 \cdot 0$. It can also be shown that the first derivative of $r_{ac} - r_{bc}$, with respect to r_{ab}, is negative for all values of p greater than 1. These facts provide the justification of the double statement introducing this case.

23   When $p = 1$, then from the formulae given in Note 21 it can be deduced that

$$r_{ac} - r_{bc} = \frac{0}{\sqrt{2 + 2r_{ab}}}$$

which is zero for all values of r_{ab} except the limiting case of $r_{ab} = -1 \cdot 0$. It can also be shown that the first derivative of r_{ac} (and of r_{bc}, for the two are equal) with respect to r_{ab} is positive for all values of r_{ab} except $-1 \cdot 0$.

24   If p is defined by $\sigma_a = p\sigma_b$; and if z_a, z_b and z_c are any candidate's standard scores in the component A, the component B, and the composite C respectively, it can be shown that

$$z_c = \frac{pz_a}{\sqrt{p^2 + 2pr_{ab} + 1}} + \frac{z_b}{\sqrt{p^2 + 2pr_{ab} + 1}}$$

As p varies, so also do the denominators of the two fractions, and so also does z_c, but these two denominators are always equal. The fraction of z_a, therefore, is always p times the fraction of z_b.

   Note that when $r_{ab} = +1 \cdot 0$, which presupposes that $z_a = z_b$, then $z_c = z_b = z_a$, and that when $r_{ab} = -1 \cdot 0$, which presupposes that $z_a = -z_b$, then $z_c = z_a = -z_b$.

25 It might be pointed out that one can operate compensation without *adding* marks–as by totalling each candidate's positive and negative differences from the standards in the various topics. All we need say in reply is that a little examination of such a procedure reveals that it is no more than a very roundabout way of adding the marks themselves.

26 If the suffixes a and b refer to the two distributions, and the suffixes 1 and 2 refer to the two candidates, so that, for instance, z_{1a} is candidate 1's standard score in Distribution A, it can be shown that the difference between the two candidates' composite marks is

$$\sigma_a(z_{1a}-z_{2a})+\sigma_b(z_{1b}-z_{2b})$$

But for two 'tit-for-tat' candidates, $z_{1b}=z_{2a}$, $z_{2b}=z_{1a}$, and so the difference between their composite marks is

$$(z_{1a}-z_{2a})(\sigma_a-\sigma_b),$$

which is zero when the two distributions have equal scatters.

If, however, $\sigma_a=2\sigma_b$, the difference becomes $(z_{1a}-z_{2a})$;
    and if $\sigma_a=3\sigma_b$, the difference becomes $2(z_{1a}-z_{2a})$;
    and if $\sigma_a=4\sigma_b$, the difference becomes $3(z_{1a}-z_{2a})$;
    and so on.

27 By means of the formula given in Note 24 it can be shown that the first derivative of the difference between the two candidates' composite standings, with respect to p, is positive for all values of r_{ab}–with the exception of the extreme cases of $\pm1\cdot0$, which are irrelevant in this case anyway.

28 Basically the same point applies to the *scaling* of marks which are to be combined. Ideally, scaling should not lower the raw marks' precision, for the reasons given in the text.

29 If there are n topics, 1, 2, 3...n, the SD of the composite distribution is

$$\sqrt{\sigma_1^2+\sigma_2^2+\sigma_3^2+\ldots+\sigma_n^2+2(\sigma_1\sigma_2 r_{12}+\sigma_1\sigma_3 r_{13}+\ldots\sigma_{n-1}\sigma_n r_{n-1,n}}$$

and it can be shown that this quantity decreases as n increases, for any given values of the intercorrelations. (The calculation is simplified if the SDs of all the topics are equal.)

30 For a more detailed account see Ebel (1965, chapter eleven) and Husek and Sirotnik (1967).

31 Unlike the chance distribution for multiple-choice questions having more than two options, the chance distribution for true-false questions is symmetrical. The Mean chance score will be $\dfrac{N}{2}$ where N is the number of questions. The standard deviation is $\sqrt{\dfrac{N}{4}}$. For reasonably large numbers of candidates one may assume that the distribution is normal, and so confidence levels can be calculated by reference to a table or graph giving percentages of scores above any particular standard score.

References

APA (1966) *Standards for Educational and Psychological Tests and Manuals.* Washington, D.C.: American Psychological Association.

BALLARD, P. B. (1923) *The New Examiner.* London: University of London Press.

BLOOM, B. S. (1956) *Taxonomy of Educational Objectives.* New York: Longmans Green.

COX, R. (1969) 'Reliability and Validity of Examinations.' *The World Year Book of Education.* London: Evans Bros.

CRONBACH, L. J. (1960) *Essentials of Psychological Testing.* London: Harper and Row.

EBEL, R. (1965) *Measuring Educational Achievement.* New Jersey: Prentice-Hall.

EBEL, R. (1972) *Essentials of Educational Measurement.* New Jersey: Prentice-Hall.

ENGLISH, H. B. and ENGLISH, A. C. (1958) *A Comprehensive Dictionary of Psychological and Psychoanalytical Terms.* London: Longmans.

GLASER, R. (1963) 'Instructional Technology and the Measurement of Learning Outcomes.' *American Psychologist,* 18.

GRONLUND, N. E. (1965) *Measurement and Evaluation in Teaching.* New York: The Macmillan Company.

GRONLUND, N. E. (1968a) *Readings in Measurement and Evaluation.* New York: The Macmillan Company.

GRONLUND, N. E. (1968b) *Constructing Achievement Tests.* New Jersey: Prentice-Hall.

GRONLUND, N. E. (1973) *Preparing Criterion-Referenced Tests for Classroom Instruction.* New York: The Macmillian Company. London: Collier Macmillan.

GUILFORD, J. P., LOVELL, Constance and WILLIAMS, Ruth M. (1942) 'Completely Weighted versus Unweighted Scoring in Achievement Examinations.' *Educational and Psychological Measurement,* 11.

GUTTMAN, L. (1944) 'A Basis for Scaling Qualitative Data.' *American Sociological Review,* 9.

HUSEK, T. R. and SIROTNIK, K. (1967) 'Item Sampling and Educational Research.' *CSEIP Occasional Report* No. 2. Los Angeles: University of California.

LENNON, R. T. (1956) 'Assumptions Underlying the Use of Content Validity.' From *Educational and Psychological Measurement*, Harcourt, Brace and World Inc. (Included in GRONLUND 1968a.)

MACINTOSH, H. G. and MORRISON, R. B. (1969) *Objective Testing.* London: University of London Press.

MAGER, R. F. (1962) *Preparing Instructional Objectives.* San Francisco: Fearon Publishers, Inc.

MILLER, N. E. and DOLLARD, J. (1945) *Social Learning and Imitation.* London: Kegan Paul, Trench, Trubner and Co. Ltd.

MORRIS, N. (1961) 'An Historian's View of Examinations.' From WISEMAN, S. (1961).

PHILLIPS, A. J. (1943) 'Further Evidence Regarding Weighted versus Unweighted Scoring of Examinations.' *Educational and Psychological Measurement*, III.

POPHAM, W. J. and HUSEK, T. R. (1969) 'Implications of Criterion-Referenced Measurement.' *Journal of Educational Measurement*, Vol. 6, No. 1.

POPHAM, W. J. (ed.) (1971) *Criterion-Referenced Measurement.* Englewood Cliffs, NJ: Educational Technology Publications.

THYNE, J. M. (1966a) 'What is the Weight of an Examination Paper?' *British Journal of Educational Psychology*, Vol. XXXVI, Part 3.

THYNE, J. M. (1966b) *The Psychology of Learning and Techniques of Teaching.* London: University of London Press.

VERNON, P. E. (1940) *The Measurement of Abilities.* London: University of London Press.

WARD, J. (1970) 'On the Concept of Criterion-Referenced Measurement.' *British Journal of Educational Psychology*, Vol. 40, Part 3.

WESMAN, A. G. (1952) 'Reliability and Confidence.' *Test Service Bulletin*, No. 44. New York: The Psychological Corporation. (Included in GRONLUND 1968a.)

WILKS, S. S. (1938) 'Weighting Systems for Linear Functions of Correlated Variables When There is No Dependent Variable.' *Psychometrika.*

WISEMAN, S. (1961) *Examinations and English Education.* Manchester: Manchester University Press.

Index

References to footnotes are indicated by *fn.* after the page number; appendix notes are indicated by *n.* followed by the number of the note.